The Art of the Gut

The publisher gratefully acknowledges the generous support of the Asian Studies Endowment Fund of the University of California Press Foundation

The Art of the Gut

Manhood, Power, and Ethics
in Japanese Politics

Robin M. LeBlanc

UNIVERSITY OF CALIFORNIA PRESS
Berkeley · Los Angeles · London

Some portions of this work previously appeared in the essay "Why Women Are Representing Men in a Japanese Town Assembly: A Little Tale about Gender Politics," *Kokusai jendā gakkai shi* 2 (2004): 35–69. I thank the International Society for Gender Studies (*Kokusai jendā gakkai shi*) for permission to reprint them here.

University of California Press, one of the most distinguished university presses in the United States, enriches lives around the world by advancing scholarship in the humanities, social sciences, and natural sciences. Its activities are supported by the UC Press Foundation and by philanthropic contributions from individuals and institutions. For more information, visit www.ucpress.edu.

University of California Press
Berkeley and Los Angeles, California

University of California Press, Ltd.
London, England

© 2010 by The Regents of the University of California

Library of Congress Cataloging-in-Publication Data

LeBlanc, Robin M., 1966–.
    The art of the gut : manhood, power, and ethics in Japanese politics / Robin M. LeBlanc.
        p.   cm.
    Includes bibliographical references and index.
    ISBN 978-0-520-25916-4 (cloth : alk. paper)
    ISBN 978-0-520-25917-1 (pbk. : alk. paper)
        1. Masculinity—Political aspects—Japan.
    2. Men—Japan—Political activity.   3. Political culture—Japan.   4. Japan—Politics and government—1989.   I. Title.

HQ1090.5.J3L4   2010
320.952081—dc22   2009009148

Manufactured in the United States of America

19 18 17 16 15 14 13 12 11 10
10 9 8 7 6 5 4 3 2 1

This book is printed on Cascades Enviro 100, a 100% post consumer waste, recycled, de-inked fiber. FSC recycled certified and processed chlorine free. It is acid free, Ecologo certified, and manufactured by BioGas energy.

In memory of my father,
Robert Guy Le Blanc (1942–2005),
and with hopes for my son,
Tieran Skye McClure (2001–)

Contents

Acknowledgments

I have put off writing these acknowledgments for a long time because I have no way to clear the debts to others I acquired in the process of researching and writing this book. In fact, I am sure I will never even properly remember them all. Most important is what I owe to the men and women of my two main field sites and in several other towns where I conducted supplementary observation and interviews. I cannot mention them by name without violating their privacy. I wish my writing could in some way do justice to the contribution they made to my research, but it simply cannot. They welcomed me into their homes, shared their families, their meals, their histories, and their passion for democracy with me. Most of all they taught me things I really needed to know; only some of those things were about politics. I thank them. I miss them.

Research of the sort I do is expensive. Mine was supported by a 1999 Japan Society for the Promotion of Science postdoctoral fellowship, and a 2002 Fulbright Research Fellowship administered by the Japan–United States Educational Commission. At my institutional home, Washington and Lee University, I received funding from the Glenn Grant program for summer research, the Class of '62 grant program for extending sabbaticals, and the Nasdaq/Suntrust Global Commerce Faculty Development Grant for international research. I was welcomed twice, in 1999 and 2002, as a research fellow at Rikkyō University in Tokyo. In the fall of 2007 I finished the last bit of my research while an International

Christian University Foundation visiting professor of political science at International Christian University, also in Tokyo. At both institutions smart and friendly colleagues, effective staff, and subsidized housing helped make my time in Tokyo productive and satisfying.

I have borrowed from the intellect of any person I thought might contribute to my own thinking, including a prospective kindergarten teacher for my son. Most of my unwitting creditors cannot be listed here. However, some have been especially helpful in my work. Igarashi Akio of Rikkyō University has guided my work in Japan since my days as a graduate student. Without his advice I would never have begun a study of Japanese local politics; without his introductions I could never have done the fieldwork in this book. His personal commitment to doing research that furthers a more democratic and ethical world is an inspiration to me. Another longtime political science colleague, Ōgai Tokuku, was also very giving with introductions and intellectual feedback. So was Sasaki Yasushi, whose rich understanding of the Japanese language (and patience with its nonnative speakers) was indispensable in the early stages of my work. Mike Schneider, Sascha Goluboff, Walter Bennett, and Yumiko Mikanagi read chapter drafts with sharp eyes and generous spirits. A provocative dinner conversation with the anthropologists Bill Kelly and Karen Nakamura following a talk I gave at Yale University in 2007 challenged me to rethink my arguments about cheating in chapter 4. I probably haven't satisfied Bill or Karen, but I know my work is better as a result of their questions. Gavin Whitelaw provided me with important background information about small retail businesses in Japan. Reed Malcolm at the University of California Press was immediately enthusiastic and supportive. Jan Bardsley, Andrew Barshay, and one anonymous reviewer provided detailed, practical advice for me in the last stages. Caroline Knapp, my manuscript editor, shepherded the project through the production process with almost no pain for me, and Judith Hoover's exacting work as copy editor has greatly enhanced my prose (and my rather impoverished understanding of punctuation).

A number of staff members at Washington and Lee have contributed to providing a hospitable environment for my research. Three have been especially helpful during the course of my project. Carolyn Hammett processed countless Japanese-language receipts and yen-dollar equivalency spreadsheets to make sure I would be reimbursed for all of my research expenses. Lynda Bassett-de Maria made it possible for me to look good at my other university commitments (most notably a campuswide student research conference and a year as head of Women's and Gender Studies) while I kept working at this book, and reference librarian Dick Grefe produced important background information for my introduction. My dean, Larry Peppers, did what I think all deans should do. Even when I couldn't fully articulate what I was up to, Larry cheerfully accepted that my crazy project might someday amount to something, sent financial resources my way, and then left me to my own devices.

I tried to write this book for my students, who each day remind me that politics is supposed to be about making a better world. A few have been especially important to this project. At the beginning Brooks Hickman helped me build a bibliography of research on men's studies. His independent study in Confucian ethics became a source for my own thinking on the topic, and our discussions of power theory helped me refine my frustrations with it. Ashley Hubbard read a draft of the entire manuscript, helping particularly in my efforts to straighten out the confused elements of my introduction. Peter Kyle devoted long hours to editing the last two versions of the manuscript. Peter has proofreading skills I envy hugely, but more important he is a sober, insightful, and gutsy editor. Without Peter's sound advice I would have written a much worse book.

Other than Peter, no one has been more fully subjected to my many drafts of difficult sections than David Millon. One summer evening conversation about the banality of good helped me to, at long last, understand what I wanted to say in chapters 4 and 5. Perhaps as helpful as David's belief in this project, however, has been his penchant for enjoying a good meal. Whether we shared them at restaurants, he cooked them for me, or I cooked them for him, our meals together have been a valued respite from work and, more than once, the incentive I needed to push through a long day of writing.

On the subject of external supports, I would never have put together the disparate writing projects that became this book if it had not been for one intense week of uninterrupted writing at my brother Bill's house in Atlanta, perfectly located between the nice morning people at Aurora Coffee and the pecan chocolate chunk cookies at Alon's Bakery. I should not neglect to mention that Billy's leftover pork in mojo sauce kept me focused through the afternoons between the coffee and the cookies. I doubt any location makes a finer writer's retreat.

My son was born, my parents died, and I was divorced over the course of researching and writing this book. I have many good friends who said and did the things I needed in that difficult time. My sister, Lizzy, and my stepmother, Sarah, have offered me a regular means of connecting to the world outside myself. My ex-husband, Michael McClure, was an early supporter of this project; he continues to share his sense of irony and wisdom when I need a defense against my own doubts. My running friends, Louise Uffelman, Tom Contos, Jim Kahn, Peter Jetton, and of course David Millon, have humored me throughout. Ellen Mayock and Domnica Radulescu taught me how powerful any smart woman armed with a few choice words can be. (I just wish I had as many choice words as they do!) My son, Tieran, has every day called me to see how new, how possible, and how beautiful the world is.

As I said at the beginning, some debts cannot ever be repaid. My father died in 2005 at sixty-three of a terrible and rare disease, amyloidosis, that destroyed his digestive system and starved him. I doubt I'll ever know what caused my father's disease, but it taught me what individuals with catastrophic illness and their families can suffer.

For a number of years during my childhood, my father worked at one of the Department of Energy facilities in Oak Ridge, Tennessee, that I describe in the introduction. Those facilities leaked a range of dangerous pollutants into the environment during decades of high-security work. As the U.S. government acknowledged with the passage of the Energy Employees Occupational Illness Compensation Program Act in 2000, the pollutants at Oak Ridge facilities greatly damaged the health of some workers. I wrote the section of the introduction that is about Oak Ridge in 2003, more than a year before I knew my father was sick, and it was not my intention at the time I wrote it to speak about my father. I have no proof whatsoever that his illness was caused by his years working there. His type of amyloidosis has no known cause. Nonetheless, disease as brutal as that was certainly a possibility for many who worked in the Oak Ridge DOE facilities during the years my father was employed there.

My father did not seek to understand the source of his illness, and he complained very little about what he suffered during it. Usually my father was not a man to simply bow to the status quo. He could offer sharp critiques of American social, economic, and political values over the dinner table on any given evening. I'm sure my fascination with and suspicions about power were spurred in those childhood conversations. But my father also grew up with limited financial resources and put enormous energy into achieving the American Dream for himself and his offspring. He never resisted the notion that it was his duty as a man to be the family's breadwinner, even if that duty sometimes required personal sacrifice. My father had a gift for living the joy available in the present moment; I think that is why he often enjoyed his work. But he also looked forward to a freer time after retirement when he would get to pursue the interests he really cared about. He didn't get that time.

The Oak Ridge section of my book is barely changed from what I originally wrote in 2003. As I revised the rest of the introduction and the book in the years after losing my father, however, I began to wonder what he quietly endured in order to do what he thought a good man should. I hope that, in some way, this book both honors his memory and challenges the good men who come after him to ask more of power than it does of them.

Note on Names

All of the participants in this study are referred to by pseudonyms. In some cases, I have also changed place names or personal details to protect the privacy of the people who so willingly told me their stories. All Japanese names are written according to the Japanese practice, family name first, except where the individuals themselves commonly use the American style.

Preface

Most of the time I have to work long and hard for the insights I have into my research subjects, but every once in a while I just run into them. That is literally what I did on a hot September morning in a Tokyo suburb where I was out for a three-mile jog just before beginning a semester as a visiting professor at a Japanese university. I was doing an out-and-back course along a river, and I was on the return leg of my run when, on a wall around a small parking lot, I saw a political poster that summed up the theme of nearly a decade's worth of my work in a few tiny words. I suppose the poster was left over from Japan's July 2007 House of Councillors' election, in which the opposition Democratic Party of Japan (DPJ) won a substantial and not fully expected victory over the long-governing Liberal Democratic Party (LDP). The poster pictured the winning DPJ's leader, Ozawa Ichirō, looking up and away, his lips pressed tight in an expression of grave determination. Alongside his face was the slogan *Nihon no oyaji, ugoku,* "Japan's middle-aged men are on the move."

My unavoidably clumsy translation actually hides the richness of the slogan's combined specificity and ambiguity. *Nihon no* means "Japan's." *Oyaji* is a slang term for men, usually used for one's father or for middle-aged or older men. The term is not always a positive one. For example, sometimes *oyaji* connotes a tasteless, unrefined geezer or an "old fart."[1] At other times *oyaji* is an almost affectionate reference to a hardworking and dependable if somewhat crusty member of a close community. *Ugoku* means "to move." As Ozawa fits the age profile of an *oyaji*, the poster slogan might be a friendly reference to him, a means of connecting this famous political professional with regular people, as if Ozawa were just like any other *oyaji* but more capable of moving, of getting things done, in national politics. The poster slogan might also be intended as a reference to Ozawa's entire political party, painting the party as a no-nonsense, get-things-done organization in comparison with the rival LDP that presided over more than a decade of economic stagnation beginning at the end of the 1980s. The poster might be a subtle attempt at praising a portion of the DPJ's constituents: the middle-class, middle-aged men who have been both credited with Japan's stunning economic rise following the end of World War II and, since the beginning of the 1990s, blamed for Japan's resistance to change. Finally, the slogan might even work as a subtle exhortation, urging Japan's slumbering *oyaji* into action on behalf on the nation.

All of these possible interpretations point to one unmistakable theme. They present a contemporary sense of crisis in Japanese politics as a problem in manhood. On the one hand, the placement of the slogan alongside Ozawa's uplifted and determined face instructs us to connect national political leadership to the movement of men (not men *and* women), as if getting the nation headed in the right direction were a matter of getting the right kind of man at its head. On the other hand, the colloquial nature of the word *oyaji* suggests that Japan's political future might rest on the kind of ability and commitment ordinary Japanese men possess but do not always use. The poster stopped me in my tracks. Waiting for me on my desk when I returned from that run was a draft of the manuscript that is this book. I don't have a plan for solving Japan's political problems by getting *oyaji* moving, and I am sure that if I did have a plan for Japan, it would not be the same one Ozawa and the DPJ would offer. Still, I do think that key aspects of Japanese politics are a manhood puzzle—or maybe many manhood puzzles.

Ideas of who a good man is and what a good man does, like those hinted at in Ozawa's poster, are indicators of an unvoiced but widely used power in Japanese politics. Of course, like most claims about identity launched against a broad swath of any society, claims about Japanese manhood, even when made by powerful Japanese men, constrain the social power of the particular individuals to whom they are attached. By condemning some behaviors and exhorting others, notions of manhood sketch the boundaries of any man's self-determination, but at the same time these notions also reinforce the value of individual men taking moral responsibility for the world around them and provide significant rhetorical tools to the man who wants to claim that responsibility. Just as the poster's simple words and the picture of tight-lipped, far-seeing Ozawa suggest I should, I see much of male-dominated political life in Japan as men's struggle for agency in a complex and obstinate environment. In that struggle "manhood" is a multifarious, inescapable and yet not indomitable force, urging the combatants into battle, playing the role of stalwart opponent, and then, almost surprisingly, supplying moral resources without which individual protagonists would find themselves lost. In the seemingly ordinary, merely "natural" practice of Japanese political manhood, we can witness three central elements of any democratic political endeavor: the elusiveness of power, the resilience of individuals, and the abiding importance of our moral commitments.

The Power Remainder

POWER'S MIDDLE MANAGERS

In his essay "The Power of the Powerless" Vaclav Havel argues that even in a totalitarian political system, responsibility for power is located in ordinary individuals. He offers the example of a greengrocer who displays in his window the slogan "Workers of the World Unite!" Even though the greengrocer might never think very deeply about his behavior, Havel says, posting the slogan expresses a choice to participate in the process of compelling others to accept, at least on the surface, the political system's dominant ideology. "The slogan really is a *sign*, and as such it contains a subliminal but very definite message. Verbally it might be expressed this way: 'I, the greengrocer XY, live here and I know what I must do. . . . I am obedient and therefore I deserve to be left in peace.'"[1] Havel suggests that although the greengrocer would not want to have to examine the "low foundations of his obedience," he puts the sign in his window because it serves his interests as a greengrocer. His gesture of conformity to the demands of a corrupt regime leaves him free to pursue his business (28). Alongside his imagined greengrocer, Havel adds an office worker who hangs a similar slogan in the corridor where she works. Neither the office worker nor the greengrocer pay much heed to each other's posted slogans. Yet as Havel explains, in their efforts to be left in peace, the office worker and the greengrocer are acting in ways that create the "anonymous" power of the totalitarian state. "Their mutual indifference to each other's slogans is only an illusion: in reality, by exhibiting their slogans, each compels the other to accept the rules of the game and to confirm thereby the power that requires the slogans in the first place. Quite simply, each helps the other to be obedient" (38). Havel's point is that even massive, totalizing structures of power are implemented by ordinary individuals who are thus in some sense responsible for the oppression they suffer. Havel was speaking to the subjects of totalitarian communist systems, but conceivably, people like the greengrocer play an important role in any of the fields of power we study. I think of them as power's middle managers, people who did not shape and do not control the power structures they serve but who are still charged with the responsibility for displaying (or in Havel's thinking, refusing to display) the signs that command the obedience of others.

Early in the spring of 1999, in one of the field sites where I did research for this book, something my informants said reminded me of my hometown, Oak Ridge, Tennessee, and of a man I have come to think of as a power greengrocer in a democratic regime. My memory of Oak Ridge was evoked by a discussion about political corruption I was having with two leaders of a powerful new group in politics in the small Japanese town of Takeno-machi, population 30,000.[2] The first was a man in his midfifties named Baba-san, the owner of a sake shop. The second was Baba's cousin, Ota-san, an accountant in his midforties. A few years before I first met them, Baba and Ota had worked side by side with others from their town to build a group called the Referendum Association. The group was organized to demand a popular referendum on the building of a nuclear power plant in Takeno-machi. Ota had been a nuclear power opponent for decades. Baba had tried to avoid involvement in local politics, especially any kind of activity as strongly associated with leftist citizens' movements as nuclear power opposition. By the time I met him, however, Baba's work as a Referendum Association founder had placed him at the front of a citizens' movement and in the very center of Takeno-machi politics.

The conversation during which Baba and Ota reminded me of Oak Ridge took place on what started as a lazy Sunday afternoon. Baba, who worked long hours at his shop six days a week, was relaxing in front of the television. Ota had come over to chat and drink tea. I was renting a room from the Baba family for the two and a half months of my stay in Takeno. The weather was cold and rainy. Baba's house, like most Japanese houses, had no central heat, so I ended up in front of the TV too. We all put our legs under the *kotatsu* table (a low table with a quilted skirt around it and a heater under it) to keep warm while we lounged about on cushions and watched a marathon race in some faraway city. I was tired from the intensity of living among my informants.

The Referendum Association was gearing up to run candidates in the local assembly elections, which meant that Baba, Ota, and other leaders in the group lived long days. Several of them met at Baba's home nearly every morning before work and then again afterward, talking well into the night about campaign strategy. Because I wanted to hear what they had to say, I kept the same hours, often retreating to my room after midnight to spend an hour or more writing field notes. Although my sole reason for being in Baba's home was to learn what he and his fellow activists thought about local assemblies and other community power structures, I made no effort to get the men talking about politics on that Sunday afternoon. I was watching a marathon. Yet as the race wore on, Baba and Ota slipped into conversation about their town's politics, shifting through a range of topics about the election and about the planned power plant. For a while I was just a lucky fieldworker scooping up unsolicited insights into my informants' worldviews, but Baba and Ota eventually insisted on hearing something from me in return.

Like other members of the Referendum Association, journalists who reported on Takeno politics, and even the politically uninvolved locals I met during my fieldwork, Baba and Ota had remarkable stories of the corrupt practices of the power company that was seeking to build the nuclear power plant. The stories included plant officials secreting supportive assemblymen to out-of-town assembly sessions for decisive votes, wining and dining Takeno-machi elected officials in Europe to educate them about the benefits of nuclear power, and bribing anyone and everyone in Takeno-machi, including minors ineligible to vote. Ota and Baba said they were especially disturbed by the notion that Takeno's political leaders—men who were fathers and grandfathers, men who had reputations as good, community-minded citizens—would take bribes to push the building of a facility Ota and Baba saw as inherently dangerous to townspeople for generations to come. As I asked questions about their stories, Ota-san finally turned to me in an almost accusatory manner. He said he doubted that, from my American perspective, I could wholly imagine the way something like a nuclear power plant project could deform the politics of a small Japanese town. But I thought I did have some sense of what he was talking about. As a child in Oak Ridge, also a town of nearly 30,000 people, I had watched a scandal unfold that I now thought bore real similarities to the Takeno-machi stories, even though Oak Ridge and Takeno-machi were in two different countries with two different political systems. I don't think I did a very good job of explaining myself to Baba and Ota that Sunday afternoon, in part because my own memories of Oak Ridge politics were fuzzy. Only later, as I began to write about Takeno, did I look up the details of that scandal I had all but forgotten.

In 1983 Oak Ridge was the location of three major Department of Energy (DOE) nuclear facilities: a nuclear weapons plant, Oak Ridge National Laboratory, and a nuclear fuel enrichment plant. The facilities were managed for DOE by Union Carbide Corporation, a company with a less than blemish-free pollution record.[3] Most of Oak Ridge had been built during World War II. As the U.S. government built plants to produce fuel for the atomic bombs, the population had soared from fewer than 100 residents to a wartime high of nearly 75,000 in just two and a half years.[4] Even in the 1970s and 1980s, when my family lived in the much smaller, postwar Oak Ridge, most of my friends' fathers worked for one of the three government facilities; for a time mine did as well. Most who worked at the facilities possessed some sort of government security clearance, and children did not expect to know more about their father's work than his official title, such as Nuclear Physicist 2 or Computer Specialist 1 (something like my father's title). On the major roads leaving our town government advertising on billboards urged the protection of secrets with graphics and slogans that rivaled anything produced during World War II, and perhaps would have recalled for Havel the slogans of communist Czechoslovakia. We Oak Ridgers proudly saw ourselves as the front line of the cold war. In this spirit one of my best friends in junior high pinned an ugly bumper sticker to the wall of her frilly pink bedroom: "Better Dead Than Red."

In the early 1980s, not long after my friend hung up her bumper sticker, the citizens of Oak Ridge learned that throughout the 1950s, in the rush to beat the Soviets to the end of the arms race, the DOE facilities had dumped an enormous amount and variety of toxic waste into the local environment. The first of these wastes to really cause a public stir was mercury. Over a period of almost thirty years more than 2.4 million pounds of mercury were released into local creeks. Yet the real scandal was not that these very dangerous wastes polluted the streams and flood plains of the area. The scandal was that, even though officials with DOE and Union Carbide knew about much of the pollution for decades, they kept the information secret. The story didn't become public until nearly two years after an Oak Ridge National Laboratory scientist named Steve Gough followed a hunch in 1981 and got his brother, a scientist with the U.S. Geological Survey in Colorado, to help him take some samples of plant life and water and analyze them independently at a USGS lab.[5]

When the samples revealed very high levels of mercury pollution, Gough expected to be encouraged to conduct further studies. Instead he was reprimanded by his bosses for challenging the system, taken out of line for a promotion, and generally encouraged to go away.[6] Gough's bosses also threatened to reach out to his brother through their government contacts and demanded the samples from the USGS lab, which they then stored away without a proper public record.[7] Gough left Oak Ridge for employment elsewhere, but his unauthorized sampling started the dominoes falling. I won't recount the whole story here, but about a year after Gough left, earlier reports about the pollution were declassified in response to a Freedom of Information Act request by a neighboring town's paper. The local media reported the problem, the U.S. House of Representatives held hearings, and, in the fullness of time, Oak Ridge began its new life as a Superfund site, a toxic waste dump in recovery.[8]

As a sixteen-year-old I was mesmerized by the issue. First of all, it was readily apparent to me that some of the fathers of my classmates might have known about the pollution for years before the public did. That was astounding in itself, considering that one of the places polluted by the mercury was the campus of my junior high school. Here were fathers (I would never know which ones) who, in some benighted understanding of "security," had kept secret from their families the potential dangers to which their work exposed their own children. Yet in the mind of an adolescent whose first introduction to politics was the moment of Richard Nixon's disrobing (and who was thus forever cynical about men and power), these silent fathers were not the most compelling aspect of the mercury incident.

More fascinating to me was the case of Steve Gough. What had led him to violate the proud code of Oak Ridge secrecy, to challenge the system, to risk his own future by asking an unauthorized question? For nearly three decades many other highly skilled scientists who must have had similar hunches about toxic waste leakage from the facilities had managed to keep their mouths shut. Why couldn't Gough? At sixteen I was especially sensitive to the enormous power of peer pressure in protecting the secrets of Oak Ridge and likewise in awe of the sort of man who could brook the pain of resisting that power. In Havel's terms, Gough had refused to display the sign that compelled his and others' obedience. Even today I wonder what special resource he possessed for facing power. Was it unavailable to the other men of his community? Why was Steve Gough different?

This is not an investigation of the psyche of Oak Ridge scientists who worked on the front of the cold war. This is a book about two Japanese men active in their local communities' politics at the turn of the twenty-first century. One of the men is Takeno-machi's Baba-san, and the other is Takada-san, who, when I met him, was a thirty-seven-year-old conservative LDP candidate for the assembly of the Shirakawa Ward of Tokyo.[9] I tell the story of Steve Gough because when I pulled the Oak Ridge mercury scandal from my memory in response to Ota's insistence that I could not possibly understand the corruption of men in a small Japanese town, I inadvertently changed my entire way of seeing Takeno and the project that drove me to choose Takeno as a field site. The things that Baba and Ota led me to recall about the equally small American town where I had done the bulk of my growing up stuck in my head. Once I had made the connection between Oak Ridge and Takeno, I couldn't seem to let it go, and new questions floated toward the top of my research agenda.

What had been a fairly vague concern with how power is structured in Japanese politics became a set of questions with a specific moral bent. Given the many opportunities for and the persistence of corrupt practices in Japanese towns like Takeno and American towns like Oak Ridge, what makes it possible for some people to do the right thing? If ordinary people—power's greengrocers or middle managers—sometimes do persist in fighting and even partially succeed in stopping corrupt uses of power, shouldn't social science have a way of recording their stances and their successes? In fact, I finally asked myself, aren't social scientists responsible for more than that, responsible not just for recording an individual's ethical response to power but also for knowing (and thus perhaps teaching) a little bit about why and how power's middle managers can come to resist corruption?

Seeing Power through Japan's Local Assemblies

I didn't immediately understand the importance of the Oak Ridge story I told Baba and Ota because I didn't originally go to Takeno with the intention of investigating the ethical choices of power's middle managers. Instead I was working on a study I called "Citizens and Assemblies." My research goal was to examine how institutions (local assemblies) and organizations (political parties and electoral movements such as Takeno's Referendum Association) more generally structured citizens' opportunities to engage in political life. My first meeting with Baba in January 1999 was only one of a series of interviews I hoped to conduct in Takeno to better understand constituency mobilization prior to the upcoming local assembly election. I had no plans to stay in Baba's home. Only when I realized that the town did not have short-term apartments did I ask if I might rent a room from him. I knew, through his wife's chance remark, that one of the Babas' rooms was empty because their oldest child had recently moved out of the house to be closer to his job in a neighboring town. My interview with Baba was not supposed to be the beginning of a concentrated examination of his role in community leadership. My study of the Takeno Referendum Association's effort to elect its members to the Takeno Assembly was supposed to be only part of the second of two cases in a larger study of Japanese local assemblies.

Before I began my fieldwork there, Takeno-machi interested me because it was one of several Japanese towns that had experienced a sort of democratic revolution in local politics during the mid-1990s. In 1998 alone, movements in nearly twenty Japanese localities, mostly rural towns and regional cities, petitioned their local assemblies to hold citizens' referenda on controversial public works projects or plant sitings. In many of these towns citizens' movements pushed aside some of the conservatives who had dominated local politics throughout the postwar period, replacing them with new groups and greatly altering the demographics of leading political actors by bringing in those who would otherwise never have participated in their community's politics.[10] By 1999 Takeno was among the leading communities in the representation of women, young people, and nonaligned progressives in local-level electoral politics. In short, although Takeno-machi is far from the center of Japan's political authority in Tokyo, and although the region surrounding Takeno-machi is reputed to be a bastion of Japan's traditional patron-client political culture, the town modeled striking new political practices springing up across the nation.

The movements and changes that distinguished Takeno-machi politics in the 1990s took place during a period of economic stagnation and policy paralysis in Japanese national politics widely known as the "Lost Decade." The Lost Decade, actually closer to fifteen than ten years long, stretched from the late 1980s into the first years of the twenty-first century. Across the country real prices dropped, economic growth stalled, and unemployment expanded. Japan's banking system nearly collapsed, and public debt rose to enormous levels. Meanwhile, beyond the nation's borders, markets grew increasingly competitive for Japanese producers, and the world seemed to grow less and less stable. National politicians and bureaucrats struggled to put forth economic policies that would inspire consumer and investor confidence, but their efforts were regularly punctuated by revelations of political and bureaucratic scandal that cast doubt on the leaders' claims of progress.[11] Throughout the period the aging of Japanese society continued without relent, but the government remained unprepared to fully pension or care for the growing proportion of elderly in the years to come. By 2005 the fertility rate was 1.25 children per woman of childbearing age, far below the population replacement rate of 2.08 children.[12] The constant repetition of the demographic trend rings like a funeral dirge for the more prosperous decades of the 1960s, 1970s, and 1980s.

Although new political parties came and went like grass fires on an autumn prairie throughout the mid-1990s, the conservative LDP continued to dominate the national government, as it has since its formation in 1955, excepting only a very brief break from power in the second half of 1993 and the first half of 1994. Even as I write this, the LDP controls the government, despite enduring some challenges from the DPJ, which controls a majority of seats in the upper house of the Japanese parliament, the National Diet. Citizens have been either unable or unwilling to hold the LDP accountable for years of dull performance at the national level. Nonetheless, the events in Takeno politics in the 1990s, like those in a number of other peripheral localities, suggest that the Lost Decade was not as stagnant as it appeared from the center of the Japanese political system. In fact, political ferment in towns such as Takeno provoked many observers to suggest that the real problem in the Japanese economic and political systems was the overweening power of the central government. Some argued that if local governments were given more autonomy Japan would find in them the political ingenuity necessary to pull itself out of the slump.[13]

My Takeno-machi case study offered me a chance to examine how the relationship between Japanese citizens and their political institutions might be evolving on the local level. But to learn more about the persistence of "traditional" LDP politics in spite of the bad news of the Lost Decade, I chose a second field site, urban Shirakawa Ward in Tokyo, with a population of 240,000. The LDP has dominated politics in Shirakawa Ward over essentially the same time period that it has controlled the national government. Shirakawa Ward has experienced its share of political conflicts, but it has never been as intensely divided as Takeno-machi came to be over the years of the nuclear power plant standoff. Both ends of the Japanese political party system, from the LDP to the Japanese Communist Party, are represented in the Shirakawa Ward Assembly; however, the new nonaligned citizens' groups, groups such as Baba and Ota's Referendum Association, that changed the entire political landscape in Takeno-machi have yet to make an appearance in Shirakawa Ward. In the "Citizens and Assemblies" project I planned to examine how the different local political environments of Takeno-machi and Shirakawa Ward affected citizens' engagement with political life by looking closely at how local assembly members and candidates interacted with citizens to form constituency support groups.

Local assemblies are still a barely tapped resource for the study of Japanese electoral politics, perhaps because local-level institutions have so much less power than national-level institutions. Japan is a unitary state. This means that neither prefectural governments nor town and city governments are independent of the central government in the ways that states and cities are in the United States and other federalist political systems. The basic rules governing the numbers of local elected officials and the method of electing them are set by laws passed by the National Diet. Japanese prefectures do not have their own constitutions, and Japanese municipalities do not display the rich variety of approaches to self-governance seen in American towns. Moreover Japanese local governments depend on the national government for much of their financial basis. Most of the time local assemblies and executives find themselves occupied with small adjustments to community housekeeping, education, and social welfare programs that follow broad contours set by national policy makers, whether the issues are trash collection, park maintenance, or day care for children or the aged. Many local officials, including some I interviewed for this study, believe the most important work they can do for their community is buttering up national-level elected officials and bureaucrats and acting as a "pipe" directing public works projects and subsidies for community industries and programs from the national level down to the local community.[14]

But Japanese local governments are sometimes much more than national-local pipes. The admitted limits of their power notwithstanding, Japanese local governments have also long been a place from which change in the practice of Japanese politics historically emanates. The leadership of the LDP has managed the central government throughout the entire postwar period, but local governments have displayed a much wider range of leadership approaches. In some localities partisan competition barely exists, whereas in others local parties, networks, and groups experimenting with new means of enhancing citizens' power vis-à-vis central government bureaucrats and the LDP proliferate. Throughout the postwar decades progressive approaches that challenge conservative policy, from polluter regulation to public provision of health care for the elderly, have originated in local governments and later been reworked and adopted by the LDP at the national level.[15]

Importantly, from the prefectural level to the village level, Japanese local governments are organized differently from the parliamentary system operating at the national level. In the national-level parliamentary system there is no separation between executive and legislative institutions. The parliamentary structure emphasizes the power of the leading elite in each of the most well-established parties. Governments below the national level, however, are presidential in structure; that is, local executive and legislative institutions are formally distinct. Governors and mayors are elected separately from assembly members, so chief executives can never be completely certain that local assemblies will do their bidding. Many Japanese towns do not experience political conflicts like the nuclear power plant conflict in Takeno, but when conflicts do arise the formal separation of executive and legislative bodies provides a greater number of access points for citizen participation in those conflicts than does the Diet, where the chief executive is also a member of the parliament and leader of the party with the most Diet seats.

Japanese municipal assemblies are fairly large, at least in comparison to the American town councils with which readers may be familiar. This is especially true in Japan's small towns. For example, the assembly in Takeno, with a population of 30,000, had twenty-two members, whereas in Shirakawa Ward, with a population of 240,000, the local assembly had forty members.[16] The city council of Oak Ridge, with a population approximately the size of Takeno-machi's, has seven members. Oklahoma City, with twice the population of Tokyo's Shirakawa Ward, has an eight-person city council.[17] As I explain further in later chapters, the fact that Japanese local assemblies meet during the day on weekdays is a barrier to engagement for citizens employed full time. Nonetheless the large number of seats in a Japanese local assembly means that, especially in towns the size of Takeno, competing for a seat or two may be a realistic strategy for a small group that seeks to establish a public platform from which to voice its concerns. Winning a seat in a local assembly is not a guarantee of power in local politics, but once the path to a single seat has been exploited groups often find it possible to increase their visibility and expand their ambitions. This is, in part, what the Takeno Referendum Association was trying to do in the 1999 general elections.

Aside from the fact that Japanese local governments can be surprisingly dynamic fields on which to watch political conflict unfold, I had some good practical reasons for taking on the "Citizens and Assemblies" project when I did. Since the late 1990s the Japanese national government has been working to restructure local governments; it is simultaneously pushing for annexations and amalgamations to reduce the number of small towns and working to increase the autonomy and fiscal responsibility of local governments in policy areas such as health and social welfare by devolving some powers from the central government to the local governments.[18] The devolution push has encouraged activists, scholars, journalists, and others to reexamine the possibility for political innovation at the local level. That increased interest in local government provides a fertile environment in which to conduct research. Even in relatively stable localities such as Shirakawa Ward, local politicians expressed interest and concern about possible changes in the role of local government in the political system as a whole. I thought that environment of change would make local leaders more open to my questions, and as it turned out, I think they were.

The year I began my fieldwork, 1999, was also a Unified Local Elections year. Most elections for local assemblies and executives are held at roughly the same time every fourth year in April; that is why they are called the Unified Local Elections. By spending winter and spring in Japan during a Unified Local Elections year, I was able to observe elections in multiple communities at the same time. The heightened constituency outreach activity surrounding the elections gave me rich opportunities for watching how citizens engaged in politics. When I began my project I did not anticipate focusing on the way just a few men thought about the ethics of local power contests, but I did plan to interact closely with a relatively limited number of informants through participant-observer fieldwork, joining up with campaigns and observing how they built their constituency over a period of months.

In Tokyo I interviewed and observed a number of local assembly candidates of all political stripes, but I closely followed the election campaigns of two conservative LDP candidates for the Shirakawa Ward assembly: Shibata-san, a woman in her late fifties, who was a several-term veteran, and Takada-san, who is one of the two men about whom I write here. Eventually I dropped my fieldwork in Shibata-san's campaign to focus more fully on Takada-san. However, by keeping in touch with her periodically, I was able to broaden my understanding of the wider political environment of Takada's career. When I met him Takada was a novice trying to win the seat his father had held in the Shirakawa Ward Assembly for twenty-eight years. I attended Shibata-san's campaign events, watched her in assembly committees and on the assembly floor, and interviewed leaders in her supporters' organization, but I ended up spending more time with Takada-san than with Shibata-san. In Takeno I followed the campaigns of candidates connected with the Referendum Association and other groups that were allied with the Association in demanding the Takeno nuclear power plant vote and pushing for its result to be enacted as local policy. I spent the greatest share of my time with Baba-san, who had not only helped to found the Referendum Association but also served as its chief election strategist.

The campaign organizations in Takeno and Shirakawa contrasted nicely with each other. The Takeno Referendum Association and its allies emphasized transparency, inclusiveness, and expanded opportunities for citizen input into local decision making, whereas Shirakawa LDP leaders tended to interpret their role in local politics as that of expert mediators between citizens and national-level leaders. Politicians in the Shirakawa LDP expressed few worries about making their organization more transparent, but I saw that they worked hard to stay connected to LDP officials at higher levels of government and regularly demonstrated those connections to their constituents by inviting higher level officials and their representatives to attend ward-level constituency events. Takeno Referendum Association leaders openly scorned such efforts to make connections to higher level officials in established parties.

How My Focus Moved from Assemblies to Men

Before I moved into Baba's home in Takeno in March, I spent two months in Tokyo, following Takada-san as he prepared for the assembly elections in April. My main focus during those two months was the question of how assembly institutions structure citizen participation in politics. I still assumed the primary value of my informants in my project was in the larger trends they *represented,* not in *who they were as individuals.* In Tokyo I developed a rapport with my research subjects, particularly with Takada-san, whose bid to follow his father interested me at first because second-generation politicians are a distinctive and important part of the Japanese political landscape, especially in the dominant LDP. As far as I can determine, no one has collected figures on the percentage of *local* politicians who have inherited their political base from a relative who retires from office and asks his constituency support group to give its allegiance to a relative. However, in the late 1990s nearly 35 percent of LDP members of the national House of Representatives had inherited their political base from a relative. If we include politicians who were preceded by relatives into politics but were unable to use the constituency base of those relatives (perhaps because they represented different electoral districts or served at different levels of government), the percentage of second-generation politicians would be much larger.[19] In a gathering of Tokyo-area LDP politicians who were alumni of Takada's university, almost half were second-generation politicians in this larger sense.

Because Takada-san was an LDP-endorsed candidate, and because he sought to pursue his father's career in an assembly seat, he fit a category of Japanese politicians well-recognized by scholars. The time I spent with Takada-san in the early part of my fieldwork largely served to confirm what I already knew to be true about the LDP's candidate-centered campaign strategy. In my first meetings with Takada-san I did not have trouble seeing him as a mere product of a set of political structures I had been studying for a long time. I liked Takada. I would have been sad for him if his ambitions had been disappointed in the upcoming election. Nonetheless I was sure of my identity as a social scientist without a horse of my own in his race. To me the outcome of the Shirakawa Ward Assembly election was, quite literally, purely academic.

When I first went to live in Takeno I felt a similar sense of detachment from the candidates I met there. I sought out Baba-san only because he was one of the founders of the Referendum Association and therefore a likely source of further contacts to politicians and activists. As I said earlier, the Referendum Association played a key role in getting the Takeno local assembly to pass an ordinance to hold a popular referendum on the nuclear power plant project. When the referendum was held more than 60 percent of voters (in a turnout of nearly 90 percent) voted against the building of a plant within the municipality. Before the referendum movement Takeno had been represented by politicians who had, in large majorities, expressed support for a nuclear power plant; after the referendum it was clear how far the politicians were from the people they claimed to represent. The Takeno nuclear power plant was facing what seemed to be a classic not-in-my-backyard (NIMBY) resistance movement.[20] Just as Takada-san, in his bid to win his father's assembly seat for the LDP, represented a widely recognized and significant category of Japanese politicians, the nonparty politicians of the Takeno referendum movement represented a widely recognized kind of political activism. I had clear social science reasons for studying them and their leader, Baba.

Eventually I came to see the categories that first justified my studying candidates in Takeno and Shirakawa as merely a sort of launching pad for investigations of a different nature: into how a man's notion of himself as a man is related to his understanding of his responsibility for doing good. My Sunday conversation with Baba and Ota about Oak Ridge and Takeno began the thought process that drove me to shift from a more general examination of citizen engagement with local assembly politics to the struggles of two particular men to make ethical sense of their engagement with political power. To explain how this shift came about, I have to say a little bit more about Takeno-machi's nuclear plant conflict and Baba's role within it.

The nuclear power plant project in Takeno was first announced in the late 1960s, and over more than two decades only a minority of Takeno residents openly opposed it. In the 1970s and 1980s the town assembly and the mayor's office were dominated by independent conservatives with close ties to LDP politicians in the prefectural assembly and the National Diet. The Takeno-machi assembly demonstrated support for the nuclear power plant on several occasions over the years not only by voting to approve it, but also by voting to approve public works projects such as roads that made building and operating the plant easier and by using "cooperation money" provided by the power plant company, Tosho Power,[21] to fund town projects. Still, the plant wasn't built because the mayor's approval was required to sell a small piece of municipally owned land inside the site boundaries to Tosho Power, and over the years mayors had not been forthcoming with that approval.[22]

Because all the mayors in office during the time between the announcement of the project and the rise of the Referendum Association were conservative and LDP-affiliated, one might think they would have supported the nuclear power plant. After all, the project was in line with the policy of the LDP-controlled central government and the views of most members of the large and also LDP-affiliated majority in the Takeno Assembly. However, factional divisions within the LDP that reached from the national to the local level led to fierce conservative competition for the mayor's office. Controlling the mayor's office meant having access to a variety of political spoils for distribution to loyal supporters. Important among these was the mayor's influence over the awarding of lucrative public works contracts, many of which would undoubtedly be associated with the building of the nuclear power plant. The politicization of public works contracting is one of the most widely practiced forms of political corruption in Japan,[23] and from the accounts of Takeno-area journalists and a number of political leaders I interviewed *across* party lines, it was a leading form of corruption in Takeno.

Fierce competition among conservatives for control of the mayor's office dampened mayoral candidates' enthusiasm for projects of uncertain popularity. The citizens of Takeno did not openly protest the nuclear power plant in great numbers, but candidates nonetheless seemed to judge that most voters had trepidations about the facility. Because mayoral candidates wanted to appeal to the broadest base of voters while differentiating themselves from conservatives already in office, conservative challengers usually promised voters they would delay groundbreaking on the nuclear power plant while they conducted further safety studies. Once in office, conservative mayors (and their factional allies in higher levels of government) did their best to make use of the spoils available for distribution to conservatives who needed to be rewarded for advancing the faction's position in the electorate. Because distributing spoils in Takeno invariably meant accepting cooperation funding from the power plant company and pushing for plant-related public works projects, most incumbent mayors were eventually revealed to be nuclear power supporters. When that happened, conservative challengers who seemed more hesitant about nuclear power usually beat the incumbent in the next election.

The faction system that had shaped Takeno politics began to

change at the national level in conjunction with a change in the House of Representatives electoral system in 1994. In conjunction with the national change, the factional divisions among conservatives in local Takeno politics that had long helped to stall the nuclear power project also ended. Prior to 1994 three House of Representatives seats were elected from the Takeno area in a single, multiseat district; two of those seats usually went to LDP members who represented different factions. But in 1994 reforms at the national level divided the multiseat districts into single-member districts.[24] After 1994 only one elected official—in other words, only one LDP member (and hence, only one faction)—held a Takeno district seat at the national level. Key retirements among LDP Diet members from the Takeno district allowed conservative rivalries in the district to draw to a close. Thus the standoff over control of the mayor's office that had prevented a final decision on the nuclear power plant in Takeno-machi ended.

The mayor in office at the time the conservatives ended their standoff announced that the nuclear power plant would be built, and citizens who had opposed the plant began to panic. The Referendum Association stepped into the breach, demanding that citizens be allowed to express their preferences on the plant directly in an official referendum. The political maneuvers needed to compel the local assembly to pass a referendum ordinance were complicated but finally successful. In the process almost half of Takeno assembly seats were won from conservatives by new sorts of politicians from grassroots organizations that had not been involved in assembly politics before. A recall petition signed by slightly more than half of all registered voters in Takeno forced the LDP-affiliated mayor to resign. He was replaced by a member of the Referendum Association in a by-election. Citizens who had never before taken part in local politics had suddenly made a new role for themselves. The political changes in Takeno beginning in the mid-1990s had been truly extraordinary, and I thought they would provide a compelling contrast with the stability of conservative control in Shirakawa Ward. Any good political scientist would want to know why Takeno's citizens had changed town politics when citizens in most localities, Shirakawa Ward, for example, had not been similarly mobilized.

When I looked up Baba in January 1999 I was confident that the data I should seek in answering my question were the kind social scientists would expect. I collected statistics on the changing economic and demographic structure of Takeno. For example, I looked for data on the rise in the numbers of citizens who lived in Takeno but worked outside of the municipality. Some change of this sort seemed to be occurring. In 1975 the daytime population of Takeno was actually *larger* than the evening population by about 1,000 people, but by 1995 the reverse was true: well over 1,000 people, about 3 percent of the population, were absent from the town during the day. Town data also showed a steady increase in the conversion of agricultural land to residential use, a shift I could easily see as I bicycled around neighborhoods of new, single-family dwellings.[25] I further investigated the effects of the changes in the electoral system. I looked into the memberships of the Referendum Association and various groups long active in nuclear power plant opposition and conservative groups, and I began to posit theories about the political influence of democratic values fed to the postwar generations in the public schools. As I went about Takeno interviewing various participants about the events of the mid- and late 1990s, I patiently endured their tales about the contributions of specific individuals involved in the referendum movement, listening instead for the general themes that would help me to trace the institutional, economic, and perhaps ideological shifts that had brought about a new citizens' politics.

I would never deny that demographic, political, and cultural trends not unique to Takeno were factors in the changes in the Takeno power structure. For example, as the chronology I recounted earlier demonstrates, institutional changes, especially the changes in the electoral system for the House of Representatives of the National Diet, played a very important role in bringing to a head the nuclear power plant conflict in Takeno-machi in the second half of the 1990s. However, I no longer see such institutional factors as the most significant part of the change because, after Ota's questioning led me to remember the role Steve Gough had played in exposing a corrupt power structure in my own hometown, I began to listen more carefully to what my informants were saying. They were telling me about the capacity of one or two seemingly ordinary individuals to change everything. Moreover no matter where they stood on the nuclear power plant issue, my Takeno informants agreed that one man in particular had played an enormous role in changing their town: Baba. I know it's social science heresy, but I have come to believe them.

Social Science and the Man Who Makes a Difference

Baba is one of Takeno's greengrocers of power. He owns a small sake shop that has been owned by his family for more than 100 years. When

I met him he was in his late fifties, and for most of his life he had not pursued any role in local politics. Like Havel's greengrocer, Baba said he tried hard to appear generally supportive of whoever was in charge of local politics in the hope that he would be left alone and his business would thrive. In fact, because he sold sake and beer gift certificates that were popular among conservative politicians for use as small bribes to voters,[26] Baba walked a fine line each mayoral election period. He had the opportunity to make money as political purchases boosted sales, but if he sold to a losing candidate he risked losing future profits if the winner and his cronies decided to do their business elsewhere. Baba's strategy was to sell to both of the top candidates. Then, Baba explained, he could tell the winner he had been pleased to help with the winning effort and he could ruefully apologize to the loser for his insufficient efforts, stroking the egos of both men.

In the mid-1990s this go-along-to-get-along man changed. When it finally looked as if the nuclear power plant would be built, Baba gathered a few close friends (locally known as the Seven Samurai) who each contributed about $10,000 to establish the Referendum Association. As Baba tells it, he simply could not stand the idea that a nuclear power plant would be built when the citizens had never had their say. The politicians bribed the voters to win pro-plant majorities, he said, but the voters never thought of themselves as bribed. They thought, "Why not take the sake or whatever else was on offer in exchange for a vote that would not have changed anything anyway?"

Prior to the mid-1990s there had never been sufficient numbers of antiplant candidates running for the Takeno Assembly to allow voters to select an antiplant majority, nor had any viable mayoral candidates who did not belong to one of the LDP-affiliated factions presented themselves. Plant protesters had run for the mayor's office, but they had been poorly funded and affiliated with the far Left. But, Baba said, if the plant might really be built, then the citizens ought finally to have the right to voice their honest opinion. In the past all plant opponents had been branded as dangerous Reds by the local conservatives. Indeed even in 1999 some conservatives I interviewed insisted that Communists and Socialists were the driving force behind the referendum movement. Baba reasoned that, as he had spent most of his career supplying the sake for the bribes used to smooth the plant's progress, no one would accuse him of having always been a plant opponent. Because his children had finished their education, he and his wife believed they could take the hit to their business that standing up to the conservative hegemony would mean. Baba became the face of a new movement. He had been one of Havel's quiescent greengrocers supplying the obedience of the local community, and then he changed his mind.

Even local leaders who opposed the referendum and denied the validity of its result offered me a similar picture of Baba. His leadership of the referendum movement made it possible for voters who did not want to associate themselves with the Left to take a stand against nuclear power. At one point in the past, in fact, Baba had marched with a merchants' association in favor of the plant, something not only he but also one of the local Social Democratic Party leaders recalled for me. When an upstanding community businessman who clearly had no ties to the leftist organizations that historically opposed nuclear power demanded that citizens be given an opportunity to make their opinion of the plant project known, the conservatives lost the war to keep the plant debate out of the mainstream of local politics. As Steve Gough had done in Oak Ridge, Baba, an insider in the ruling establishment, opened a door to a serious challenge to a power structure three decades old.

THE POWER REMAINDER

Following Ota's probing questions on that rainy Sunday, I came to see my memories of Steve Gough's revelation of pollution secrets in my hometown as relevant to my understanding of Baba's leadership of the nuclear power plant referendum in Takeno-machi. Then I suddenly saw that, if Takeno were my home, I would probably have to agree with my informants who insisted that the individual moral wherewithal that finally drove Baba to take up leadership of the referendum movement was hugely important—not that he alone changed the town, but that his stance compelled others to make a sort of ethical reevaluation of their own. Baba's stance made obvious what, according to Havel, most power greengrocers (and social scientists) don't usually acknowledge: that the potential for a person of middle-range privilege to encourage resistance to a power structure is as real as the likelihood that he or she will reproduce that power structure by modeling obedience to it. Baba's ethics, I thought, really mattered.

My social science training, however, told me that Baba was simply lucky enough to be riding a wave not of his making. Politics had evolved, and his conversion was merely a symptom of that evolution. Neither Baba nor any other individual could be credited with the force for change. To think otherwise was to risk missing the forest for the trees, as my social scientist colleagues would tell me (and have told me). What, therefore, was I to do with the problem posed by my informants' confidence that a single determined individual can play a significant role in large structural changes? How was I to insist that the greengrocer of Havel's anticommunist polemic was a significant site for social science investigation?

For years I have wandered through this problem in utter frustration. I have chipped away at describing those parts of Takeno politics that were, in fact, shaped by big structures on which it is hard to find the mark of any particular individual. Part of my work in this book is to highlight the extent to which Baba, Takada, and those with whom they worked in pursuit of power in local politics were all bound by structural forms of power that could not be controlled at the local level. In this, the Tokyo case of Takada's LDP campaign helped greatly because, despite the difference in the two localities and in the power structures I found there in the 1990s, many similarities remained. Some of the key structures in both Shirakawa Ward and Takeno-machi, such as the Japanese party system, the electoral system, the demographics of ageing, and the contemporary trends in national and even global economies, played a powerful role in the fields in which the local-level political actors I studied operated. The operation of these structures has certainly not gone unseen by students of Japanese politics who have written widely on such topics.[27] Even sustained attention to such structures in the cases of Takeno-machi and Shirakawa Ward would not add much to the existing literature.

However, I have focused considerable energy on highlighting one persistent structural dimension of political life in both Shirakawa and Takeno-machi that has received little attention by political scientists: male gender. Japanese politics is unambiguously male dominated; hence most students of politics would find utterly without controversy the notion that the political opportunities of Japanese women are constrained by their gender identities. In fact, in my earlier research on Japanese housewives, I actually had to work hard to argue that, despite their sex, Japanese women playing home-centered gender roles could also play a role in public life.[28] Political scientists are doing a better job of describing the ways structures of gender shape political constraints for women,[29] but we have not studied gender as a big structure that constrains the power of political *men*. Men's studies more generally is a growing field in Japan, and some work has been done to trace how masculinist ideologies shape images of the Japanese state.[30] However, as far as I know, little research has been published that directly addresses the effect of male gender on Japanese men's political opinions or participation.[31]

Nor has there been much study of masculinity and politics in other nations. The social scientist Seungsook Moon does pay careful attention to the gendered political constraints on men in *Militarized Modernity and Gendered Citizenship in South Korea*. Moon traces some of the ways the postwar Korean state used financial incentives, threats of punishment, and especially a discourse of honorable Korean manhood to mold men into soldiers and workers to advance the state's agenda for rapid growth. She also argues persuasively that, even as Korea democratized and men once subjected to the state's pursuit of militarized modernization began to assert themselves against the state as democratic citizens with rights, they constructed their citizenship ideals and built their resistance movements in forms that made use of elements of military manhood practice and discourse from the authoritarian era.[32] Moon's work suggests that we should see discourses about masculine gender and the political system as shaping and constraining each other just as gender expectations constrain and shape women's engagement with political life.

The "Citizens and Assemblies" project that brought me to Shirakawa and Takeno-machi was not originally focused on gender. But I was interested in how citizens sought power in their communities through local assembly politics, and because of that I spent much of my time with male informants, the people in my field more likely to be in control of key decisions. Because I had studied women in politics as a young researcher, I was at first surprised by the extent to which the men I observed in Shirakawa and Takeno felt and described themselves as constrained in their choices *simply because they were men*. Even Baba, whom his fellow activists viewed as powerful, felt this way. Most of the time these men were like Havel's greengrocer: they were just doing what they thought was necessary to avoid trouble. They considered avoiding unnecessary trouble to be a fundamental requirement for being a grown man, one who could meet his primary responsibilities, which were usually characterized as those of a breadwinner and head of household. As I describe in more detail in later chapters, Baba often talked of the extent to which his movement was challenged by the fact that many of its strongest supporters had to "work for all they were worth" to maintain their family. In Tokyo Takada mused that men's obligations as breadwinners constituted a sense of mutual understanding among them, and sometimes a barrier to making rational choices about public policies.

As I was following political men and women in both sites, I was able to see that activist men (despite having the upper hand in terms of numbers and authority) described themselves in terms of constraint much more often than did activist women. That might be in part because women involved in political movements or running for office have already consciously decided that, for some reason, the constraints that are assumed to generally keep women out of politics don't apply to them. At any rate, the irony that the very men who seemed to have power were quick to dismiss such a claim with a reference to ever-present constraint made me want to know more about how this constraint worked.

Because I do think that preexisting power structures are highly determinative of any individual's choice for action, I work here to delineate some of the subtle ways in which social expectations about masculinity, a crucial system of constraints heretofore little remarked upon by students of politics, operate to shape the choices of my informants. Focusing on notions of masculinity as a power structure in local politics also offers a view into the operations of other structures that political science more commonly examines, such as political parties and markets. For instance, I observed that Takada was most likely to give specific form to the masculinist expectations placed on him or others when describing the challenges he confronted working his way up in the LDP. And conservative men in Takeno-machi sometimes explained their support for nuclear power as a way to support fathers whom they conceived of as struggling to make ends meet in a domestic economy challenged by global markets and hamstrung by Japan's lack of natural resources. Correspondingly, the pro–nuclear power conservatives characterized opponents of nuclear power as young, naïve women manipulated by extremist leftist outsiders. In fact masculinist rhetoric so permeated practices such as coalition building and was so often employed as a means of simplifying complex debates (including the one in Takeno about the possible effects of a nuclear power plant on the surrounding community) that I now believe it is quite hard to talk about political power structures without discussing the politics of masculinity that are mobilized to help keep those structures together.

My study focuses on men who are bound by their own and others' notions of what good men are, and are then embedded in the constraints of the institutions provided to them in Japanese local politics at a time of general constraint in the Japanese economy, at a moment in which the future seems altogether more constrained by the combined elements of Japan's ageing demographics and global competition. These constraints come out richly in the ways my informants— Takada and Baba and the men and women they work with in their communities' politics—describe the challenges of pursuing the politics they admire. But my informants are not satisfied to simply accept the constraints. In different contexts and to varying degrees, they think about and conceive of a use for that part of their way of being that is not entirely shaped by power structures seemingly out of their control. In fact they see making good use of this small portion of power as their responsibility. I think of this sense of responsibility as an ethical sense, and I will try to show how my informants respond quite differently to power, with significantly different effects on the political life around them, based on their different conceptions of what it means to be a good man.

Searching for power structures that shaped politics in Takeno-machi and in Tokyo's Shirakawa Ward, I came to focus on masculinity in particular. But in the end a part of the story was left unexamined, a remainder that could not be wholly explained by structure, even by a structure as subtle and pervasive as a hegemonic notion of gender identity. Explanatory formulae in the social sciences always have this remaining, unexplained element. Mostly social scientists ignore it; the remainder is likely to apply only to a specific case, and thus is of little use in the formulation of general hypotheses about how social processes work. But thanks to Baba and Ota's insistence that I think about Takeno-machi in relationship to my own hometown, and to the voices of the many Takeno activists who credited or blamed Baba in particular for the political situation in which they found themselves, I now believe that as social scientists, as teachers, and as students we must leaven our theoretical commitment to general trends and big structures with a measure of attention to the idiosyncratic capacities of ordinary individuals.[33]

That said, contemporary power theory's bias against the individual presents a serious challenge to the intellectual usefulness of my focus on the practical and ethical choices of particular men. Therefore, in the following section I briefly leave the men in my field sites in order to examine the theoretical ground that can be laid for my attention to individual-level choices about how to manage power. Following the late twentieth-century work of theorists such as Foucault, social, political, economic, and discursive structures replaced individuals as the dominant objects of analysis in studies of power. In other words, researchers shifted their attention from individuals caught up in power relationships to the larger social phenomena that predetermined many of the dimensions of those relationships. I agree with these structure-oriented theorists that looking beyond individuals for the dimensions and sources of power significantly expands our critical reach. But I also believe we must be careful not to neglect the small but significant spaces for individual moral agency that remain even in the almost over-whelming web of constraining structures.

If we tell the story of the Oak Ridge mercury scandal or the Takeno-machi referendum movement through their structural elements, as if Baba and Gough were not especially important, we leave out evidence of what Havel would call the "power of the powerless." If we describe the persistence of conservative traditionalism in a ward of Tokyo as if Takada were merely evidence of trends rather than a creator of them, we miss a chance to understand the process by which structural power is made and remade on an individual level every day, another view of the power of the powerless. At the heart of structural power opera-tions are individuals who make choices about what they think is right or, at any rate, best to do given the circumstances. Those choices then thwart or reproduce aspects of structures that constrain the fields in which those individuals live. The unexplained remainder is the loca-tion of ethical being. Capturing the power remainder as it is real-ized through the often stopgap actions of individuals enmeshed in the contingencies of their daily lives requires attention to small individual differences and statistically and historically "insignificant" events to a degree that is disquieting to social scientists. Yet if our scholarly accounts of power ignore the remainder, we inadvertently suggest that the power remainder—and the ethical opportunity it represents—do not matter.

How the Individual Got Lost in Power Theory

In 1957 political scientist Robert Dahl attempted to synthesize the state of modern power theory at that time. Dahl described power as a type of relationship, and his definition of that relationship was simple: "*A* has power over *B* to the extent that he can get *B* to do something that *B* would not otherwise do."[34] The case he chose to test his method was an examination of the influence U.S. senators exercise over their colleagues. Although Dahl pointed out that power was operative only in the context of specific relationships that vested some individuals with more power than others (e.g., teachers and students), he assumed that the locus of our attention should be on choices made by individuals with authentic and strategic preferences in those relationships. For example, to determine the relative power of different senators, he developed a rough means of measuring which senators were better able to compel other senators to vote differently from their original preferences. Dahl is certainly not the only student of power who has centered his analysis of the power relationship on individuals' preferences, but his formula for the power relationship epitomizes the way of thinking against which many contemporary power theorists now direct their critical force. Since the late twentieth century the study of power has gradually shifted in focus, first away from Dahl's political elites, then away from individuals altogether.

Clarissa Rile Hayward's *De-Facing Power,* written half a century after Dahl offered his definition of power, leaves behind the study of individual actors' power, as do most of the power studies produced by her contemporaries. *De-Facing Power* examines how power shapes the experiences of teachers and students in very different social and economic circumstances. The power Hayward seeks to understand and highlight is built into big structures such as cultural concepts of race, legal systems that support discrimination in markets, and notions of discourse that mark some uses of language as good and others as bad. Hayward argues that these structures have a profound influence on an individual's consciousness about his or her situation, and thus preempt the possibility of Dahl's A to either clearly know or pursue preferences for B.[35] For Hayward, a privileged A is as subject to power as is a less privileged B, even when A is more likely than B to benefit from the effects of power. "I propose reconceptualizing power's mechanisms," she says, "not as instruments powerful agents use to prevent the powerless from acting independently or authentically, but as social boundaries (such as laws, rules, norms, institutional arrangements, and social identities and exclusions) that constrain and enable action for all actors."[36]

Hayward's view of power as located in "faceless" social expectations, laws, or institutions rather than in an individual "with a face" is in itself quite a change from Dahl's formulation; Hayward also chooses different phenomena for investigation. Dahl wanted a power equation by which we might measure how one senator shapes the behavior of another. But Hayward's concerns are far from the chambers of the U.S. legislature. Instead, like many of her social scientist contemporaries who share an interest in power, Hayward wants a theoretical perspective that will help us to see how those with little access to the social and economic resources available to Dahl's senators are subjected to power. She needs a framework for studying subjection because she wants to explain the barriers to success faced by teachers and students in struggling public schools, not the resources senators have for squeezing cooperation out of colleagues.

Like that of many of her contemporaries, Hayward's reconceptualization of power owes much to Foucault's work on subjectivity. Foucault's understanding of the role of power in shaping individual identity drives Hayward's and others' claims that the most important questions about power are not the questions Dahl asked about *A*'s and *B*'s differential preferences and resources. Foucault insists that the acquisition of a subjectivity—in other words, the sense of self that drives *A*'s desire to get something from *B* that *B* does not want to provide—is, even in the case of a powerful *A*, a kind of submission to the sorts of social and institutional structures Hayward lists.[37] Foucault declares that power "is exercised only over free subjects and only insofar as they are free"; yet he also claims that those who conceive of themselves as free subjects have already been subjected to the workings of power on the most intimate level.[38] In Foucault's view, Dahl's questions about the extent to which any *A* can impose his or her preferences on a *B* who would have chosen otherwise if he or she had not been in a power relationship ignore more pressing questions about how the desires of both *A* and *B* were shaped in advance of their specific power relationship by other, larger power operations. According to Foucault, even the idea that we should view power as something one individual imposes on another is the product of our subjection to a particular mode of power, the discourse that teaches us to conceive of a person as an *individual* with a coherent identity and set of preferences. That individual-oriented discourse is the product of modern institutional arrangements.

In the modern state political and social institutions employ a form of "pastoral power" that evolved from the Christian church to regulate its subjects. So writes Foucault in the mid-1980s essay "The Subject and Power," in which he offers a summary of his thinking about power.[39] In the same way that the Christian church uses institutional structures and discourse conventions (such as orthodox interpretations of scripture) to help individuals choose to mold their lives around a direct relationship with an omnipotent God to whom all human beings are equally subject, modern states use social and political institutions, ideologies, and discourses to shape, categorize, and document the modern individual. In Foucault's reading, modern claims of autonomous individuality placed against a state (even when placed by a political elite A) are ironically *dependent* on, or *subject* to, the existence of a state that recognizes and thus makes cognizable that individuality, just as Christianity teaches that God gives men free will with which they may to choose to acknowledge their dependence on His omnipotence.

According to Foucault, pastoral power is an expansive "form of power which does not look after just the whole community but each individual in particular," and it "cannot be exercised without knowing the insides of people's minds" (422). Both our body and our consciousness are subject to institutional power managed according to pastoral visions and in accordance with state standards: "This form of power applies itself to immediate everyday life which categorizes the individual, marks him by his own individuality, attaches him to his own identity, imposes a law of truth on him which he must recognize and which others have to recognize in him. It is a form of power which makes individuals subjects" (420). Individuals may be conceived of as "free subjects" to the extent that they have "several ways of behaving" (428), but they are not able to constitute themselves *free* of the determining effects of power relations: "There are two meanings of the word 'subject': subject to someone else by control and dependence; and tied to his own identity by a conscience or self-knowledge. Both meanings suggest a form of power which subjugates and makes subject to" (420). Our subjectivity is the object of complex structures of power, and therefore our subjectivity is not any more our agent than it is an agent representing and reinforcing within us power whose sources are located outside of and beyond us.

Foucault's view of power broadened the scope of the study of power in important ways. His followers have looked far beyond the question of the extent to which A could impose his will upon B to ask how big structures shaped the way A came to see himself as an A and to ask how the structured subjectivity of B facilitated and often legitimized A's efforts to extract compliance from B. For example, for Hayward, the student of power in American schools, the Foucauldian turn in power theory means that locating power in the classroom requires looking beyond the intentions of individuals, such as teachers, whom we might ordinarily assume are powerful actors: "A teacher might invoke a rule of grammar to produce an intended effect on her student's speech and writing. But, as Foucault and others have argued, even conscious social action that effects intended results interacts with and is shaped by norms, conventions, standards, identities, and other institutionalized forms of action: codified actions that are, at times, historically remote, and the effects of which are unintended."[40] Students might think the teacher applying a rule of grammar to her judgment of class work is exercising power over her pupils, but in Hayward's analysis the seeming power relationship between teacher and student is only an effect, probably unintended, of the operations of larger structures, in this case a social norm that educated people adhere to a certain sort of language usage. The norm itself is shaped by and reinforces preexisting power inequalities such as race or class differences. In another example of the structural power Hayward provides, zoning laws and social practices constraining the real estate market options for inner-city nonwhites also constrain the tax bases from which local schools are funded and thus restrict the resources with which teachers operate.[41] Guided by this Foucauldian notion of power that makes no presumptions about the significance of individual intentions, Hayward is able to provide important insights into the puzzle of why schools and classrooms in different places perform differently, even when teachers are commonly dedicated to serving their students well.

The emphasis on structure in the study of power means that students of power dynamics have paid increasing attention to the ways social, economic, and political dynamics can privilege some groups and disadvantage others even while the participants in the advantaged group are certain in their own consciousness that they are not exercising power over others. This changed agenda in the study of power has allowed us to do a better job of tracing the subtle ways in which exclusions and hierarchies come into being. Another inheritor of this approach to power, the Japanese power theorist Sugita Atsushi, operates from a bibliography that overlaps a great deal with Hayward's and proffers examples of power in the real world that similarly direct us to the pervasiveness of structure in the formation of individual identity.[42]

Sugita examines the penetration of power into citizens' subjectivities through their acceptance of nationalist ideologies that helped to justify Japan's domination of East Asia during World War II (78). He points out that state-supported notions of Japan's "national language" constrain even power-critical discourse because the discourse must be expressed in a shared language already overburdened with meanings drawn from the use of the same language in prior contexts (89). In Sugita's view, asserting an identity is, by definition, a form of attachment to power operations beyond one's control. For example, seemingly liberating universal categories such as "we citizens" are burdened with contradictory meaning from the moment of their construction. Even in social contract societies the biological children of citizens have much greater access to citizenship than children of noncitizens, regardless of whether they claim allegiance to their society's fundamental social contract (66–69).

The structure turn in power theory has also encouraged scholars to seek the ways that marginal subjects, such as housewives and tenant farmers, can occasionally manipulate structure to their advantage. The political anthropologist James C. Scott has produced classic studies of the possibilities for resistance that highly structured social interactions afford the oppressed and marginalized. As a participant-observer in Southeast Asian agrarian communities, Scott painstakingly collected evidence of the "weapons of the weak" such as poaching by peasants on the estates of the powerful. He has also explored how oppressed groups such as slaves are able to use the strategies of joking or excessive, dramatic politeness, what he calls "hidden transcripts," to safely criticize those in power.[43] I have described how housewives who became active in the public sphere sometimes used their gendered identification with (and hence structured subjection to) the housewife role as a shortcut means of highlighting their critical, alternative politics and "ordinary person" point of view. Most of the time, being seen as a housewife disadvantaged women in politics, yet sometimes the very stereotypes that seemed to justify a view of women as unqualified for power served instead to make them seem less corrupt and more caring than male competitors.[44]

Yet although we are ever more discerning about the subtle means by which power conditions the terms of human relationships and determines the grammar of resistance, post-Foucauldian power theory remains problematic in two big ways. First, we have difficulty accounting for how an individual can exercise a structure-changing agency despite the fact that Foucault himself argued that the existence of power assumes resistance. Even when we study resistance we tend to emphasize (as both Scott and I have) its structural dimensions. We study, for example, the patterns of resistance discourses that make them effective against oppressors. Second, although our attention to the ways structure *subjects* individuals has encouraged us to take the study of power beyond Dahl's influential senators to my politically marginalized housewives or Scott's peasants and slaves, we have overlooked an enormous field of power: the world of political, social, and economic actors who are neither national elites nor marginalized subalterns. This is the not-quite-elite, not-quite-marginal field in which individuals like Baba and Takada—well off, male, and sometimes influential in local politics in a rich nation—find themselves.

Post-Foucauldian power theory helped me to see why most housewives do not run for public office (and even why women feel compelled to call themselves housewives). It helps Hayward and Sugita to see why historical inequities among racial and gender groups that began in outright discrimination can be sustained by reference to "impartial" notions of belonging.[45] Similarly, contemporary theory has helped Scott trace the irrepressible urge for agency demonstrated in the creative (if highly constrained) use subaltern groups sometimes make of their structured identities. But structure-oriented power theory does not do a very good job yet of talking about whether individuals with some access to structural privilege—such as Baba and Takada, who use their resources as well-connected, affluent community members to seek power over their local polities—have the capacity to make structure-changing choices about their use of power, even as they draw from existing structures the privileges that give them power to act in the ways they do and notions of selfhood (their subjectivities) that tend to naturalize their privileges.

The paradox of applying Foucauldian approaches to the study of power is that, on the one hand, structuralist approaches effectively broaden the field in which we might look for the operations of power while, on the other hand, considerably narrowing the theoretical ground on which to base a claim of authentic resistance. As the anthropologists Nicholas Dirks, Geoff Eley, and Sherry Ortner explain, this paradox has been especially troubling in areas such as gender study, where producing a foundation for effective resistance to oppressive power is one of the main motivations behind seeking a richer understanding of power in the first place.[46] "We can learn a great deal about the mechanism of sexual oppression . . . by conceiving of the subject as a cultural project," says Linda Alcoff, describing the usefulness of Foucauldian theory for feminists. Nonetheless Alcoff also asserts that Foucauldian deconstruction of the troubled notions of a female subject poses a dilemma: "You can not mobilize a movement that is only and always against: you must have a positive alternative, a vision of a better future that can motivate people to sacrifice their time and energy toward its realization."[47]

Sugita wrestles with a similar problem. He reminds us that Foucault always assumes that the subject constructed within power relations is never *completely* constructed by those power relations; cases in which a subject enjoys no possibility of resistance Foucault considers domination, something very distinct from "a power relationship."[48] But Sugita also acknowledges that many students of social life feel frustrated by the Foucauldian claim that even at the moment of resistance we can never escape our constitution by and dependence on structural power. Some, Sugita admits, see this part of Foucault's view of power as more likely to induce political apathy than resistance. Yet Sugita insists that real resistance is a possibility. He offers Japan's local citizens' initiative referendum movements, including the kind of movement that took place in Takeno-machi, as examples of how citizens assert agency while enmeshed in structures that control them. In the referendum movements, he explains, citizens turn state structures to unexpected uses and challenge how the state understands and to whom the state assigns the costs of meeting basic social needs such as water management, energy, and security. At the beginning of these localized confrontations with power, citizens may understand themselves through subjectivities that have been shaped by the power structures they are fighting, but as an effect of their confrontations with power they begin to elaborate new subjectivities (90–91).

Sugita extends post-Foucauldian power theory by directing us to the ways freedom can be culled in the midst of power relationships through "localized," "individualized," and "heterogeneous" resistance movements. He draws on a number of examples from contemporary Japanese politics, indicating that his readers should contemplate how they might act on his insights into power and resistance in their own local "power spaces" (90, 101–102). Beyond briefly referencing news-making controversies, however, he does not tell us how, as social scientists, we might study (and teach) these heterogeneous efforts at asserting human freedom within and among the power structures that shape us. Sugita's theoretical push beyond Foucault to the promise and uncertainty of individualized resistance is compelling, but surely we need richer data than a list of protest movements to understand exactly how structured subjectivities can transform themselves into free agents. Just as Sugita argues for the importance of the "concrete" and "local" qualities to effective resistance, I would argue that we need more concrete, more "individualized" social science writing about power.[49]

Accounting for Agency

One inheritor of Foucault's theoretical legacy, social theorist Michel de Certeau, insists that the reason we do not see much attention paid to the "localized" and "individualized" aspects of agency is because power theorizing is bound up with institutionalized, "scientific" concepts about what constitutes scholarly knowledge, and those concepts militate against careful examination of particular individuals' engagements with power in specific situations. Certeau describes the difficulty theorists of power face when they try to see how power is threatened in everyday life by positing the problem of capturing the "operation" performed by people who consume a potentially dominant mass media discourse: "Once the images broadcast by television and the time spent in front of the TV set have been analyzed, it remains to be asked what the consumer *makes* of these images and during these hours. The thousands of people who buy a health magazine, the consumers of newspaper stories and legends—what do they make of what they 'absorb,' receive, and pay for?"[50] The answers to Certeau's questions are important for our understanding of how fully our research subjects are subjected to hegemonic discourse structures, for example, but the sort of evidence that works best in meeting social scientific standards does not help us get those answers.

Social scientists are especially wary of misinterpreting broad social phenomena by placing too much importance on the experiences of a single, inevitably unique individual. Mostly this wariness makes sense; knowledge about social life that applies to only a handful of people can dangerously bias our accounts of our research subjects. And the audience for our work might quite reasonably worry about the usefulness of the perspective of a distinct few, particularly if those few are not recognizable as extraordinarily influential elites. Social scientists commonly feel more confident about the accuracy of claims about the social world that can be supported with statistical evidence, demonstrating a high probability that a given claim would be true in many cases. Even when statistical data are not available social scientists usually work to emphasize the fact that the cases from which they are making generalizations are, to the extent possible, representative of larger populations. As I explained earlier, when I justified (both to myself and to granting agencies) my choices of Takeno-machi and Shirakawa Ward as locations for my original fieldwork on citizens and assemblies, I did so on the basis of the fact that the two localities represented important phenomena visible throughout Japan: the persistence of LDP dominance and the growth of threats to that dominance taking new forms such as citizens' referendum movements.

Such claims of representativeness require and validate at least a simple practice of counting, even if they cannot be grounded in anything resembling statistical significance. Yet although counting offers a social scientist basic reassurance that her work is social science, Certeau still argues that it should not give her confidence that her work has accounted for all of the significant elements of a power relationship. "What is counted is *what* is used, not the *ways* of using," he says (35, emphasis in original). Certeau argues that ordinary individuals' "ways of using" structures around them, such as the imagery of the desirable self that is presented time and again in health magazines, involve "ruses" and "tricks," a *"polytheism of scattered practices"* that allow individuals to subvert the power that would otherwise subject them (38–41, 48, emphasis in original). But of course those ruses against mass media imagery often take place at the level of individual readers and are, by their very nature, not representative of wider trends.

When power theorists look for evidence of resistance, as I did with my previous study of housewives and Scott did with his studies of peasants and slaves and Sugita did in his listing of localized social movements, we do capture some of the practical tactics Certeau points to—or at least we capture evidence that some of those tactics have successfully interfered with the reproduction of preexisting power structures. In his work, for example, Scott explicitly acknowledges Certeau's perspective.[51] Conceivably, if we are willing to push even further in our investigations of our informants' ways of using the structures around them, we can yet deepen our understanding of the resources that any ordinary person, Havel's greengrocer or my political activist of medium privilege, for instance, can mobilize to press his or her moral agency through or against structure.[52] However, Certeau's illustrations of this more ambitious search for the scattered power practices of individuals highlight the difficulty we will have in making a full account of ways of using structure if we stick to social science expectations that our work remain above the level of the idiosyncratic individual.

As an example, Certeau offers a schoolchild who draws graffiti on his textbook despite the fact that he will be punished for doing so;

the student marks through his use, or consumption, of the book the symbol of institutional power (the textbook) with his own assertion of authority (31–40). Unfortunately, Certeau says, social scientists seek a knowledge they can "transfer" from its field to an accepted academic practice of analysis, what Certeau calls the social theorist's "laboratory," and so theorists do not record these small subversions (20). Certeau's textbook example is especially sharp for me because Baba actually used recollections of resistance in school, including marking up his textbooks, as means of explaining the source of his later resistance to Takeno's conservative political establishment. Most social science approaches to explaining the referendum movement in Takeno would ignore Baba's stories of his textbooks, in the way I first tried to ignore my informants' focus on the personalities involved in the Takeno conflict. Individuals' personalities and histories of high school graffiti are seen as irrelevant to the general pattern of political events that social scientists are usually aiming to explain. But what is merely surrounding confusion to a social theorist may be the source of a political actor's notion that it is his destiny to defy the community of town fathers to which he has belonged for decades; that notion of destiny may be what encourages him to pay the personal costs of his defiance.

If we believe that society's power structures are daily reproduced by the actions of individuals who are themselves the product of those structures, then when we are confronted with the defection of an individual who has been a faithful reproducer of the structures around him we should want to know why he defected. We should be especially curious when the defector, like Baba-san in Takeno-machi, is a power middle manager, both generally well served by the power structures that have shaped him and far too ordinary to hope to dominate them on his own. Similarly, we should want to know why others, like Takada-san in Tokyo, develop narratives that help them to continue their participation in the reproduction of power structures about which they feel, quite self-consciously, ambivalent. Pursuing the extent to which even the men who are at the heart of public life in the communities of a rich and powerful nation are themselves constrained, we can appreciate how small any man's share of power may be. But by moving on beyond the constraints to take account of how individual men work to make use of their bit of power, we can also see that some space is left for an individual's mark. As we follow Baba and Takada as each seeks to understand the mark he ought to make, we can see something more: how tremendously important are an individual's particular ideas of what constitutes good.

Of course Baba's and Takada's differing notions of what it means to be a good man are not drawn on blank slates. Both men borrow proudly from what each believes constitutes the best of the traditions of Japanese manhood. Thus in energetically pursuing the idiosyncratic attempts of two individuals to come to a personal conclusion about the proper way to seek and wield power, we come back to the universe of structures, this time discursive structures, in which they seek to be responsible individuals. Perhaps such an investigation cannot tell us which is more determinative, preexisting power structures or the wherewithal of a self-conscious and committed individual. Nonetheless we can see here two models of how the tensions between circumstances and ethics can be managed.

What I have here is only my understanding of the way two men think about what it would take for them to be good men who do good through politics. I chose the men from field sites I saw and still see as representative of important aspects of contemporary Japanese politics. The pictures of them I draw here are based, as will be obvious in the chapters to come, on countless hours of conversation and observation over months of political activity. Between my first work in 1999 and the writing of this book I visited again with these men, asking them to answer more questions about their political involvement and even asking them directly to define for me who a good man is. My view of these men is doubtless not the view they would offer of themselves; it is, at any rate, limited in severe ways even I can see: by the qualities of my own personality, by the time in politics and in their lives that I knew them, by the vagaries of their memories and my own (however much I struggled to support mine by writing field notes in the wee hours of the night). Yet if, with an imperfect record of two idiosyncratic individuals, I am unable to offer a definitive new direction for power theory, I still offer this account as the beginning of a new library of tactics for using the ethical remainder of structure's operations, a library from which I hope power's middle managers might seek insights.

WHAT FOLLOWS

The rest of this book is divided into five chapters. In chapter 1, "Breadwinners," I use the Takeno-machi case to investigate the way widespread expectations that men will be family breadwinners often suppress men's political engagement by classifying political activity as a hobby for those men who have already secured their family's economic well-being. Chapter 2, "The Inheritor," moves to the Tokyo field site, where I explain how ward assembly candidate Takada escaped the need to establish his breadwinner credentials by portraying himself as the filial heir of a Takada family tradition of self-sacrificing manhood. In chapter 3, "The Paradox of Masculine Honor," I describe how the notions of filial duty and honor that sustain Takada's political career also constrain him to deference to masculine hierarchies in ways he sometimes finds troubling.

I move back to my Takeno fieldwork in chapter 4, "Cheating as a Democratic Practice," where I follow Baba's narrative of his midlife turn to politics, paying particular attention to his assertion that his resistance to the conservative male hierarchies of Takeno-machi, though justified by the circumstances, is also a kind of defection from the demands of responsible manhood. Throughout the book I work to point out where the experiences of Takada and Baba overlap or present clear contrasts, but in chapter 5, "The Art of the Gut," I look at the two men together. I describe men's uses of strategic silence, or the "art of the gut," to manage power. Then I explore how the effectiveness of the art of the gut helps to explain why even men who are self-consciously working against some masculinist hierarchies hold fast to their male gender identities. My conclusion, "Salad and Cigarettes for Breakfast," returns to the themes I address in this introduction. I describe how badly a tight focus on one or two individuals endangers a social scientist's sense of appropriate distance from the subjects of her study, and I explain why running such a danger is also sometimes a democratic project worth the risk.

CHAPTER I

Breadwinners

Takada-san looked weary and sounded miserable. It was an unusually warm Saturday morning in January, still almost three months before the beginning of the official campaign period for the 1999 Shirakawa Ward Assembly elections in which Takada-san hoped to follow in his father's footsteps. As is commonly the case in Japanese elections, Takada-san's efforts to win endorsement from the Liberal Democratic Party and round up supporters for his bid had begun the previous fall, when the legally recognized, ten-day public campaign period was more than half a year away. Takada-san described the emotional strain he was feeling as we chatted in the campaign office he had set up in the home he shared with his parents.[1] We were planning to go together to the neighborhood association's *mochi-tsuki* festival, a traditional New Year event where highly glutinous *mochi* rice is made into chewy cakes by pounding boiled rice in a large wooden container with a huge wooden mallet until it turns into a springy-sticky ball, which is then cut into pieces and used for making sweets and soups. Because the mallets are so heavy, they are usually wielded in turns by the neighborhood men, the way an old-fashioned ice-cream maker might be passed from person to person, each turning the crank for a few minutes at a time. The festival was an opportunity for Takada-san to show himself to his neighbors as a strong and earnest young man committed to preserving community traditions, and therefore the festival was a good place to drum up support for his campaign.

Takada-san and I sat chatting in his office before it was time for him to appear at the festival. His father was phoning Takada-san's key campaign advisors. One of these advisors had heard that the local television station, which broadcasts ward news on a local-access cable channel, was going to film the event. They couldn't decide what Takada-san should wear to the *mochi* festival. A suit would look professional but might convey an unwillingness to join the volunteers in the sweaty work of pounding the *mochi;* more casual clothing risked portraying Takada-san as insufficiently serious for elected office. At last they settled on the combination of suit pants and shirt, topped with an athletic-looking windbreaker bearing his university crest. Takada-san told me he was getting weary from the seemingly endless round of events he attended in search of supporters. Still, he dressed obediently in the outfit his father and advisors chose, and we set off for another event at which he would have to grin *niko niko* (as if he were overflowing with happiness) and present himself to his potential constituents more convincingly than his grim outlook warranted.

At the *mochi* festival Takada-san seemed to have worn the right clothes, and contrary to the morning's glum start the event worked very well for him. Only two others wore suits, one an advisor of Takada's and the other a female incumbent of the ward assembly, a member of the Communist Party. As expected, the local television station focused on the two candidates for ward seats. The Communist assemblywoman gamely took up the mallet and attempted to pound the *mochi*. But she managed its weight as awkwardly as did I and, I'm sure, most of the women who tried it. Once she finished her brief effort at pounding she was without a task or companion. Most of the other women were wearing aprons and already very busy preparing and distributing the food, and the assemblywoman did not seem to have many friends among the men in attendance. Takada-san, on the other hand, managed the mallet beautifully. He was then in his late thirties. At about six feet he is quite tall for a Japanese man, and with his even features he is better looking than average. He was younger and taller than most of the men present, and he swung the mallet hard, hitting the wooden bucket with a steady, sonorous rhythm. His athletic-style college jacket accentuated his youthful prowess. Everyone, especially the women, murmured approvingly.

Counting both the seniors who waited in the warm gymnasium for their *mochi* and the few children who had been brought to the event by their parents, the average age of the festival attendees was around fifty. As the organizers explained to me, the attendance was not what it had been in times past. As one put it, the idea of previous generations, that one should engage in a community activity because "it will make everybody happy," had been replaced by a more self-centered vision of spending free time on "things that are fun." No one said it directly, but it was obvious that thirty-something Takada-san, swinging a heavy mallet with ease and enthusiastically slurping up large quantities of the women's pork and *mochi* soup, represented the possibility that younger generations would return to the spirit of community about which older men had spent the day reminiscing. Takada-san simply looked like a man who should represent his ward.

Some workings of masculinity in politics are easy to see. In Japan, and in most countries, the most obvious of these is the overwhelming number of elected offices held by men. In 1999, when I was first doing fieldwork for this book, the rural town of Takeno became one of the national leaders in the percentage of assembly seat holders who were women: 26 percent. Women hold fewer than 10 percent of the seats in typical local assemblies, and female representation in rural assemblies is even lower on average. During the April 2007 Unified Local Elections, three election cycles after the election I observed, women won a total of 8.4 percent of seats in town and village assemblies nationwide, an increase of more than 2 percentage points over the result of the previous elections in 2003.[2] The story of Takada-san's appearance at a traditional New Year festival represents another of the obvious ways masculinity often seems to be at work in politics. He used his masculine appearance and his physical vigor to connect to constituents who worry about the well-being of their community and its traditions as people's habits change and society ages. In the festival setting Takada-san had obvious advantages over the female incumbent. He was comfortable playing a man's role in a highly gendered setting; she couldn't both play the woman's role and present herself as a competent community leader. Actually, given that she couldn't really swing the heavy *mochi* mallet, she seemed, at least in this setting, unable to be *either* a proper woman *or* a community leader.

If we couple Takada-san's demonstration of his masculinity as a symbolic resource with statistics describing the dominance of men in elected office, the gendering of Japanese politics seems clear. Men can do things in politics that women cannot. The statement is true enough, yet describing Japanese politics as simply male-dominated eliminates important elements of gendered power from our analytical view.[3] Because Takada-san uses a masculinist performance to seek recognition and ultimately political power from his constituents, his success in politics seems at least in part dependent on his being male.[4] It is tempting to conclude that he is mobilizing a resource that all men have to some degree, that the only difference between him and another man who might not be able to best Takada-san in a *mochi* display would simply be his possession of fewer of Takada-san's "manly" traits—insufficiently strong arms or an insufficient sense of duty, for example. In fact, as we stood in the schoolyard discussing the small festival attendance, the organizer who had mused about the changed habits of young people gestured up at a high-rise apartment building across from us. The organizer said that he didn't know the sort of young people who lived in the building and that he had no way of meeting them. He suggested that young people had chosen not to pursue their connections to the community because they had other, more enjoyable (and selfish) things to do. Arguably this presumption that the young people in the high-rise lacked a will toward community offered a contrasting background against which Takada-san's performance of traditional masculinity was especially attractive to the festival-goers.

Yet the assumption on the part of the festival organizer that Takada-san had a sense of (manly) duty that the young people in the high-rise did not have may not be quite fair. Most men are as excluded from political life as are most women. Men's political exclusion is not the result of their inability or unwillingness to do their manly duty. Nor is it the result of a general breakdown of cultural expectations about community obligations or masculine roles, although changes may well be occurring. Actually, the problem is quite the opposite: most Japanese men are not involved in politics because they are too encumbered by the expectations placed on them *as men* to engage their citizenship in an active way. If most young men cannot share in Takada-san's pursuits, then their turning out to watch him swing the *mochi* mallet is much more important to Takada-san and his campaign advisors (who are looking for every vote they can find) than it is for the young men themselves, who might quite rationally view the festival as just one of many potential opportunities for pleasure on a Saturday morning.

In Tokyo I focused on Takada-san's campaign, which played itself out through a range of community activities, and so I was daily immersed in a world of men who are sufficiently privileged to manage a full engagement with political life. From that perspective, the festival organizer's complaint about the poor community values of disengaged young people was quite persuasive. However, in Takeno-machi, as I followed the efforts of Baba-san and his fellow Referendum Association leaders seeking to round up candidates to fend off the power of conservatives similar to Takada-san in their local assembly election, I came to a fuller understanding of the problem of men's political disengagement. I watched the Referendum Association leaders enter into a head-on confrontation with how the expectations of masculine duty, in particular a man's duty as a breadwinner, constrain men's citizenship. In fact, young and middle-aged men were so generally marginalized in Takeno-machi's political world that, as male-dominated groups of local activists tried to stop the building of a nuclear power plant, they found themselves forced to rely on the electoral muscle of women, in some cases their wives and daughters. In the second half of the 1990s women became the standard-bearers in elected office for the challenge to conservative hegemony in Takeno-machi. Although prior to 1995 only a single woman had ever served in the twenty-two-member Takeno Town Assembly, by 2004 seven women held seats and Takeno had become a leading example of women's advancement into formal political power. These women brought into politics not only opposition to the nuclear power plant favored by the town's conservative leaders, but also the "care" agendas and anti-organization constituency networks that they used to distinguish their contributions to politics as particularly female. Accordingly, because men involved in Takeno antinuclear politics could not take office themselves, they ceded to women both formal political power and some of the symbolic advantage we might have thought would be the privilege of community-minded men.

In the past decade Japanese female politicians have received enormous attention for their growing presence in local politics and for their demands that politics focus on issues neglected by the postwar conservative regime. The voices of these new women politicians are often summed up as the *kurashi* or *seikatsu* (daily life) perspective. Making creative use of the widely accepted stereotype that women are closer to the home than men are, these women emphasize the importance of an ordinary citizen's voice in politics, focus on quality-of-life or "care" issues, and pursue constituency mobilization strategies that downplay organizational hierarchy and professionalism in favor of what is often called the "handmade" election. In my own work I have called this sort of politics "bicycle citizenship" to contrast it with the largely male world of established political parties characterized by institutionalized hierarchies and considerable resources (which I have called "taxi politics").[5] Just as there are places, in the midst of traffic jams and down narrow streets, for example, where bicycles are a more effective form of transportation than cars, the home-centered, female politicians I call bicycle citizens can do some sorts of political work more effectively than the elite men of taxi politics.[6]

Unfortunately nonelite men cannot as easily use their outsider status as a symbolic ground from which to resist the political status quo and demand a new politics with greater emphasis on broad participation, ethical clarity, flexibility, and sensitivity to the needs of the weakest members of society. Like bicycle citizen women, nonelite men are excluded from the centers of political power in a variety of ways; however, the source of men's political exclusion differs from that experienced by women. The limit of a nonelite man's political participation is often powerfully influenced by gender expectations about men's work outside the home as household breadwinners. Determination to meet these expectations constrains nonelite men's capacity to voice complaints about the terms of their exclusion from politics. In fact, when political involvement threatens their breadwinner capacity, men may be at least as constrained by the culture of gender-role expectations as women are. Further, Japanese men cannot draw on their sex as a shortcut symbol of their challenge to status quo politics in the way that women can claim to represent the viewpoint of a daily life nurturer simply by being women. It is easy to see how gender expectations contribute to women's exclusion from politics. Men's gender-based exclusion is comparatively harder to see but persists nonetheless. Japan's political system is male dominated, but *most* Japanese men, unable to play either the taxi politician or the bicycle citizen role, are not likely to play a part in it.

Students of gender and politics have documented how widely accepted notions of womanhood affect or are affected by women's participation in politics but have neglected to think about the ways gender conditions men's participation.[7] Japanese female politicians are using their experiences as housewives and mothers to justify themselves as spokespersons for ordinary citizens on issues such as care for the aged, consumer and environmental protection, and freedom of information. That story deserves attention because the policy questions on which women's voices have been effective are important ones, and the growing involvement of women in the political process demonstrates a significant change in gender-role expectations for women.[8] However, as paradoxical as it may sound, the focus on the rise of women's "caring politics" as an achievement of *female* politicians obscures the fact that even where women are gaining a new political voice, men's voices remain curiously controlled. The growing field of men's studies has done much to uncover the ways gender expectations constrain men's life choices, sometimes to the extent that men must fight employers and social norms in order to fully participate in some aspects of life to which they would seem to have a natural right, such as fatherhood.[9] Nonetheless, social scientists make little effort to examine how men's actions in politics are shaped by notions of masculinity.[10]

Social scientists' silence on the connection between masculinity and politics means we ignore the ways men in politics are constrained by their gender; by association we imply that a politics that does not include women is not lacking in anything other than female bodies, that women's use of the politics of bicycle citizenship is simply their attempt to substitute for a more whole politics they could practice freely if they were men. But is that true? By looking at how gender kept some men in Takeno-machi from running for office in a challenge to postwar conservative hegemony, we can see how the gendered notion of men as breadwinners works to keep men from practicing the politics of bicycle citizenship even when that is precisely what they wish to do. If men, because they are men, find it difficult to practice certain kinds of important politics, then a political world in which few women participate is gravely distorted—not only because women's voices are missing but also because gender expectations repress men's ability to speak for the full diversity of political needs *men* have. As a structure of social expectations that predetermines which sorts of behaviors are normal and good, gender places remarkable constraints on the men in my two field sites. The evidence that what is possible in democratic political life is reduced by the connection between the gender identity of the men who dominate politics and the choices of men more generally to engage or resist engagement with community politics should provoke a larger reexamination of the marginal status social scientists have given to the study of gender in political life.

WHEN MEN'S POLITICAL OPPORTUNITIES SUFFER IN COMPARISON TO WOMEN'S

To understand the sort of politics men's voices have often been excluded from, we need to know something about the role some women have played in the Japanese political system. As bicycle citizens, women have made their way into politics precisely where cynicism about the policies and practices of postwar leaders has been at its highest. Since the late 1970s increasing numbers of women have entered formal political arenas. Despite the generally low levels of women's representation in elective office across Japan, in population-dense prefectures such as Tokyo, Saitama, and Kanagawa women have occupied more than 10 percent of local assembly seats for the past couple of election cycles.[11] Following the 1999 local elections in Saitama, women took 14.2 percent of all city (as opposed to village, town, or prefectural) seats.[12] In Osaka women's move into politics is attracting attention.[13] These trends have continued in the most recent elections. Women made news from Ōiso, Kanagawa Prefecture, in June 2003 by capturing 50 percent of the seats in the town assembly.[14]

The rise of the number of women in elective office in disaffected urban areas is not the only significant aspect of women's growing participation in politics. Just as the growing numbers of female elected officials attract attention, so does their tendency to justify their claims to power on the basis of their capacity to make quality-of-life concerns central to public life. Where quality-of-life challenges to conservative dominance spring up, so does the political participation of women. Most of the Ōiso female politicians got their start in a citizen's movement advocating environmental protection.[15] Similarly ten women were elected to the thirty-six-member Tokorozawa City Assembly in suburban Saitama Prefecture following the 1999 scandal over dioxin-contaminated spinach caused by trash incineration in Tokorozawa.[16] The election of these ten women was an increase of nearly half again on the previous historic record of seven women. Of course scattered episodes such as the rise of women in the Tokorozawa Assembly during a local environmental crisis or the rise of women in politics, even to the status of mayor in Zushi City during a dispute over the disposition of forest land there,[17] cannot decisively prove that quality-of-life challenges are avenues for increasing women's participation in formal political arenas. But the coincidences are more than a little provocative.

In each election cycle, reports from around the country document the slow but steady advance into formal political arenas of women bearing a bicycle citizen's message. For men, however, the story is different. As the changes I followed in Takeno-machi illustrate, women find success with quality-of-life challenges to the postwar political establishment more easily than men do. Notions of masculine power provide men with some political benefits, but the breadwinner expectations that come with masculine power are also disabling, especially for men in similar middle-class positions as those occupied by the female bicycle citizen activists. To put it more baldly, Japanese men who want to mount a quality-of-life or "ordinary citizens'" challenge to the underpinnings of the postwar policy consensus and political power structure are often dependent on women to do it for them.

TAKENO'S NEW GENDER REGIME

As I explained in the introduction, in Takeno in the mid-1990s citizens' groups defeated a long-serving mayor and an overwhelming conservative majority in the Takeno Town Assembly to bring about an official (local government-sponsored) referendum on whether a nuclear power plant should be built in their municipality. Other attempts to stop the power plant in the nearly three decades prior to the rise of the referendum movement had been unsuccessful. Anti–nuclear power groups had sponsored several different men as candidates for mayor, but these candidates were branded Reds by the conservatives, who dominated local politics from the end of World War II until the late 1990s. Moreover antiplant groups could not amass sufficient campaign funds to compete with the notoriously well-funded and corrupt conservatives with ties to the power company that planned to build the plant. When the two local factions of conservatives that had competed to control town politics joined together, the company planning to build the nuclear power plant took the sitting mayor, who had spent several terms "considering" nuclear power plant safety, on a power plant "study tour" to Europe. After his return the mayor announced that he now considered the plan a safe one. He declared he would seek approval from the pro-plant local assembly to sell the remaining piece of municipal land necessary to build the plant.

When it appeared that the plant would finally be built, two different groups tried to defeat the incumbent mayor in the next mayoral election. Baba-san represented the first group, a loose gathering of self-declared pragmatic men who approached another conservative and offered to back him for mayor if he would agree to hold a referendum or a substantial electorate survey on the plant after his election. A second group banded together as the Green Association, dominated by young families that worked in surrounding cities but had moved into new suburban housing developments in Takeno. They chose to run their leader for mayor. He was a declared nuclear power opponent, in contrast to the conservative candidate of Baba's group, whose only public statement on the plant was his agreement to offer citizens some means of sharing their opinion on the project. The contest for mayor became a three-man race. In the end, the combined total votes for the two candidates who had expressed either clear opposition or at least no explicit support for the plant outstripped the votes won by the incumbent mayor. The voters could be said to have voted against continuing with the plant project; however, they had split their votes between two candidates, so the pro-plant mayor won the greatest number of votes. Therefore, representing a minority of the electorate, the pro-plant incumbent took office once again.

Disturbed that the plant might get built despite opposition from the majority of the voters, the two groups opposing the sitting mayor joined forces. They approached the mayor and requested a citizens' referendum on the nuclear power plant. When the mayor refused to grant the request, Baba-san and the other Referendum Association founders, known collectively as the Seven Samurai, contacted every town resident on the voter rolls, hired an accounting firm to manage secret ballot proceedings in an impartial, secure manner, and held an unofficial referendum. Forty-five percent of the local voters turned out to vote in the *unofficial* referendum. Still, the conservative assembly and the conservative mayor refused to hold an official referendum.

In response, the pro-referendum citizens' groups banded together to elect representatives to the local assembly, hoping to replace a number of oppositional conservative assembly members with new people who would pass a referendum ordinance ordering the local government to offer citizens the ballot on the plant. Baba's Referendum Association took an officially neutral position on the building of the plant but demanded an official town referendum be held and that the town's elected leaders abide by its results. The Referendum Association was joined by two groups that had taken public antiplant stances: the Green Association, which was fighting the plant primarily for environmental reasons, and a group of socialist independents. These nonparty, progressive groups became what I call the "referendum alliance." Other groups that had long led plant opposition provided support as well, but nearly all of their members had overlapping membership in one of these three groups. In the 1995 assembly election the referendum alliance groups succeeded in electing four new representatives to the local assembly. The Social Democrats and the Communists, which held one assembly seat each, pledged their representatives to the referendum cause. The alliance also persuaded four conservative incumbents who had won reelection to pledge support to a referendum bill in the assembly. After a complicated series of events, including the threatened recall and eventual replacement of the pro-plant conservative mayor, the referendum was held. Sixty-one percent of voters in the referendum said no to the nuclear power plant (turnout was approximately 89 percent), but nothing in Japanese law makes a local referendum of this sort binding on the actions of local officials.[18] A new assembly majority could legally disregard the referendum results and vote to sell the municipal land inside the proposed plant site to the power company or act in other ways that would make it easier to build the plant. Therefore in 1999 the referendum alliance once again ran candidates in an effort to make sure the city assembly continued to act in line with the referendum results.

In both the 1995 and 1999 elections in which the referendum alliance ran candidates, they were most successful with female candidates, despite the fact that men held most of the formal and informal leadership positions in these groups. In 1995 the referendum alliance put up six candidates for the twenty-two-seat assembly, two men and four women; three of the women and one man won seats. (The term "referendum alliance" does not include the pro-referendum conservatives, the Social Democrats, or the Communists, who also opposed the plant and ran only male candidates.)[19] In 1999 the referendum alliance offered voters seven candidates, two men and five women. This time all five women were elected, while the two men failed to win seats, including one who was an incumbent, the single referendum alliance male elected in 1995. By the end of the election cycle in Takeno in 1999, three citizens' groups in which men were the formal leaders, key decision makers, and chief fundraisers found themselves dependent on women for public representation. Takeno, a town formerly known for its corrupt, conservative (and masculine) politics, became a leader in its prefecture and the nation for the proportion of its elected offices held by women.

HOW BREADWINNER STATUS KEPT MEN OUT OF POLITICS

In Takeno in 1995 and 1999 male referendum alliance activists who had no intention of challenging contemporary gender-role expectations backed a history-making number of women's campaigns for local office because they could not get their male friends to run.[20] The forty-something and fifty-something men who dominated the referendum alliance were dominated in turn by their family breadwinner role. Thus they experienced real limits on their capacity for political involvement, despite the fact that they shared an intense desire to bring a voice to politics they believed had been ignored by the conservative men of older generations who had long dominated the mayor's office and local assembly.[21]

Research by sociologists and historians documents the force of the family breadwinner expectations placed on Japanese men. Even men of the postwar "bubble generation" who claim to believe that men and women should share equally in the home and in work outside the home usually find themselves playing out a traditional breadwinner role, devoting themselves first to the needs of their employers, leaving the duties of home and community to their wives.[22] According to Amano Masako, "Until now, the number one condition of a man being a man has been his taking on the economic responsibilities of the family. In this way, to 'do something for oneself' and to 'do something for one's family' have been seen as largely the same thing."[23] Even when men have seen the gendered division of labor as problematic, most have chosen not to rebel against it.[24]

When men choose not to fulfill the role of family breadwinner, they are often obliged to justify their claims to a masculine identity with the self-conscious construction of an alternative narrative that replaces the predominant image of dedicated salaryman. For example, they might choose to describe themselves as independent loners whose spirits cannot bow to family demands.[25] Alternative narratives might help men who have eschewed or failed at the breadwinner role find peace in private life. However, in Takeno-machi public life, commitment to the breadwinner role was a prerequisite of a man's participation because his family was usually dependent on his earnings in paid employment and because a man's reputation as a good man, the sort of man one would want to elect to office, was dependent on his reputation as a hardworking and uncomplaining breadwinner. The employment and reputation demands placed on men often knocked them out of contention as candidates, and thus referendum alliance members were forced to ask women to take their voices into politics. By the end of the 1999 election season, all the members of the Takeno-machi assembly backed by nonparty referendum alliance groups were women.

After the 1999 elections the Referendum Association women who had succeeded in winning assembly seats joked that the Association was now represented by "three mere women." The joke played up the distinction between the Association's male decision makers and its female public officeholders, but it actually understated the importance of "mere women" to the public face of the larger and similarly male-dominated referendum alliance. Following the 1999 elections the alliance was represented in the assembly by five women (the three from the Referendum Association and one each from the Green Association and an independent socialist group) and supported by four men who were elected to office with more traditional party bases (two conservatives and the Social Democrat and Communist representatives). The fact that women were so prominently placed in the referendum alliance is surprising given the history of extreme underrepresentation of women in the political institutions of Takeno and the rest of Japan.

What is more surprising is that, unlike groups such as the progressive, female-dominated consumers' network, the Seikatsu-sha (or Ordinary Person's) Network, that have had notable successes in electing women to local office, the groups in Takeno that pushed women to the fore of electoral politics were unabashedly male in their leadership. At the Referendum Association meetings the discussion was managed by Baba-san and his male friends and otherwise dominated by men's voices. Other sorts of work were also divided by gender. Women prepared and served refreshments at meetings and group events while men formulated strategy, designed fliers explaining the group's principles, and did their best to assess campaign progress. Men formed the bulk of the group that discussed the names of potential candidates and approached the named individuals with requests that they run. Men were the contacts with the many journalists from around the country seeking to understand the movement.

The male leaders of the Referendum Association, the Green Association, and the independent socialist group that shared in the alliance expressed no desire to remake the gender power structure of their town, and they made few efforts toward gender equality in their own organizations. During my fieldwork I stuck as close as possible to Baba-san and other male alliance leaders in order to get the best inside view of the organizations driving Takeno's anti–nuclear power politics. As the election date grew closer, the meetings I attended with these leaders became more and more male. This was especially true in the Referendum Association. At the most sensitive meetings discussing projected vote counts or the delicacies of the Association's alliance with other antiplant groups I was often the only woman. Perhaps there was no greater symbol of the men's preeminent position than the fact that they

sat huddled around the kerosene heater in the center of the prefabricated building the group used as their headquarters. The women kept
to the chillier outskirts of the room, not an enviable spot in a northern
Japan winter.

When I visited meetings of the Green Association and events at the
campaign headquarters of the female independent socialist Kagawa,
men occupied center stage in similar ways. The Green Association did
include women in strategy discussions, but men who also happened
to be academics tended to dominate, using their specialized skills of
analyzing and presenting information to control the discussion. At the
office opening party for Kagawa-san, women were so marginalized
that most of them sat in a different room from the male representatives
of supporting organizations and the Social Democratic Party who gave
the speeches that preceded the main event.

Women ended up representing their organizations in public office
because gender-role expectations got in the way of men's running for
office. Even though many of the female members of alliance organizations worked at least part time, the primary breadwinners in nearly
all of the families with members involved in the antiplant movement
were men, and movement members generally believed that holding an
assembly seat was incompatible with male members' role as breadwinner. This belief may be surprising given that, prior to 1995, all but one
assembly seat had always been held by a man. But as Baba-san and
several others, male and female, explained, those seats had long been
viewed as "honorary positions" (meiyo shoku) for men who were either
retired or so advanced in careers such as farming or running a small
business that they had the time to devote to the weekday assembly
meetings. According to the town's official report for 1999, the previous
year the assembly had met for sixty-five days out of the year, divided
into four regular sessions and two special sessions that were only four
days long. Because forty-five of those days were devoted to committee
work, it is likely that not all days would have required the work of all
assembly persons. The basic assembly person's salary was 246,000 yen
per month (slightly less than $2,400 given the exchange rate at this
writing). On meeting days, assembly members received an extra 1,000
yen, and seasonal bonuses were also paid. The assembly speaker and
committee chairs received a slightly higher base salary.

Given the amount of time required on weekdays and the constraints
of the salary, it is not hard to understand why men in their prime
breadwinning years would find it inadvisable to run for a seat. Men

employed at large companies or institutions were particularly poorly situated for elective office. They may not have had sufficient vacation time to cover absences that the assembly meetings required, and they were subject to frequent transfers. In fact, I knew two men who were very active in the antiplant movement who were transferred to work in other cities during my time in Takeno. They used their vacation time to return to their hometown and campaign for the female candidates who represented their groups. During the 2007 Unified Local Elections the *Asahi Shinbun* newspaper reported on a new phenomenon: companies that give salarymen leave to pursue elective office. But the newspaper also recounted the persistence of strong doubt among many workers and employers that an employee taking leave to run in an election would or should be welcomed back to his job.[26]

Members of the referendum alliance included representatives of all sorts of professions: plumbers, farmers, independent business owners, schoolteachers, bureaucrats (on the sly), engineers, and lawyers. But on the whole, in terms of age (averaging in the low forties for the Green Association, the high forties for the Referendum Association, and the midfifties for the independent socialists) and work situation, the men of the antiplant group differed from typical assemblymen. Indeed all but three of the conservative assembly members were older than sixty, and those who were involved in assembly politics prior to reaching retirement age were either farmers or small business owners, capable of controlling their own work schedule to some degree. The Social Democrats' single representative was a retired postal worker. The Communists' representative was an exception; he supported himself on his assembly seat salary and by doing party work, as his father, a former assembly member, had before him.

With the assembly election, scheduled for the end of April, slightly less than two months away, the leaders of the antiplant movement were still searching desperately for enough candidates to allow them to present the voters with the possibility of electing a pro-referendum majority to the local assembly. Baba explained why they had some faith they could elect a pro-referendum majority if they could field the necessary number of candidates. In 1995, when they threatened the mayor with a recall election, they had been able to collect signatures in support of a recall from a majority of registered voters. Moreover, when the threatened mayor stepped down, the Referendum Association candidate was handily elected. When the referendum was finally held in 1996, more than 80 percent of voters had turned out to vote, and a clear majority of voters had voted no on the plant project that most of the conservative assembly members had long supported.

In the April 1999 elections the Referendum Association hoped to put up six candidates. With the support of representatives elected from other alliance groups, as well as the Social Democrat, Communist, and two pro-referendum conservative assemblymen, the pro-referendum, antiplant groups could control the assembly majority. If the Referendum Association could get at least five candidates into office, the pro-plant and antiplant forces in the assembly would be tied. Supposing the conservatives put their own man up for the speaker's seat (a likelihood, given the traditional prestige and extra compensation attached to the position), the pro-referendum groups would have a working majority on most votes because speakers in Japanese assemblies traditionally refrain from voting. By the end of February 1999 the Referendum Association knew it would be able to run at least three candidates, but it struggled to add more to the list before the April election. Eventually Association leaders had to content themselves with only five candidates. Two of the five were men; one, Takahashi-san, had won a seat in 1995, when the Association had sponsored two male and two female candidates and elected one male and one female. The other male candidate, Yanagi-san, was running for the first time. Both men lost.

The other three Referendum Association candidates were women; all were wives or daughters of men whose breadwinner obligations had prevented them from considering a bid for office. One was the incumbent Aoki-san; her husband was a founding member of the Association who had run for mayor of Takeno in 1982 as a representative of the nuclear power plant opposition movement. Another, Toda-san, who lost as a Referendum Association candidate in the 1995 assembly elections but won in 1999, was the daughter of a deceased former assemblyman. Originally her father had been a conservative supporter of the power plant, but in later years he had decided the plant was a bad idea. The third Referendum Association woman, Miura-san, was the daughter of one of the original group of Seven Samurai who joined Baba-san in contributing financial support to the Association's self-administered, unofficial referendum. Two other women who represented the alliance, the Green Association's Sakata-san and the independent socialists' Kagawa-san, were running in place of their husbands, who were leaders of the groups backing the women's bids for office.

Baba and other alliance leaders actively sought more male candidates, but when they approached men they thought would be strong candidates they were repeatedly told that work obligations would not permit the potential candidates to run. The husbands of Aoki-san and Sakata-san were clear cases of this problem. As both men had run for mayor in the past, they were likely choices for assembly candidacy. Sakata-san's husband was the 1994 antiplant mayoral candidate, and Aoki-san's husband had run for mayor in 1982. In their respective bids for the mayoralty, each man had captured far more than enough votes to win seats in the assembly. However, breadwinner duties made running for the assembly hugely impractical. The men were midcareer professionals who might have managed on a mayor's salary of 818,000 yen per month (approximately $8,000) but who would not ask their families to try to squeeze by on the fraction of that amount paid to assembly members. The husband of the independent socialist candidate Kagawa-san had been active in the Social Democratic Party since his youth. He certainly had the political connections to build a campaign, but he too could not countenance the salary cut he would have to take if he won an assembly seat. The more poorly paid male members of the Referendum Association might have found the assembly salary acceptable, but they were least able to take the risk of taking time off from their current jobs to campaign for an uncertain new one. Tellingly, all three of the men who did run for seats as representatives of the Referendum Association in the 1995 and 1999 elections were independent workers in one way or another. One had a small travel business that was very busy in only a couple of short seasons, one was a rare full-time farmer, and the third was part owner of a car repair business he shared with his brother, who was willing to work harder to make up the difference during assembly sessions.

The difficulty of fielding young or middle-aged men who did not have especially propitious financial circumstances was highlighted by the case of yet another man, Abe-san, a full-time farmer in his thirties who at first agreed to run as a Referendum Association candidate and later withdrew. Abe-san was a vocal opponent of the planned nuclear power plant. He had even posted huge signs in his fields expressing his opposition. Early in 1999 he agreed to run for an assembly seat as a representative of the Referendum Association, but just about the time I settled in Takeno group leaders began to be concerned that his candidacy would fall through. One night we all assembled in the cold prefab building where the referendum group made its office in order for Abe-san to sit down with the group leaders and discuss his campaign strategy. But Abe-san never made it to the meeting. He called about a half-hour after it was to start and said a cold kept him from leaving home. A week later we gathered again. This time Abe-san showed up, and in his humble posture and words he made a good impression on some of the group leaders. But when Baba-san asked him what his wife and parents thought about his run for office, Abe-san said in a soft voice that his family suffered from the same cold that had kept him home, and, in this spate of ill health he had not found a convenient time to mention his candidacy to them.

"Daijobu da kai? Omae? Daijobu kai? [Is that okay? Are you sure?]," Baba asked, his agitated voice ringing with the local dialect. The young man bowed his head and said everything would be okay. Abe-san worked with the incumbent assembly member Aoki-san to create a one-page leaflet. Together they printed thousands of copies on the copy machine, and he gave her the information she needed to make business cards for him. He collected his leaflets and left, ostensibly to attend an organization of young farmers in his village. Later that evening, at Baba-san's home, those of us who had been at the meeting told Baba-san's wife of the discussion with the new candidate. The conversation went like this:

Baba's friend:	What kind of man is it who doesn't tell his wife and parents that he's running for office?
Baba:	He's a good man. He put up those opposition signs when he didn't have to. And they say he's in the youth association, and he pulls his weight in the village. He participates.
Baba's friend:	But he seems like he doesn't have it all together. What kind of a campaign will he run?
Baba:	Perhaps his parents or wife would oppose him running, but he knows if he just gets out there and does it, they'll back him. He has a responsibility. He's the sort of man who would not shirk the responsibility.
Baba's friend:	But when you went to ask him to run, what did he say? Are you sure he said yes?
Baba:	He said, "Hai wakarimashita" [I understand]. He said he would do it. He knew he had a responsibility.
Baba's friend:	But what did he mean when he said "Wakarimashita"? Maybe he's just got a weakness for the word *sekinin* [responsibility].
Baba:	He's a grown man. He said "Wakarimashita." He will stand. He just has to work out his family issues.
Baba's friend:	They say he's a flaky farmer. Insists on going to Tokyo to sell his rice by himself.

At this point in the conversation, Baba told his wife to call a friend who was familiar with the young man's village. She made the call, then she told everyone what she learned. "There are rumors that the young man will run for office, but that's it. No bad story about this young man has ever entered the man's ears." The analysis of Abe-san continued.

> Baba: He's a hard worker. He wants to do things the right way. He has ideas. But that's okay.
>
> Baba's friend: I've never known a man like this [*Konna otoko wa inainda yo*].

With this point we all agreed.

Abe-san's business cards were printed, and the Referendum Association organized a small kickoff party the following weekend for the candidates it had recruited by that point (four of the six it hoped to eventually field). Abe-san did not make it to the party. Instead, only a few hours before the party, his young wife went to the home of a referendum group leader with a new baby strapped to her back. "Please don't make my husband run," she begged. The leader she talked to came to the party certain that the young man would not run, and a pall was cast over the whole party. If Abe-san decided not to run, the group would need to find three more candidates.

The group members didn't give up on Abe-san immediately. A small group of them traveled out to the young man's village. But as Baba said, he could not properly press the man on his responsibility to the referendum group and to its goals for the town while the prospective candidate's wife sat nearby with a newborn at her breast. Group members could not agree on what the abandoned candidacy said about the young man's character, but they knew it said something. Baba was accused of having been too optimistic a judge of character. Abe-san was obviously flaky. No agreement could be reached on the quality of the wife's behavior. Had she undercut her husband in a grotesque way by going around him to the group leaders, by the doubt she expressed about his ability to manage both farming and political life? Was she thus an inexcusable sort of wife? Or was it his fault? Was he weak? If Abe-san had been a better husband and father, would his wife have stood behind him? Should he have run for office despite her protest and found a way of quieting her? Did he have a responsibility grounded on that "Wakarimashita" he had uttered to Baba when Baba asked him to stand? Was he a good man simply victimized by the fact that the world of politics made demands that ordinary men, mere middle-class husbands and providers, could not meet—the demands his character made of him unanswerable in a political world that was designed to exclude his sort? How much should a family endure for the sake of a town? Where must a good man draw the line between saving some comfort for himself and his family and standing up for those principles in which he believes?

The Referendum Association leaders relinquished Abe-san, and they managed to persuade another man to run in his stead, Yanagi, the man who shared a car repair business with his brother. By late March 1999, less than a month from election day, the Referendum Association had lined up four candidates: incumbents Takahashi and Aoki, new candidate Yanagi, and Toda-san, the woman who had run and lost in 1995. At this point Baba-san suggested that five candidates rather than six would be sufficient, but the Association struggled to find even one more. After being turned down by several prospective male candidates, Baba-san, his cousin Ota, the friend with whom he had debated Abe's character, and Takahashi-san at last began to talk about searching for a young female candidate. When Baba-san's friend first suggested that a young woman might make a good candidate, the other male leaders resisted the idea. Baba-san said he worried what a run for office might do to the reputation of a young woman (a worry I never heard him or others express when discussing potential male candidates). Eventually the men reasoned that a young woman would be hard-pressed to find better career options elsewhere and that the freshness of a young female face might make the campaign attractive to voters otherwise disaffected. Thus they settled on Miura-san, the young daughter of a founding member of the Referendum Association. Miura-san was a controversial choice, and I discuss the issues surrounding her candidacy and the masculinist strategy Baba pursued to resolve them in chapter 5.

Breadwinner obligations deterred otherwise seemingly viable male candidates from standing for the referendum cause, but that was not the only effect of men's breadwinner identities on antiestablishment political engagement in Takeno-machi. In another, more insidious way, men's roles as breadwinners prohibited their fullest participation in the antiplant movement. Men who worked in businesses that were owned by or served supporters of the plant project had much to lose if they expressed their opposition openly. As elsewhere in rural Japan, construction firms were powerful locally. Their owners were conservative, and they expected to be the likely beneficiaries of public works projects that would come with the building of the plant or because of the subsidies the national government would pay the local government for accepting the plant.[27] A close male friend of Miura-san was an employee of an area construction firm and, as a result, could not do much to aid her campaign. A key female leader of the Green Association was married to a carpenter who did not dare show his face at any Green Association activities because he feared that construction firms in the area would stop hiring him. Several women I met at Referendum Association meetings attended without their husbands because the men feared the economic consequences of being associated with the plant opposition movement. Leaders of the Referendum Association who operated restaurants or stores knew how real such threats could be; their businesses had been boycotted by supporters of the power plant. Baba-san had his long-term Lions Club membership revoked by the other members, who were supporters of the plant project, and, as I witnessed myself, a local police detective stopped by Baba's shop to ask him "friendly questions" about his politics on more than one occasion.

Of course, a curious puzzle remains: Why was a wife able to brave a reputation as opposition activist without adversely affecting her husband's workplace interests? I think one might find the answer in what a conservative assembly member said to me about losing the referendum to the antiplant activists. The loss, he said, was the result of "young mothers" being emotionally swayed by schoolteachers who claimed that the nuclear power plant would endanger their children. The opposition activities of women were, in this man's estimation, the understandable result of their emotional involvement in motherhood. He did not blame the young mothers. In fact, he blamed the male schoolteachers and later the "activists from outside" for preying on vulnerable subjects. Because the conservative plant supporters did not think women were capable of making reasonable decisions in the face of pressure from men, they did not see women's political behavior as the appropriate object of sanction in the way they saw the behavior of male business associates and employees. Comments I heard from other conservatives who blamed men for upsetting mothers or failing to calm them support my reading of the constraint that expectations of masculine responsibility placed on men's behavior.

The men in the referendum alliance were quite aware of the fact that their role as breadwinner constrained their activities in politics. They empathized with those men who were unable to back up conviction with action by standing for office when those men were perceived as having responsibilities, such as supporting a wife and young children. Interestingly, alliance men did not describe the political constraints they struggled against as gender-based despite the fact that, arguably, that is exactly what they were. Because men in some positions could participate in politics, the general assumption was that politics was a hard place for women but not for men. Viewed from another perspective, however, politics was in some ways actually harder to enter for *most* men than it was for some women. Consigned to the role of family provider in the gendered division of labor, men were much more at the mercy of those who could affect their income.

Moreover, men in the ranks of Takeno's referendum alliance judged each other as men in large part on how well each seemed to maintain his breadwinner status. Men interested in participating more in the alliance's activities could not simply make the choice to reduce or change their employment commitments because such choices would tend to make them appear less than men in the eyes of their fellow activists, who might, in turn, be less inclined to share with them in political endeavors. This breadwinner reputational constraint was not merely a judgment of a man's earning prowess. For example, Baba-san had great respect for some men believed to have low incomes. When they turned down his urging to stand in the elections because they felt unable to take the financial risk, he praised them as men who worked *isshōkenmei* (with their whole life's effort) to maintain their *seikatsu* (daily life).

Of course a man's earning prowess was not entirely irrelevant to his reputation; after all, the men who provided the initial financing for the referendum group were known as the Seven Samurai: men's men. Correspondingly, men who simply did not fit the role of breadwinner were not welcomed into the group. I listened as alliance members derided one man, Yano-san, who frequently came by Baba's shop to join morning chats about politics. As one said, Yano-san was able to stop by and join conversations about the group's political objectives because he was a mere "thread" of a person. When I asked Baba-san what the comment meant, he told me that the man's family relied primarily on his wife's larger income, which the man supplemented by working nights at the local supermarket. The man had the perfect schedule to run for and serve in local office without damaging the family income, but that schedule gave him an unmanly reputation that kept group leaders from considering him as a potential candidate.

Quite conscious of the breadwinner burden borne by their fellow movement members, leaders of the referendum alliance told me they did not feel they could ask typical salarymen to run for office because the leaders could not guarantee victory and the salarymen did not want to jeopardize their jobs. Ironically this led the Referendum Association to turn to exactly the same sorts of retired and well-off men who formed the conservatives' candidate pool, the men whom alliance members slightingly described as "honorary" representatives or people "who just like to be in elections" (*sukide sukide shouganai*). But when the Association approached these men problems developed. Either alliance members suspected the strength of the men's commitment to the alliance cause and disagreed strongly about the prospective candidate, or the prospective candidate turned down requests to run, sometimes pointing out that running under the alliance's banner would be a hard way to win an election.

WHY GENDERED CAMPAIGN STRATEGIES GAVE WOMEN ADVANTAGES OVER MEN

The three men in the Referendum Association who did become candidates over the 1995 and 1999 election cycles suffered handicaps related to their responsibilities as family breadwinners. Worse, the fact that they were men prevented them from effectively using some of the clever underdog strategies employed by female candidates. As men they found that differentiating themselves from conservative male candidates was more difficult than it was for progressive female candidates. Thus for the Association men, selling themselves as true fresh faces with real reform agendas was made more difficult by their gender. Part of this was the effect of the reality that, because women had been almost entirely excluded from past political practices that were widely accepted as thoroughly corrupt, female candidates' claims to represent a new politics was true on its face. Part of the problem for male candidates was that their natural support base, networks of friends and colleagues, had often already been mobilized by leaders in the conservative political establishment that had dominated Takeno-machi since the early postwar era. For men, mobilizing friends usually meant reversing the mobilization that had already occurred. For women, mobilizing friends often meant asking for active support from women who had never been directly asked to support a friend; it meant asking a woman to change a vote she cast as a favor to a husband or father or some other male who had been the direct beneficiary of the old, male-centered mobilization practices. I'll treat the first problem for men, the image problem, and then return to the second problem, the mobilization problem.

Given the policy role of local governments, it is not surprising that both male and female candidates in the antiplant, pro-referendum groups presented relatively similar concerns in the fliers, postcards, and government-sponsored advertisements they circulated to potential voters. In 1999 all of the circulated materials from each of the anti-plant alliance candidates stated prominently that the candidate would work hard to make sure that the results of the 1996 referendum in which voters had displayed their opposition to the nuclear power plant would be reflected in town policy. Connected with this pledge was usually a pledge to protect Takeno's natural resources, such as clean air and water. Beyond that, most antiplant candidates claimed a desire to improve social welfare services such as care for the aged and disabled and the children of working mothers. Several candidates, male and female, promised to represent farmers' voices in the assembly.

The antiplant, pro-referendum candidates' self-presentations did differ markedly from the presentations made by most conservative, pro-plant candidates. For example, most conservatives produced no fliers and made only the barest effort to use their allotted advertising space in the government-sponsored election newspaper. A couple of candidates actually used hand-lettered statements in that official publication. One of these was so poorly lettered—illegible, small, and crooked in the box—that I could have prepared a better looking one. (And my hand-written Japanese is ghastly.) A few relied on a slogan on a business card. One 1999 conservative male candidate had run in 1995 as a supporter of the referendum, then turned against the referendum cause after winning and consequently suffered a recall at the hands of referendum-supporting voters. When he sought a return to office in 1999, he circulated a full-color, professionally produced flier, but its main feature was a photo of him in athletic gear kicking a soccer ball. Journalists and referendum alliance members I spoke with suspected that this man got funding from conservatives at higher levels of government. Most of the conservatives emphasized economic redevelopment as their key issue. Only one of the conservatives admitted in a publication that he was still a supporter of the nuclear power plant, despite the fact that, when asked by researchers and journalists, the pro-plant candidates were perfectly willing to admit that what they meant by "economic redevelopment" was accepting the nuclear power plant.

Male and female, the candidates from the referendum alliance could
fairly argue that their campaign literature, in style and substance, dif-
ferentiated them from the pro-plant conservatives. However, viewed
in a larger context, the female candidates' literature may have seemed
especially distinctive to voters. For example, although men and women
mentioned social welfare and education in their fliers and other methods of presentation, the women were able to add language that capi-
talized on the special expertise as family caregivers that voters were
likely to assume traveled with their gender markers. One female candidate began her flier by addressing a question about street safety to
"those of us in the middle of child rearing." The four other female
candidates used pink prominently in their circulated materials; three
used it as the background color for a flier or postcard, and one used
a painting of a cherry tree in full bloom on the front of her postcard.
The candidate with the cherry tree postcard was widely known as the
operator of a child and elder care center. One of the candidates with
a pink flier, a full-time housewife, specifically mentioned household
garbage problems in her discussion of environmental concerns. As this
and other research I have done has shown, women believe that they
are especially able to speak about garbage problems because, in Japan,
managing household garbage is usually women's work.[28] Another full-
time housewife simply declared on her pink postcard that she would
use her "clean" (*migakiageta*) housewife's perspective (*shufu kankaku*)
to "refresh" (*rifureshhu*) politics.

Obviously the male candidates could neither capitalize on housewives' previous exclusion from corrupt politics nor declare themselves
hands-on garbage experts. In fact, declaring themselves garbage experts
might have been dangerously effeminizing. Worse, the men occasionally
had to settle questions about why they were involved in politics when
it might make their breadwinning role harder to perform. The man
who lost in 1995 was not seen as a potential candidate in 1999, despite
the fact that the Referendum Association was desperate for candidates.
Baba-san told me this was because the man had gotten divorced since
the previous election, and it was widely said that he did not fully support
his ex-wife and daughter. His small travel business that required sales
work only during a very limited part of the year and maintenance work
during partial days the rest of the year was not seen as a sound financial
means of supporting his family. Ironically the irregular work schedule
meshed nicely with the assembly demands, and with the assembly salary he would have earned if elected he could have better supported his

wife and daughter. But just as his fellow male movement leaders had ugly words for men who were financially supported by wives earning higher salaries, they were dubious that, given his family and employment circumstances, he could appeal to enough voters to make a second run for the assembly.

Yanagi, the man's replacement in 1999, actually tried having his picture for his official campaign poster taken in the crisp work coveralls he wore to his job; he believed it would strengthen the impression that he was gainfully employed. Baba, Takahashi, Ota, and a few other of the group's core leaders decided that the work coverall photo would look too odd next to photos of other male candidates in jackets and ties. In a revealing paradox, the farmers, small businessmen, and independent contractors who could scrape together the time to get engaged in politics did not look "right" on campaign posters if they did not present themselves in the jacket, starched shirt, and tie that they hardly ever wore, whereas the salarymen who regularly donned such a uniform simply did not have time to run for office. In other words, men who run for political office must present themselves in the clothing of men whose work prohibits their running for office. Of course, because this convention of public appearance compels all political leaders to present themselves as salarymen, it becomes literally impossible to *see* that salarymen are, on the whole, excluded from most forms of engagement with political life.[29] Thus while female candidates could complement their claims to provide a fresh voice in politics with simple references to their femininity, the men who wanted to challenge the town's pro-plant, conservative establishment had to contend with the psychological noise caused by the assumption that politics was an activity for dilettantes who had either retired or were not serious about earning their family's living. Moreover conventions of male self-presentation as responsible breadwinner citizens encouraged the men to portray themselves in a narrow salaryman image that obscured both visual symbols of resistance to the dominant political men and the way the men actually did earn their family's living.

I cannot be certain that voters read these messages as I did, but I do have some clues that my analysis is not completely wrong. Because I was in Takeno during the prefectural assembly elections as well as the town assembly elections, I was able to observe how my research subjects were approached about voting in an election in which the pro-plant/antiplant divide was not operational. In that election relatives and neighbors active in the various prefectural assembly candidates' campaigns would stop by Baba's home or shop to drop off candidates' fliers and talk about the candidates' qualities. I collected quite a lot of prefectural election fliers by sitting in on the visits, and I was able to listen in as the information on the fliers was translated into specifics about the candidate's work history or gender. I frequently heard comments such as "He just waited around until he could get his seat from his daddy. He's never done anything," made about one candidate. Yet whereas judgments of male candidates for the prefectural assembly usually included some reference to whether the men were perceived to have been gainfully employed prior to seeking a position in politics, discussion of female candidates seldom centered around their work histories. I certainly never heard anyone make a claim about a female candidate's ability to financially support a family (or her inability to do so). Also, female candidates were uniformly associated with freshness—not a guarantee of victory but an asset for candidates who hoped to challenge incumbents.

We might think that in a relatively small town like Takeno, where connections with other political leaders, whether with one's politician father or with a mentor involved in politics at a higher level of government, were seen as integral to the campaign process, men would have an advantage because they would, on average, be members of more politically influential circles. But in Takeno only some men, members of the long-term conservative political establishment as well as the Socialists and the Communists, had such benefits. The Referendum Association's male candidates who wanted to challenge the conservatives from outside the Social Democratic or Communist camps (neither of which had ever held more than one Takeno assembly seat anyway) were disadvantaged in comparison with women. Over the years the conservative establishment had so penetrated most local, male-member organizations in their efforts at voter mobilization for elections to all levels of government that male challengers seeking a new voter base had to work with men who already had histories of loyalty to other candidates or to higher level elected officials supporting particular local candidates. Takeno's elections were historically known by journalists for the prefectural paper as among the most corrupt in the prefecture. In fact journalists, taxi drivers, even conservatives themselves referred to them as *nomase, kuwase senkyo,* or "let them eat, let them drink elections."

Even in the Referendum Association leadership, I knew of only one man who had never been included in the *nomase, kuwase* elections prior to 1995. He had been an antiplant activist since his college days and commuted to work in a larger city. The small shop owners, farmers, and employees of local businesses I met had all been out drinking with local political bosses at some point in their lives, as members of the chamber of commerce, the neighborhood youth association, or the area farmers' cooperative. Most had been out repeatedly over the years. Some had even prepared or delivered the food or drink served at the events. For some it had been a typical source of social life in their youth. Salarymen living in newer housing developments might not have been tapped by the old boy networks, but they also lacked the time and connections in the area to develop alternative networks. So, for the Referendum Association's male candidates, campaigning among their same-sex networks meant doing a lot of explaining, and doing it without sake and sushi.

Women, on the other hand, had not traditionally been the direct targets of these mobilization efforts. The men in politics, including Social Democrats and Communists, admitted that they had never thought to try to reach women in a special way, assuming husbands, brothers, or fathers would carry home a ballot message. Certainly, my imperfect sample of women voters explained to me, women did pledge loyalty on the basis of these indirect relationships, but when their female friends asked them to reconsider their votes they were more open to doing so. Not surprisingly, the female candidates from the referendum alliance relied very heavily on same-sex networks in their mobilization efforts, turning to PTA friends, mothers who had used the same day care, old schoolmates, and neighborhood housewives. The surprising effectiveness of the female candidates' same-sex mobilization strategies in 1995 was rued by the conservatives and praised by the longtime (male) nuclear power opponents for the same reason. As the Social Democrat who sat in the Takeno Assembly pointed out, everyone had assumed that the women's votes were tied up by their male connections until women candidates went out to seek the votes themselves.

As a result of the serendipitous rise of women to the forefront of the referendum movement in Takeno, gender expectations for women in politics were altered noticeably. What did *not* happen was a change in gender expectations for men. The fact that some male candidates lost to women proved that women could win elections, but it was not viewed as proof that men could not. After all, sixteen of the twenty-two assembly seats were still held by men. Yet a more careful examination of those seat holders would tell a different story. Men younger than retirement age did not have seats, with the exception of the single Communist, two conservatives who owned their own businesses, and the conservative with the professionally produced campaign flier. He was a full-time farmer, which probably meant he had a considerable degree of flexibility with his schedule during assembly terms, but his flier also suggested to me (and to several journalists with whom I discussed it) that the man's political endeavors were probably well financed by some larger conservative interests. Middle-class salarymen, those who would write their occupation *kaishain* (company employee), were not represented in the assembly in any way, unless their wives count as their representatives. Nor were lower-class men. A portion of the local population had been effectively silenced, but it was not the female portion we gender scholars usually assume it is. Instead, the silenced were men who might easily be characterized as "ordinary" men: middle class, middle-aged, not aligned with either the left or right ends of the political spectrum—the core of the Japanese workforce. They went to work and stayed out of politics. Their acceptance of a gendered division of labor ensured that they did.

GENDER AS A FUNDAMENTAL CONSTRAINT ON MEN'S POLITICAL BEHAVIOR

The effects of gender expectations on male participation in politics that I observed in Takeno were not unlike those I observed following Takada-san in Tokyo or in interviews with members of local assemblies in other areas of Japan. In metropolitan Tokyo the growth of lifestyle politics in groups such as the Seikatsu-sha Network, represented entirely by female politicians, has attracted a great deal of attention because of its connection to the expansion of women's presence in elective office. Yet the success of women in the Seikatsu-sha movement is, ironically, also evidence of the exclusion of most men from the politics of their communities. The cooperative movement that led to the rise of Seikatsu-sha politics was founded by progressive, nonparty male activists who could not figure out a way of establishing a foothold in suburban Tokyo other than reaching out to its female residents. Responsible for housework and children, women were more likely to be at home and active in their neighborhood than their husbands who commuted to full-time jobs usually located outside the residential district.[30]

In conservative politics too, which continues to rely primarily on men to fill elective office, the powerful constraints of breadwinner expectations are apparent. For example, as Takada-san's grim mood on the morning of the *mochi* festival demonstrates, even men who are socioeconomically well situated to pursue politics struggle with the gendered dimensions of presenting themselves to their constituents. Because Takada-san's only previous paid employment had been in his parents' real estate firm, some people, even some conservatives, described him as a Botchan, the title character of a famous Japanese novel about a privileged and naïve young man.[31] One of Takada-san's closest supporters explained to me that, even though he was a young man, Takada-san could run for office because he was "very rich" and did not need a salary. This supporter explained that Takada-san's wealthy family had an obligation to represent the local neighborhood, and in presentations to his supporters Takada-san seemed to echo such thinking by talking about himself as taking on a role of public service that men in his family had assumed for generations. In his dealings with male constituents in his ward, Takada also confronted the power of the breadwinner ideology.

After he had been elected to his second term in the Shirakawa Ward assembly, I asked Takada-san how he thought gender affected the way assembly members performed their jobs. He gave me a curious answer. He began by telling me a tale about a budget meeting members of the LDP in the Shirakawa Ward assembly had held for their supporters. He said the meeting was the best example of how masculinity operated in politics. In the slow-growth economy, the ward budget was tight, and Shirakawa Ward suffered from a terrible debt problem. As LDP supporters came in with their various budget requests (including, for example, requests for continuing certain local subsidies for home renovations that would help to guarantee work for struggling local contractors and architects), Takada-san keenly felt the enormity of the demands LDP supporters made compared with the constraints of ward resources. Many of the requests seemed disappointingly self-serving. "We say we'll look into it seriously," he said. "But we want them to understand the financial situation of the ward." He went on:

> As we're listening to these stories I think, well, if you're really suffering that bad, couldn't you change to another line of work? When there are so many other kinds of business, why do you have to come to this point [of demanding subsidies from us]?
>
> I think that, but they can't change professions or they are staying in this one—Well, in the case of men, well, there are assembly members who have built relationships in these business sectors, and then, I do understand a man's desire to stick with the line of work he started in. Up until now, in Japanese society it was always men working outside the home and

women doing the housework—and if you think about it along those lines, you can see how male assembly members, how they say to these requests, "I understand what you're saying," and why they end up saying "We'll do what we can to help you out."

As I explain in greater detail in chapter 5, Takada-san argued that the male constituents' entreaties were particularly hard for male assembly members to ignore because male members were manipulated by the expectation of mutual understanding, what Takada-san called the "gut" ties between men.

Until very recently students of politics tended to assume that gender scholarship could be reserved for those whose primary interest was increasing women's participation in the political sphere. But the case of the citizens' movement in Takeno-machi as well as the work I have done in Tokyo suggest that gender is a powerful structure shaping political life for all participants. Of course if we cite gender identity as one factor influencing why women's political engagement lags far behind that of men, we necessarily imply that political men are beneficiaries of their gender identity. However, gender identity does not work in a symmetrical fashion. Some men may well experience their gender as politically empowering, but the very same masculine identity that seems to naturalize one man's political engagement also tends to suppress the engagement of many others. Without a careful analysis of how men's gendered identities are formed and maintained, we cannot account for the heterogeneous effects of apparently similar social expectation. Certainly we cannot fully understand which men participate and why they participate in the way they do. We would also find it much harder to see what might be most accurately described as class differences at work in the political arena. Importantly, these class differences in access to power are managed through the common participation of nearly *all* men, regardless of class, in playing out and thus reinforcing a gender role that makes *some* men politically more powerful than others. Breadwinner expectations constrain men and do so effectively in part because men are both proud to be breadwinners themselves and willing to judge their fellow men in terms of their commitment to the breadwinning role. As with all structures, however, masculine gender identity is not entirely determinative of its bearer's choices. In Takeno progressive men who could not take an official role in local politics because they could not relinquish their breadwinner role at home still chose to assert themselves against the constraints of gender discourse. They worked hard to change the terms of political life—for women.

CHAPTER 2

The Inheritor

In Takeno-machi many of the Referendum Association men with whom I talked were cynical about elected officials. Along with the terms they used to describe local politicians as people who craved position (*sukide sukide shōganai*) or who were seeking a sinecure and a feather in their cap after completing their life's more serious work (*meiyo shoku*), I often heard residents repeat a local saying that went something like this: "If you can sell one rice paddy, you can run for election." The point of the saying is that, given how expensive it is to campaign for office, especially when corruption is rampant, an office seeker would either have to be so well off he could afford to part with a producing field or so irresponsible that he thought nothing of selling his resources out from under his household. The Referendum Association activists sought to change the terms of Takeno's "let them eat, let them drink" elections by recruiting new kinds of people to run for office, running transparent and inexpensive campaigns, and touting the fact that they tried to convince voters with ideas rather than sake and sushi.

Given that the Referendum Association succeeded in getting an official referendum held, electing some of its members to office, and finally stopping the building of the nuclear power plant, its members often argued they had evidence that a clean politics approach to elections could work. Still, in the April 1999 election season the difficulty of finding candidates and the failure to get two of them into office seemed to remind members of how high the barriers to office could

be for most people. In the days after the 1999 assembly election Baba
and the others shook their heads and muttered rumors they had heard
about conservatives' lavish (and illegal) gifts to voters and repeated
their old refrain about the difficulty and expense of politics for regular
townspeople.

As the Takeno Referendum Association members considered and
reconsidered the various reasons they had failed to elect their whole
slate, Takada-san won his 1999 election to the Shirakawa Ward Assembly quite handily. In many ways Takada-san and his campaign for a seat
in the Tokyo ward assembly where his father had served for twenty-eight
years were emblematic of precisely the sort of politics that Baba-san and
other Referendum Association members frequently criticized as beyond
the means of ordinary people. Takada-san was born into a family that
had been involved in politics for generations. According to his father,
they had also been landholders in their area since the Edo era. In fact the
family business still consists of managing the income from their land,
on which they have apartment buildings and parking lots. The Takada
family home is large, even by American standards, and surrounded by
a proper garden and hidden behind high walls; in their densely packed
Tokyo neighborhood the house is enormous. Although Takada-san has
worked for his parents' real estate management business, his primary
career has always been politics. Before he ran for office himself, he
worked in his father's campaigns and in the campaigns of politicians
in the Liberal Democratic Party. When I described my fieldwork in
Takada's campaign to Baba-san, he was intensely cynical; in his eyes
the Japanese political world had been tailor-made to serve the interests
of people like Takada who did not have to do any real work to get
ahead.

But Takada-san himself often described the process of getting elected
to the Shirakawa Ward Assembly as grueling. During the campaign he
was repeatedly glum, as he had been on the morning of the *mochi* festival. He described his move into the political world of Shirakawa Ward
and the dominant Liberal Democratic Party not as an easy exercise of
inherited power and position but as a complicated play of deference
in an intensely hierarchical world. Indeed to me as well his campaign
looked much like a demonstration of deference. In the previous chapter
I made the point that men's acceptance of the duties of breadwinner has
the effect of obscuring the way the pursuit of masculine gender by most
men works to provide selective political benefits to a few men. The
salaryman image that candidates cultivate in their campaign posters

provides a good example of how this works: a few men, who are most likely not salarymen, run for office while sporting the image of men who are slaving away as breadwinners for family, company, and country. The diligence of most men in attending to their manly duties keeps them out of politics, but it also burnishes the general image of men that provides a powerful resource to those who do not need to be diligent in the same way. Ironically, taking receipt of the selective benefits of generalized masculine duty is not easy precisely because the benefits are selective. For the few men who can parlay the benefits of generalized masculinity into a political resource the image of dutiful manhood is something useful for getting valued work done, and it deserves protection. Newcomers to the world of politically dominant men are potential threats in part because they might make a mistake that would undercut the notion that dominant men are dominant because they are the best representatives of dutiful manhood.

As Takada-san's experiences as a newcomer to the world of LDP politics demonstrate, proving one's fitness as a user of the selective benefits of generalized masculinity means proving that one can do one's duty toward other men. So Baba-san is wrong; men like Takada-san do not win political power in their communities without work. Takada-san works very hard, but at a different type of work. While the majority of middle-class breadwinners are so consumed by their masculine duty to work for wages that they cannot easily engage directly in political life, men like Takada-san who seek to enter political life as a form of masculine duty are consumed by deference to the idea of duty itself. By seeming to embody dutiful manhood in public performances of deference to tradition and family, Takada-san secured benefits for his political career. In turn, a significant part of the political career won for him by his demonstrated dutifulness consisted of loyally serving those senior to him in the LDP. Certainly as a representative of Japan's most powerful political party, Takada-san became a *representative* of the kind of power against which Baba's Referendum Association struggled. However, the effectiveness of the same masculinist strategies that made Takada-san a success at events such as the *mochi* festival was sustained at a price. That price was sufficient to complicate any attempt to define Takada as *individually* more empowered than the "ordinary" men whose interests Baba defended. The "easy" power Takada-san achieved by leading a sufficiently privileged life to obtain elective office was also an enduring constraint on his self-determination.

THE HARD WORK OF DEMONSTRATING DUTY

On the morning of the *mochi* festival Takada-san was glum. He talked about how troubled he was by his failure to squeeze into the already overscheduled previous evening a meeting of a neighborhood group devoted to maintaining the portable shrine used in the fall festival. Originally he had thought it necessary to skip the meeting in order to make it to the gatherings of two other groups he hoped would lend him support in the campaign. Later he decided the portable shrine group meeting would have been an important chance for his campaign, and worse, because he had obligations as an official member of the shrine group, he might have injured his reputation by skipping its meeting. Takada-san thought missing the shrine group meeting might have been the first real failure of his campaign. He told me he had slept poorly because he was worried about the issue, and that confession led him into more general comments about the negative way the campaign was affecting him.

> I think I have gotten to the point where I can't remember what I like about myself. But I know what I hate: it's becoming another person. It's not my character [*seikaku*] that is changing. It's my style. But I've had to develop a "sales face" [*eigyō kao*]. I worry about things I never used to worry about. I am making some greeting remarks, and I see someone standing. He's probably just coming back from the bathroom, but I wonder if it's a sign that he's not supporting me. I used to be able to make these sorts of remarks for my father's elections, but now I worry about everything everybody else is doing. It really wears me out, in terms of my spirit, my nerves, to have to go around and pour sake and smile *niko niko* [in this case, the implied meaning is "ingratiatingly"], when I didn't used to worry about that stuff.

Takada-san hoped that once the election was successfully concluded, this tension-inducing role-play would come to an end and "everybody" would relax. It must end. He couldn't keep up the pace for the four years of an assembly term, he said. He'd die.

In part out of necessity, in part as a matter of personal inclination, Takada-san's first bid for office was not grounded in an effort to plead a policy position or any relevant experience. Instead the campaign was about who he was as a young man, and what promise his manhood held for his community. In a way Takada-san's campaign was a "festival of manhood," and that was the source of both its sustaining and defeating aspects. He believed the success of his campaign for office was dependent on his ability to tap into the practical and symbolic aspects of a masculine power structure grounded in the conservative Liberal Democratic Party and its local supporters. And many of the frustrations he expressed with the process of running for office originated in the ways he felt oppressed by the same masculine power structure he relied on for the resources he needed to win an assembly seat.

Takada-san explained that he saw the politician's pursuit as an ethical project.[1] In one of our first meetings he wrote the two-character word *jingi* in large, balanced strokes on a piece of yellow scrap paper and gave it to me. He explained that this term signified the feelings of duty and honor that bound politicians as representatives of the people and in their relations with others. *Jingi,* as I explain more fully in chapter 3, is a quintessentially Confucian moral term. In fact the term is so stereotypically Confucian that at first, no matter what he said, I was quite dubious that *jingi* could have any power to explain the political motivations of the thirty-something, trendy, and election-savvy Takada-san. I initially thought he might simply be trying to impress his new American friend with his inscrutable Asian ways. Yet after years of following his political career and getting to know him as a person, I have changed my mind. The worldview evoked by Takada-san's use of words such as *jingi* is important to him. He works hard to a build a political identity in congruence with a traditionalist ethic that makes self-conscious use of notions of honorable manhood from Japan's Confucian and samurai pasts.

But Takada-san is not simply a Confucian gentleman caught in a modern Tokyo ward assembly. He struggles to maintain his ethical identity against his own cynicism, a cynicism born of his practical understanding of how much of his ethics must be compromised to satisfy his political ambitions. The problem for Takada-san is that, although the masculine power structure in which he has grounded his career has been instrumental in providing the vocabulary and images he uses for describing his ethical identity, that same structure constantly threatens to expose itself as a sham. Takada-san himself tells stories of how the values of selfless service, loyalty, honor, and duty pointed to in the conservative, masculinist vocabulary are often overwhelmed by a crass competition for power that he condemns, even though he feels compelled to participate in it. As Takada-san acknowledges, the tradition of masculine politics in which he participates sometimes makes unattainable the very goals it teaches him to hold dear, leaving him and his observers with perplexing questions about the place of masculinity in democratic life.

Although Takada-san sometimes talked about the performance of this traditionalist manhood identity as if it challenged his ability to be the sort of man he admired, he remained unwilling to surrender his attachment to the masculinist and traditionalist dimensions of his political identity.[2] As he successfully concluded his first campaign and began his career as an assembly member, he continued to struggle, sometimes dispiritedly, to make ethical sense out of his undertakings. During his first term in office he reexamined the vision of traditional masculinity that shaped his notions of duty and honor and tried refitting it into a more satisfactory political identity. A traditionalist or Confucian manhood came to be the practical and ethical ground from which Takada-san launched his bid for elective office, and the practical uses of this Confucian manhood deeply frustrated him, perhaps in part because he took the ethical claims of his Confucianism so seriously. His efforts at revising his notion of Confucian manhood in the midst of power politics made such revision a daunting challenge.

Like his father before him, Takada-san is a member of the Liberal Democratic Party. In 1999 his father was retiring from public life after twenty-eight years of unbroken service in the ward assembly, and Takada-san hoped to follow him into office. Technically speaking, Takada-san was not running for his father's seat. Elections for ward, city, town, and village assemblies in Japan are run in at-large districts. Therefore the seats are not officially attached to specific geographic locations within the municipality. Any voter who lived in Shirakawa Ward could vote for any candidate seeking an assembly seat. Takada-san planned to use the substantial organizational resources his father had built up over the years to return a seat to the Takada family. Because voters could easily have taken their support elsewhere, especially after the assembly member with whom they had long had a relationship retired, Takada-san needed to appeal to his father's voters as the bearer of his father's tradition of service. If he won he would be known in Japanese by the term *nisei giin*, "second-generation politician," the same status that would lead him to a successful campaign.

Second-generation politicians are a common phenomenon, especially in the LDP, because having a readymade constituency organization as well as contacts with party leaders is a tremendous advantage in running a first campaign. At times second-generation politicians have held more than a third of National Diet seats.[3] During Takada-san's elec-

tion race, having his father's organizational base was particularly helpful. As part of the ongoing attempt to streamline local governments,
the Shirakawa Ward Assembly was being downsized from forty-four
seats to forty. The aim was to reduce the portion of local government
budgets dedicated to maintaining the local assembly. Ward assembly
members' salaries vary depending on the size and level of the local
assembly. Town assembly salaries in Takeno-machi were not especially
grand, but in Shirakawa Ward the annual salary of an assembly member below the level of vice speaker is approximately 9,360,000 yen
($93,000 when 100 yen equal one dollar).[4] Some assembly members,
such as Takada-san's father, were retiring, which meant that, in theory,
incumbents need not be deprived of their seats. Yet even established
politicians were complaining that the reduction in the number of available seats was likely to make getting elected more difficult and thus
required expanded and more costly campaign efforts.[5] New faces were
therefore entering a more intense race than usual, increasing Takada-
san's dependence on the organizational resources his father could make
available. For Takada-san, becoming a second-generation politician
meant appealing to his father's ageing, conservative support base and
doing so by emphasizing his one natural connection to them: as the
dutiful son of their long-term representative.

The performance of filial duty before an elderly and conservative
crowd therefore won a central place in the Takada campaign. Without
his connection to his father, Takada-san would most likely have found
it difficult to mount his own campaign. Occasionally he would openly
question his own desire to run for office and expressed great distaste
for the process of doing so. More important, some of his supporters
explained to me that Takada-san was running because he was a rich
kid whose family had always been involved in local politics. The "rich
kid" impression might have easily overwhelmed Takada's efforts to
construct a more positive image if it weren't balanced by the impression
of his dedication to self-effacing service modeled in his humble filiality.
As I mentioned, given their home and substantial local landholdings,
Takada-san's constituents were likely to see him as distinctly better off
than they were. His father told me their ancestors had owned land in
the area since the Edo period, and another politician in the same party
described the family as "able to participate in politics because they
are big landholders." Following military service during World War II,
Takada-san's father had divided his time between managing the family's real estate resources and being a ward assembly member. He had

studied law briefly, thinking it would help him in some postwar legal disputes about his inheritance, but he had held no other paid employment. It was not hard to see why some supporters thought a political career was an easy option for the privileged son of this privileged man. At times even Takada-san agreed with this view.

For one thing, Takada-san did not seem personally ambitious about a career in politics, or for that matter in anything else. In fact he had little work experience of any kind. He had spent the slightly more than a decade since his college graduation studying to take a national bar examination and "helping out" in his father's business. He had failed the exam several times. (His failure was not considered a reflection on his fitness for political office. Between 1980 and 1990 the number of law graduates per year increased from 27,000 to 38,000, but the number of examinees allowed to pass the bar remained a constant 500.)[6] At any rate, Takada-san had given up on the idea of becoming a lawyer. At first I imagined that working in his father's real estate business might have required more effort than Takada-san's description of "helping out" seemed to denote. But when I pressed him for examples of what he had done for the business, he offered only that he had pulled weeds at apartment buildings his parents owned. The bookkeeping was done by another relative; his mother dealt directly with clients.

Moreover Takada-san could not describe a single local-level policy issue or political problem that motivated his quest for a public role. Other than "helping out" in the campaigns of his father and a couple of other politicians, he had no prior political experience. The problem was not that he was apolitical. He enjoyed discussing with me the twists and turns of the hotly contested Tokyo governor's race and had read widely about politics in Japan and elsewhere, including both popular and theoretical texts. He had little specific to say about what role he might be willing to play in the political process, however, because he believed his own views on the matter were either entirely irrelevant or even dangerous to his pursuit of office.

Winning an election, Takada-san declared, had little to do with either a candidate's real character or the sort of policy promises he might make to voters. Instead a candidate's win or loss was predetermined by the number of powerful community and organizational leaders who signed on to support him or her. In Takada-san's view, unorganized voters were unlikely to go to the polls, and the fewer than half of all eligible voters who were actually likely to turn out for a ward assembly election in Tokyo would be moved to vote in whatever way

these local leaders suggested.[7] Much of Takada-san's daily schedule
in the months running up to the election was composed of meetings
with local interest groups or their leaders who might consider lend-
ing him their support in the campaign. He talked about these crucial
decision-making processes with words like "closed" and "secretive,"
and he described the decisions these groups made to back a candidate
or withhold support as essentially arbitrary. Sometimes he was darker
than that, implying that political alliances carried dangers with them,
some even including the possibility of threatening encounters with the
Japanese mafia. He never offered specifics, and I was left on my own to
determine how seriously to take his mysterious remarks. But his father
also told me stories about local politicians he had known who had
accused their opponents of passing money around the neighborhood
after dark or using personal ties in the police to get campaign workers
arrested for campaign rule violations. Without a doubt, Takada-san
himself had heard stories of campaign alliances in which right-wing
organizations or the mafia played a role.

Takada-san clearly saw the electoral process as a structure full of
empty symbols. Power was held by interest-mongering groups from
trade associations to organized crime, and it was managed behind
closed doors. But Takada-san also argued that most voters understood
little of that truth. Like the leaders of the organizations that could help
get out the vote for a candidate of their choosing, voters worked from
a fairly arbitrary sense of their likes and dislikes. Given his reasoning
about the nature of building organizational and electorate support,
Takada-san's reliance on the filial son image is unsurprising. The image
of a traditionalist following obediently in his father's footsteps cast his
"little rich boy" qualities in a different light for voters, and the deference involved in the constant reenactment of his filiality might suggest
a promising obedience to community leaders looking to have their own
man in office.

THE FILIAL SON

On the wall of the home office he had set up for running his bid for the
Shirakawa Ward Assembly, Takada-san hung a poster from his father's
last run for office, four years earlier. On the poster his father's face had
been cut out and replaced with Takada-san's more youthful mug, as if
Takada-san was literally seeking to become his father. On a gray, cold
January morning I watched him enact this connection to his father as I

followed Takada-san and his mother through his *jimoto,* or home territory, as he passed out name cards and offered New Year greetings to his father's list of local supporters, much the way his father must have done over the years with his wife at his side.

Most of Shirakawa Ward lies within the Yamanote train line that loops around the heart of Tokyo. Shirakawa is a diverse ward. It is a densely populated area, despite the fact that the population has declined over the past two decades.[8] At the center of the ward is a major train station surrounded by a substantial shopping and business area. The ward contains big department stores and hotels and an active entertainment district with a wide assortment of restaurants and nightclubs. More than one university falls within the ward boundaries, and the quality of residential housing ranges from expensive high-rise condominiums to ageing public apartments to the largish single-family dwellings that dominate the area that Takada-san thinks of as his *jimoto.* As assembly elections are run in a single at-large district, Takada-san could expect votes from throughout the district, even from the area near my apartment, a twenty-five-minute walk away. In practice, however, LDP members have tacit—and sometimes even explicit— agreements that divide up the territory of the ward into different *jimoto* for different members of the party. Small bits of campaigning across the lines of one's *jimoto* are done regularly, but it is not acceptable to simply pursue votes across the entire ward. Members of the LDP are expected to respect each other's distinct territories because that mutual respect helps divide the LDP vote in the most efficient way possible, keeping the most popular candidates from eating up the votes that could be used to elect others in the same party.[9]

Takada-san was undertaking the New Year greetings because they were one of the few means of introducing himself to the area residents who would form his constituency in the April election. Given the at-large district system for the ward assembly elections, Takada-san would actually be competing with members of his own party for votes. He could not count on simple partisanship for support, and because ward assemblies govern geographically constrained areas and election advertising rules are extremely restrictive, he could not expect to succeed with a mass-media attempt to reach voters.[10] He needed a personal connection to them, and he intended to build it by using his father's network of supporters, based primarily in the neighborhood surrounding the Takada family home. Takada-san's parents had sent 3,000 letters to community residents on his father's supporter list, telling them how

Takada-san had been drafted to run in his father's place by his father's
kōenkai, his political support group.[11] Now Takada-san needed to follow the letter with a personal appearance.

Door-to-door election campaigning is illegal in Japan, and at any
rate, the period during which actual electioneering is legal is a scant
week and a half before the elections. Takada-san and his mother explained to me that, as a result, he could make no clear statement of his
electoral ambitions as he made his neighborhood visits. Nonetheless
these rounds of New Year greetings offered him an indirect opportunity to remind constituents that he was running. He reminded me
more than once that these greetings were not "campaign activities";
nonetheless they were considered an absolutely indispensable part of
the total election effort. Most candidates find similar means to justify
door-to-door visits, his mother said. In my experience, which includes
observing and interviewing candidates of various parties and citizen
groups in a wide variety of electoral contexts, Takada-san's mother is
right: local assembly candidates almost universally violate the spirit, if
not the letter, of the prohibition on door-to-door campaigning.[12]

Takada-san had invited me to join him for a morning's worth of
rounds at 9:30, and I did not want to make a bad impression by being
late. I was out of breath when I arrived at his house barely on time, but
Takada-san was not available to meet me. His mother let me in and
showed me to the room set aside for the election office activities. It was
noticeably cold; no one had entered it since the previous day. She tsked
and fretted and apologized for her son as she started a heater and prepared me a cup of tea. Takada-san was not yet out of bed. His mother
chatted with me while we waited for him to rise and dress for the day's
outing. "He's tired from all of the tension," she offered, explaining that
the many meetings and events he had attended in search of support
for his election bid had taxed his energy. "He's tired from meeting all
the new people. When he gets used to it, it won't be so bad," she said.
"Until then . . . ," she trailed off.

When he finally came down to see me Takada-san explained that he
had been out the previous evening at a party of the local pharmacists'
association to celebrate the beginning of the year. The new year is an
important marker in Japan's ritual calendar, and social and professional networks usually celebrate its arrival in some way. Many groups
have end-of-year parties in December, but probably equally as many
others hold New Year parties in January. After Takada-san returned
from the pharmacists' association party there had been another call at

about 11:00, an invitation from a campaign advisor to meet a potential new supporter. So Takada-san had gone out again. He showed me the loot he had won at bingo games at various organizations' New Year parties: a hairdryer, a water purifier to attach to the kitchen faucet. Then, bearing out his mother's words, he complained of being worn out by the process of courting supporters. "The problem is they don't care what you have to say," he claimed. "They just want to decide on the basis of little things, whether you're the kind of guy they like or not [*aitsu ni ki ni ireru ka dōka*]."

Eventually we set off through the neighborhood to offer the New Year greetings, and I watched as Takada-san was presented by his mother at door after door. He bowed extremely low, and when he was offered words of encouragement for the upcoming elections he laughed in a self-deprecating manner. He spoke little himself. Neither he nor his mother wore an overcoat, despite the fact that the bitingly cold air harassed me through my full-length wool coat. I have seen other candidates in Japanese elections leave their coats behind, as if they are so warmed by their earnestness that no coat is necessary. Moving along the streets, listening intently to his mother's running commentary on the past three generations of the neighborhood's inhabitants, Takada-san seemed to have left his earlier dispiritedness far behind. Yet I would encounter it several times more before he won his bid in late April.

The New Year rounds of the neighborhood offered a corresponding performance of Takada-san's subservience to the expectations of his father's generation. To a great extent the terms of his candidacy were out of his hands. He had a single office staffer of his own choosing, a young woman who had graduated from his university. She spent most of her time converting the voluminous paper records of his father's supporters into computer data files. But the other office work—stuffing envelopes, answering phones, and, during the official campaign period, fixing snacks and lunch in the campaign office—was handled by his mother and women she knew in the neighborhood. She, rather than Takada-san, handled office staff questions about constituents' family names and addresses. Only for the rare, large events did Takada-san's own friends join the campaign staff, and then they took care of the most menial tasks, such as carrying boxes of supplies. Most of these friends lived and worked outside of Shirakawa Ward and were not eligible to vote for Takada-san.

Because Takada-san was relying on his father's constituency organization to mobilize support for his bid for office, the men and women surrounding him had generally closer relations with his father. They decided most of the details of Takada-san's presentation to the community, and he in turn played every bit the earnest and dutiful apprentice. When men with some pull in the local community, such as leaders of the neighborhood association, stopped by to offer campaign assistance or to ask questions, Takada-san's father handled them. Often the only contact these men had with the candidate himself was when Takada-san led them into the house and to the door of his father's Western-style front room or to a more traditional living room toward the rear of the house. Takada-san kept his back half-bowed even as he guided these guests through the house. Sometimes they smiled at him indulgently or offered gruff words of encouragement before leaving him to discuss his fate with his father. Whenever I joined Takada-san at events, I found that I too was pushed into the role of keen young person, as if we were both a decade or so younger than the midthirties we actually were. Just in case we misunderstood our roles, Takada-san's father briefed us in detail before each event.

Nowhere was the display of Takada-san's subservience to the older generation made clearer than at the New Year luncheon held by the women's auxiliary of the neighborhood association. I planned to tag along with Takada-san and his parents, and this time, when I arrived at their house hours before the noon event, Takada-san was awake and ready. His mother set out earlier than we did in order to make a show of wanting to help other members of the women's auxiliary prepare the food. (I say "make a show of wanting to help" because she told me that the women would probably claim they needed no assistance and insist on treating her as a guest.) His father gave us very detailed instructions on how we were to behave. We were to insist on sitting at the back of the hall, the section traditionally reserved for the least important guests and those who have volunteered to serve the meal. Takada-san's father prepared a very formal, very humble self-introduction for me to practice before leaving for the association lodge. He wanted his son to be able to present his international friend, but he didn't want the international friend to seem too foreign. Later Takada-san's father decided that I had sounded "too Japanese" in my luncheon greeting, and at other events he urged me to arrange my own words of greeting, which were always on a level more simple than is common for LDP politicians.

The women's New Year party, ostensibly a simple get-together for the neighborhood women, was really a carefully orchestrated campaign event. As expected, our insistence on taking humble seats was met with utter refusal. We were rushed to the front of the room, where Takada-san and his father, the only men in attendance, became the main attractions. In brief remarks Takada-san's father presented his son as a healthy young man who would work hard for the ward. He reminded the assembled women that Takada-san had played baseball in college (failing to note that he had given up the sport because of injury some fifteen years previously). The audience of mostly elderly women murmured appreciatively. "Yes, we must have the young people run," I heard some say.

Takada-san reinforced his filial son image in any way he could.[13] He made a few remarks of his own that began with his reflection on the fact that the women's auxiliary group used the word *fujin* for "women" instead of the more contemporary-sounding *josei,* a distinction somewhat akin to the difference between "ladies" and "women" in American English. He was surprised, he said, that the group did not use the word *josei,* as it is so much more popular today. "But," he said, "looking out at the women here, I realized that *fujin* was a better choice because it contains the meaning of tradition, of the deep roots of the womanhood [*onna rashisa,* literally, "woman-like-ness"] that overflows in this group." He followed his remarks by serving tea, then sake, and then beer to the women, one by one. Because the room was traditional in style, with low tables and a tatami-mat floor on which the guests sat on flat cushions, he had to move around and around the room on his knees, bowing and smiling as he poured drinks for each woman. As his loyal sidekick I did as I was urged, and followed clumsily along with a teapot for refills. The women chatted to his parents about their own children, occasionally asking Takada-san if he remembered a child or grandchild of theirs who would likely have been his grade school classmate.

Following lunch there was karaoke singing. Takada-san and his father each performed a number. Their voices were deep and strong, and the women cheered them, pretending to be overwhelmed by the men's charm as singers. Takada-san's song was remarkably well delivered, and the older women teased him: Had he been practicing? He blushed obligingly, and they laughed merrily. His father had set aside his meal to enjoy the whisky and water the women had brought for the men, but Takada-san, who has a low tolerance for alcohol and had been finding the long nights of drinking with supporters hard to bear, quietly turned the whisky aside and drank only warm water. He and I ate every scrap of our lunches, and later he praised me for finishing my meal. It is very important to do so, he insisted, sounding like a Japanese grandmother.

On our way back to Takada-san's home following the meal, we ran into Mizuno-san, a ninety-year-old man who ran the elders section of the neighborhood association in the next neighborhood. He had business to take up with Takada-san's father, who had an errand to run, so in the meantime Takada-san and I were to escort Mizuno-san to the Takada home to wait for him. As Mizuno-san headed down the street, Takada-san fell in about a half-step behind and, with hand motions, indicated that I ought to fall in behind him. We made a little three-tiered procession, picking up speed as Mizuno-san quickened his steps upon approaching the Takadas' front gate, just as Confucius of the *Analects* is described doing to show respect when engaged in official business.[14] Mizuno-san was bustled into the front room with elaborate courtesy, and when Takada-san's father returned he and his wife sat down with Mizuno-san for a chat about the election. Takada-san was banished to the room serving as the office to wait with me and his staffer, but he crouched in the doorway trying to make out what he could of the conversation from across the entrance hall. What we could hear most clearly was Takada-san's father giving Mizuno-san a list of established politicians who had offered Takada-san their endorsement.

THE WEIGHT OF DUTY

The challenge of recruiting younger supporters was a concern for Takada-san, but he was more troubled by what he saw as the basic demand of the campaign: that he present himself, again and again, as a man whose main purpose is to please others. The most carefully choreographed aspects of his electoral effort highlighted Takada-san as a young man conspicuous for his filial devotion to family and community. Yet playing the devoted son also caused him frustration throughout the campaign, and I heard him grumble many times about the unpleasantness of campaigning, just as he complained on the morning of the *mochi* festival. Part of his frustration was surely generated by the constant stress of presenting himself in public, but another part seemed to come from the way the play of filiality constrained the extent to which he could pursue a campaign defined by the idea of *jingi* he had originally presented to me. In its large Confucian sense, *jingi* is a rich concept of self-development. It includes a necessary element of cooperating with and serving others; it also includes a portion of individual discretion, a certain moral autonomy. However, in the practice of campaign politics, where most of the situations in which Takada-san operated were not of his making and where a premium was placed on pleasing those in any situation who might assist his career with resources or votes, the *jingi* Takada-san associated with being a "good" political man was often reduced to the minimalist "duty." By depicting the work of politics as a matter of doing one's duty as a young man and a young son, Takada-san presented politics as a place in which a man's moral worth would be tested. Yet paradoxically, because he practiced politics primarily in terms of duty, he saw the political world as offering almost no opportunity for moral self-definition. A man must do what is required of him; if he does not, he is not a good man. Yet what is required, as Takada-san seemed to understand and practice, is submission to a system that is not, in itself, good. Takada-san was stuck in a paradox: to do the duty required of a good man, he surrendered his right to choose for himself which political practices were good and which were not.

Takada-san shared some of his frustrations with me on our way home from a luncheon sponsored by a National Diet member from the Tokyo area. The attendees were Liberal Democratic Party members of either the Tokyo Prefectural Assembly or Tokyo ward assemblies and alumni of Takada-san's university. Because he had worked on the Diet member's previous campaign, Takada-san was invited to the luncheon despite the fact that he had not yet won his first election. He had served on the campaign of a Tokyo Prefectural Assembly member in the alumni group who had once served in the Shirakawa Ward Assembly with Takada-san's father. Takada-san thus had some connections with the others, but as the youngest member of the group, and the only one not yet elected to office, he was the lowliest member, a fact that seemed to have made him nervous.

He called me the night before the event to settle the terms of our attendance. The meeting would be held at the offices of Japan's Ministry of Foreign Affairs, where the Diet member had a minor vice ministry appointment. Takada-san checked that I remembered the time at which we would set out together for the luncheon, and more than once he described the likely attendees. "This event is going to be a bit *kinakusai*," he said, a word the dictionary defines as the smell of paper or cotton burning or a description for the atmosphere at the opening of a conflict. When I pressed him for an explanation he offered the alternative *yayakoshii* or, as another friend suggested, "sticky with regard to etiquette." Takada-san wanted to know what I would wear, and he seemed relieved when I told him I'd have on a proper business suit. "Don't forget to have as many as thirty business cards and to have them accessible," he reminded me, adding that I should understand that his position in the group would not be high.

But in the morning he overslept, just as he had when we were to meet for the neighborhood rounds for New Year greetings, and our departure time for the luncheon had to be adjusted with an apologetic call from Satō-san, his staff member. Despite Takada's oversleeping, we were early for the luncheon meeting; the Diet member hosting it was a half-hour late. Takada-san's position was clearly the lowest in the room. At this meeting we were not rushed to the front of the room; we had to sit in glare from the windows falling on the uncomfortable rear seats of a reception area, and we ate our luncheon at the far end of the long table. The conversation was directed by the Diet member and another senior politician. Most local elections across Japan are held on the same day as part of the Unified Local Elections, so nearly all of the alumni at the meeting were facing reelection in their own districts during the same April election period in which the Shirakawa Ward elections were being held. But little time was devoted to the election considerations of those assembled. Instead, aside from offering each of the alumni an opportunity to introduce himself, the meeting leaders clearly wanted to hear how members' constituents were reacting to the various conservatives floating their names in the press in contemplation of a bid for the Tokyo governorship. Takada-san was the last asked to speak in response to each question posed to the group. He kept his answers short and humble, and he was not encouraged to elaborate.

On the way home from the event we shared a bench on a subway train with Matsui-san, the Tokyo Prefectural Assembly member who had served in the Shirakawa Assembly. Matsui-san was also preparing for reelection, but he queried Takada-san about his campaign effort in the tone of a knowing elder. "The most important thing," he said, "is just to get out and go house to house, to bring your mother with you and work the neighborhood. That's the best thing." Matsui-san asked several questions about Takada-san's campaign office. He was especially curious about who would staff it. "Who is this person working for you now?" When Takada-san explained that Satō-san was an alumna of his institution who had helped in his father's previous campaign, Matsui-san seemed dissatisfied. "You need to have people who have been connected to your father's elections not just this last time, but the time before that and the time before that. Can't your older sister work with you?" Takada-san said he didn't know, but he thought she might be able to help out. "Your sister is the person who will be your greatest support," Matsui-san insisted. Before we parted Matsui-san again emphasized the importance of having family members central to the campaign effort. Takada-san thanked him graciously for his advice and said that he would return to making rounds in the neighborhood with his mother that very afternoon.

But he didn't. Instead Takada-san and I stopped for cake at a coffee shop near the station. He had only angry words to describe the luncheon we had just attended, calling it a "meaningless event," worthwhile only if I had gotten something out of it for my research. As if he hadn't called the previous night, nervously anticipating the challenges of making an effective appearance at the luncheon, he now offered a multitude of words to dismiss the day. It was "stupid," "a waste of time," "irrelevant," and just plain "whatever" (dōdemo ii). He had unpleasant words for the Diet member as well. "Our relationship is one of threads," he said. "He sticks his threads down to everybody below him, and they can be of use to him in elections because his district is all of Tokyo. But the only threads the ones below have to him are very long. They can't reel him in. Although everyone asked him to visit their districts, I doubt very much if he'll go to any of them," Takada-san proclaimed. "These connections have no use for me." He claimed that he had gone to the alumni luncheon only because Matsui-san wanted him there, and Matsui-san was the sort of attentive person for whom one should do such things. This was an unexpected comment given that Matsui-san's queries about Takada-san's election strategy seemed to have precipitated his irritation at the day's activity.

Because Takada-san had chosen to spend his afternoon musing over coffee instead of making more rounds in the neighborhood with his mother, as Matsui-san had suggested, I wondered if he wasn't upset as much by his inability to escape the role of dutiful son as by the idea that he was being used by a member of the Diet. As I observed Takada-san's pursuit of office, I began to think he was unsure of his own motivation. His discomfort at modeling his "sales face" at the neighborhood events and gatherings continued, and sometimes it negatively affected the tone of his campaigning. He often seemed to be performing a delegated chore less than willingly. At one point he told me that he'd rather be studying than running for office. He had spent many years after college studying law, and he enjoyed taking up new topics, such as international relations, and doing extended reading in them. In fact whenever he had a spare moment between meetings he would slip into the nearest bookstore to browse. Takada described his schedule, full of breakfasts and dinners with the local party leadership or interest groups such as the local physicians' association, as full of meaningless meals: "I just go to maintain *wa* [harmony]." Nothing of significance would be discussed, he insisted. "Everybody always thinks, 'Well, anyway, let's eat,'" he said in a dismissive tone. He speculated that American politicians led more purposeful lives. Takada-san seemed at times to be running for office merely out of boredom with his previous life as an employee at his parents' property management business. Visions of public service did not seem to occupy him. He seemed to prefer to spend his time with me and his staffer, making jokes and talking about television dramas and movie stars.

Clearly he couldn't control his campaign apparatus. That could have simply been the result of his inexperience, but I think it was also an effect of his ambivalence about the election. When we made a weekend day trip with his father's constituent group, Takada-san demonstrated little desire to refocus his father's campaign apparatus on himself. His father filled three buses with neighborhood men and women, many of retirement age and older who had traveled with him in previous years, and we bused into neighboring prefectures to make first-of-the-year visits (*hatsumode*) to significant shrines. The *hatsumode* trip is a key component of many conservative politicians' system of supporter cultivation. I had joined the *hatsumode* trip of another Liberal Democrat in Takada-san's district a month earlier, and in the bus parking lots at the highway rest stops I saw other groups of politicians and their supporters. The politicians and their secretaries were recognizable for the badges they wore on their suit jackets, even if the awkward, inflated names of the groups, names such as White Wings Association and Friendly Spirit Club, hadn't given them away.[15]

This trip was the single biggest opportunity Takada-san had to meet with a large number of his father's loyal supporters and impress upon them his fitness as a candidate so that they might recruit friends, family members, and neighbors to turn out for him. But he never seemed wholly committed to it. At the beginning of Takada-san's *hatsumode* trip, as on the other politician's trip I had joined, elected officials representing the district constituency at higher levels gave speeches encouraging support for him and speaking more generally of the importance of good public policy in economically trying times. One of those speaking was Matsui-san, the Tokyo Assembly member who had joined us at the alumni luncheon. Takada-san's father spoke about the long years of camaraderie that had held together the tradition of *hatsumode* trips, even after he had announced his coming retirement from the ward assembly. Takada-san, legally barred from asking directly for the trip-goers' votes and seemingly unconvinced that the travelers wanted to hear more about public policy, limited himself largely to repeatedly bowing and thanking the participants for coming. He spent some time passing out food and refreshments on the bus in which we rode, but he did not seek to engage the mostly elderly passengers in conversation. As the day went on and we traveled from shrine to shrine, munching and drinking between stops, many of the male travelers, and even some of the women, became quite intoxicated and boisterous. But Takada-san did not attempt to join their raucous fellowship. Instead he chatted with Satō-san and me and a couple of male high school classmates who had come along to help load and unload provisions for the trip.

When we returned to Tokyo and a small group of us went back to the Takada home with the remaining provisions, Takada-san continued to direct his attention to our small group of younger people, while his father and a few of the older men and women, still quite cheery from their afternoon sipping sake, regaled each other with funny tales of the behavior of group members who had gotten inebriated on the long bus ride. They would have gone out for more drinking themselves that evening if Takada-san's mother had not intervened with a firm suggestion that the next drink would be better begun on another day. The gap between Takada-san, who drank little, and his father's drinking buddies of many years seemed great at that moment. Despite the fact that he could be unfailingly humble and polite when a situation required him to be so, Takada-san did not seem to warm to his father's crowd in any way. When they publicly teased him, still single in his midthirties, about finding a wife, he would smile as if embarrassed and say, "I hope one can be found for me" or "Please find me a good one." Privately he joked that he was in love with a television star. Sometimes Satō-san or I asked him his opinion of single women he knew, but he usually laughingly described them as not his type. Satō-san knew some of the women he had dated, and she thought he had not married yet because he was "still playing." On Valentine's Day a neighborhood "grandma" (as Takada-san called her) delivered candy when I was working with Satō-san in the office. Takada-san passed around the box of chocolate bears. "They just keep bringing it, and I wish they wouldn't," he said.

But as we bit into our sweet bears, Satō-san asked him if he thought it was all right to express such irritation aloud. After all, the Valentine-bearing grandma was a potential supporter.[16]

Sometimes the gaps and strains in the campaign seemed to be more a result of the power of Takada-san's parents than his ambivalence. For example, as the office work grew more complicated, Satō-san ran into difficulties trying to do her job. Takada-san had told his mother that Satō-san would be managing his schedule, but Takada-san's mother or father continued to make scheduling decisions without telling her. The phone lines in the various rooms of the large home could all be observed or picked up from Satō-san's desk, but she could never be sure if she was to answer calls for family members other than Takada. Sometimes she would avoid answering the phone when she saw it ringing in Takada-san's father's office, only to be told that she should have. Often when she did answer, however, she sensed that Takada-san's parents were irritated that she had done so, as if she had intruded. When he learned about such miscommunications, Takada-san would usually say something about it to his mother, but I am not sure if he himself had a clear sense of how the campaign tasks were being managed. He could be quite meticulous about details such as the development of an informative database for campaign workers to use to make phone calls during the official campaign period. Yet at other times, such as when there were questions about how to list endorsements from other politicians on campaign literature, he would simply tell his father, "You manage that stuff." Frequently I heard his father give him very detailed instructions about how to handle his relationships with potential supporters.

When Takada-san's parents were not as closely connected to a group of supporters as they were in the case of the shrine visit, the situation actually seemed more difficult. Satō-san and I helped Takada-san to host an early evening party for some alumni of his college at a formal Chinese restaurant in the area. We were surprised by the level of disorganization. I arrived at the Takada household some hours before the event expecting to chat while stuffing envelopes and then head off to the dinner. I assumed I would play my usual tag-along role in the event. Instead, almost none of the details had been arranged. A guest roster hadn't been prepared. Seating plans had not been made. There was no established program order. There wasn't even a receipt book for presenting receipts to party guests in return for their 5,000 yen admission fee. I was roped into playing the role of a full staffer, running to a stationer's shop for last-minute supplies and helping to arrange tables and seating arrangements at the restaurant.

The evening was so disorganized that Satō-san concluded that Takada-san had no desire to run for the local assembly. She thought he was just doing it to please his father, who, in her words, had a "strong personality." She said that when she agreed to work on the campaign she had no intention of being a central figure. But now Takada-san had gotten into the habit of simply saying, "I'm leaving it to you, Satō-san." "But I can't make the decisions," she said. It was clear as we stood in the restaurant banquet room waiting for Takada-san to show up that she had little idea what he wanted from her. Asked question after question by the restaurant staff and volunteers and guests who had arrived early, she fended them off, repeating "The candidate himself hasn't shown up yet."

The evening teetered on the brink of disaster without ever going over the edge. The reserved room turned out to be much too large for those few, slightly more than twenty, who made their way through a blinding, cold rain to attend. Hardly anyone brought the congratulatory envelopes with the cash contributions often seen at such events. The emcee for the evening was a young woman with professional announcing experience who knew Takada-san from another politician's campaign. But she and Takada-san had spent so little time going over the details of the event that she made awkward mistakes as she read through guests' titles or the names of organizations they represented. Once, when she read the characters in the name of a ward neighborhood incorrectly, a guest shouted that no such place existed. Several people had been asked to offer a word or two in support of Takada-san's candidacy at the beginning of the dinner. However, few were well prepared, and one even explained sheepishly that he had nothing much to say because he had just been asked to speak shortly after he arrived at the restaurant.

In putting the event together Takada-san had received some assistance from fellow alumnus Matsui-san. In fact, the restaurant reservation was in Matsui-san's name, and some portion of the guests had come because they had been asked to do so by him. However, Matsui-san was late in arriving and quick to leave. He bustled his way through the room offering apologies for his tardiness at each table. He also made some brief comments in support of Takada-san, but he explained that he was late because he had attended the campaign event of another candidate, a woman running for the same ward assembly in which Takada-san sought a seat. Matsui-san also used his remarks as a chance to advertise his own upcoming event, explaining that he expected an attendance of more than 200 people. Finally he talked about university business completely unrelated to the upcoming elections. In the end most of what Matsui-san had to say served his own interests as an elected official seeking new opportunities to put his face before his constituents.

Simply having an established, higher level politician show up may well have served Takada-san in some sense. One message his constituents might have taken from the event was that Takada-san possessed connections to successful local leaders who could help to ameliorate his lack of political experience. However, no one at the event was a strong advocate for Takada-san himself. Even the leader of his *kōenkai* (supporters' organization) bumbled through his remarks. No one made a speech about the indispensability of supporters' efforts to victory in a tough contest. Having attended a great many campaign events for other candidates, I had assumed such speeches were de rigueur for any election-related gathering.

Takada-san's own remarks emphasized his filial son identity. Instead of saying much about the ward assembly or ward politics, he spoke about a letter written to an ancestor who had fought in the Russo-Japanese War. He explained that the letter had been written in archaic Japanese and that he had to consult a scholar in order to translate it into modern Japanese. Then he went on to share the contents of the letter. It was written to encourage the ancestor when he was a young man fighting the war; it exhorted him to fight courageously by reminding him of the "three principles" by which Takada men live. Takada men strive to be *seijitsu, chakujitsu,* and *kakujitsu,* he explained. *Seijitsu* has a variety of potential meanings: integrity, honesty, loyalty, and sincerity. *Chakujitsu* means "steady" or "surefooted." *Kakujitsu* overlaps a bit with *chakujitsu,* but it also carries the connotation of "completion." When I later asked Takada-san about the three words, he explained that his father had used them to describe his standards for himself. "These words are a tradition with Takada men," he said.

The audience seemed to find Takada-san's remarks interesting. His presentation of a conversation among men of his lineage nearly a century ago was unusual. The lines of the letter he presented in contemporary Japanese had a certain eloquence. And the letter gave weight and durability to Takada-san's political ambitions that nothing else about the disorganized, poorly attended event could provide. Instead of taking the position of the inexperienced, ill-prepared candidate for the local assembly that he looked to be next to Matsui-san's confident hustle and bustle, Takada-san used the letter to make a sort of birthright claim to the seat he sought. Alongside the image of the young soldier the letter evoked, Takada-san seemed to be a young soldier too. He sought an elected office not because he desired it for himself but because his sense of integrity as a Takada man demanded he do so. His lack of political experience (demonstrated so fully in the sloppiness of the event) was irrelevant because, as a century of Takada manhood before him had already proven, Takada-san was born to surefooted competence. The calm grace with which he told his story of the letter seemed to confirm the validity of these implications. Of course if Takada-san deserved the political position he sought by birthright, then he owed much to his father and to his father's friends. The meaning of *seijitsu* most essential to his election is "loyalty," despite his own frustrations with that fact.

When Takada-san spoke with me about his family's three principles he seemed proud of them, but he also seemed dubious of how important they would actually be to any political career he might have. He told me that his father's retirement marked the end of an era when people could take office on the basis of their family reputation. His father could simply give orders and expect others to follow them, just because of who he was. Takada-san doubted the same would apply to him. "This is the era of specialists," he said. "You've got to do something, like the environment or social welfare." I asked Takada-san what he thought his specialty would be, but he didn't offer any suggestions. "I'll have to have something, and that's why I'll have to gather experts around me," he said. In the same conversation he said he was unsure whether he was running because he wanted to run or because other people wanted him to run. He guessed that his motives were about half and half.

Not long after the awkward alumni group dinner, I left my Tokyo field site to investigate the preparations for the town assembly election in Takeno-machi. During the time I was away I spoke with Takada-san occasionally by phone, and his father called once in an attempt to get me to make some public appearances on his son's behalf. But I was unwilling to desert my new field site to play a role in a campaign that was, at any rate, an ethically dubious one for a social scientist.[17] I did return to Tokyo on the day that the official campaign period for the ward assembly election began. Takada-san's office had been moved down the street, and it was certainly more lively than it had been prior to the official campaign's beginning. His mother's friends rushed about preparing snacks for the campaign workers, and a small crowd of his father's supporters gathered in a gloomy rain to watch Takada-san kick off the campaign. He and a few campaign volunteers drove away from the office in a small sound truck to announce his candidacy throughout the ward. They would circle the ward neighborhoods many times in the ten days between the beginning of the campaign and the voting.

On the day of the campaign kickoff the office was full of busy people and family members, such as Takada-san's sister, whom I had not yet met. Until then, Satō-san said, she had worked largely alone, at last persuading a friend to help her with the preparations for the official campaign period. Even on the day of the campaign kickoff there were worries about whether there would be enough young women to staff the sound truck as *uguisujo* (the "nightingale"-voiced women who traditionally call out the candidate's name and a short message as the sound truck makes its way through neighborhoods). In the past Takada-san's father had relied on volunteers from the politics club at Takada-san's university, but this year the club had gone away on a group trip, so no volunteers were available.

A few weeks earlier I had stupidly agreed to be featured in a newspaper column about women candidates in the local elections, and Takada-san had made an enormous stack of copies of the column. He handed a copy to each supporter who stopped by the office to greet him and introduced me again and again with flattering words. Privately he complained to me that I had put undue emphasis on the cause of female candidates, but publicly he seemed to have decided to use the column to highlight his connection with an international scholar. Passing out the copies of the column was one of the only prepared activities of the disorganized morning.

At last the candidate, his father, and a few visiting dignitaries (myself included) were lined up in a parking lot across the street from the small campaign office. The supporters tried to keep out of the rain and the roadway by huddling under the building's eaves. Most of the remarks were simply short greetings and good wishes, but a secretary for the LDP Diet member who represented the district in which Takada-san's ward falls spoke at length about the importance of electing "this superb young man" to lead Japan in a new century. Unfortunately the man did not know Takada-san's given name, and he got it wrong until Takada-san finally yelled it out to him. Takada-san's father kept saying that someone ought to shut the secretary up. The leader of a medical group supporting Takada-san and the leader of the women's branch of the *kōenkai* offered brief greetings. At last Takada-san's father took the microphone to introduce his son. His voice sounded as if it might break into a sob as he thanked his supporters for their years of loyalty and their willingness to support his son. The introduction was the single truly dramatic moment of the event. Takada-san accepted his introduction, made a few very vague remarks about rising to the challenges of the twenty-first century, and the campaign officially began as he rode off in his sound truck, waving a white-gloved hand from the window.

Of course the outcome had already been secured. I poked around the office a bit before departing, chatting with the women there. One of them was the professional announcer who had emceed Takada-san's precampaign dinner with university alumni. "How do you think the election will go?" I asked her. She told me she had no worries. Takada-san would be victorious because he was so well liked by the old ladies who had supported his father. He did win quite easily. His nearly 1,800 votes put him into office comfortably toward the middle of the winners' rankings. Takada-san had captured almost exactly the number of votes his father had taken on his first run for office and about 200 more than his father had taken on his last run for office. In each of his father's several campaigns he had submitted advertisements to the circular that provide a glimpse of the evolution of policy concerns over the years he served. One year he made a promise to work to have highway projects routed underground; in other years he expressed support for redevelopment at the entrance to a large train station in the area and expanded moral education in the public schools. In his own advertisement space, however, the son eschewed his father's fine-print list of projects. Instead he had written his age beside his name and promised simply to work for a "new local governance for a new century." Takada-san didn't need to make policy promises; he was selling himself as the next-generation version of a political leader the voters already liked.

During his campaign Takada-san described the work of politicians in moral terms as a cultivation of oneself as a dutiful, humane man, a man of *jingi*, a man who was *seijitsu, kakujitsu, chakujitsu* (true, loyal, reliable, precise). He identified himself with these rather Confucian values by presenting himself in preelection events as a model of the filial son and dutiful young man, but the demands of such a self-effacing presentation frequently left him despondent and cynical about the nature of election politics. When the pressures of the campaign became too much for him, he mused that surely, once he was elected, things would get better. But when he won his seat Takada-san was encumbered by a new set of demands for his submission.

His father still played a role in his political career, and pleasing the political elders of his community was still a central part of Takada-san's daily activities. The election-night photo printed in a small newspaper circulated in the ward showed Takada-san with his arms crossed in front of his waist, his hands locked with the hands of his mother and father, who stood on either side of him. An election advisor about Takada-san's father's age stood to the side of the trio wearing a restrained half-smile. The caption read, "Continuing after his father, Takada-san is successful in his first run for office. On the report of his victory, he clasped his parents' hands tightly." Compared to most of the other shots of victorious campaigns, with crowds of smiling and waving men and women, Takada-san's victory shot was remarkably somber. With his hands crossed and locked in front of him, he looked like a man in an invisible straitjacket. Takada-san had entered the political arena well connected and well supported. He was secure. But he was not his own man.

CHAPTER 3

The Paradox of Masculine Honor

Takada-san's strategy of connecting himself to his father's constituency base worked, and he won his first election. Unfortunately for Takada-san, however, his notion of ethical identity was enmeshed with the same masculinist power structure that commanded his submission to the often arbitrary likes and dislikes of men more powerful than he. His postelection political narrative justified his acceptance of the masculine hierarchy he faced in elected office, and thus it also acted to constrain his political and ethical ambitions as an elected representative. Takada-san struggled to reinterpret traditionalist notions of Japanese masculinity into the means of defining a politician's work as an ethical and community-oriented project. Still, hierarchy and deference remained key structural elements of the political environment in which he found himself, and he argued that, to be of use to his community, he had to be pragmatic and accept aspects of the political system that he saw as ethically questionable.

Takada-san's job as a new entrant to the assembly was to do what his seniors told him to do, displaying his understanding of the limitations of his position. He was not expected to aim for any particular political good. As he gained seniority he might expect to develop some influence, but he was not given to speculating on his political future. For example, in addition to his work in the assembly, he was taking a continuing education seminar on social welfare policy in Japan's rapidly ageing society, but he did not think it worthwhile to establish specific policy goals to pursue in the assembly. He was in no position to dictate the priorities of his party delegation. In fact he was dubious about how well received his efforts to study social welfare policy would be among the senior conservatives, who might see his seminar participation as a tad socialist. Because he saw his political future as tied to the future of veteran politicians who had supported his first bid for office, he believed that pushing policy initiatives they did not favor was inimical to his career and thus, by extension, harmful to any long-term policy interests he might have.

After months among the fiercely determined political reformers I had studied in Takeno-machi, returning to Takada-san's cynical acknowledgment of the limits on his political endeavors was depressing, and our relationship became more fractious. In our conversations I picked at his realist philosophy of power and the resignation with which he accepted a subservient position in his party delegation. Only half-jokingly Takada-san suggested that I might have become some sort of communist, and he finally seemed satisfied to attribute my obstinate refusal to understand what seemed obvious to him to my Americanness. His assessment of my differences as the product of my foreign upbringing fit well with his commitment to preserving what he saw as a uniquely Japanese tradition of politics. Over time, however, it seemed that Takada-san could not deal with the limits of his position as easily as either he or I first thought. As he worked his way through his first term and on into his second and third, Takada-san expressed frustration with the submission demanded by the hierarchical political ethic of his party that in some ways echoed his frustrations with the "sales face" he felt forced to wear during his first campaign for an assembly seat.

Takada-san had always been a reader, and so he began to read more fully into Japanese history, seeking a better understanding of how notions of masculine duty, self-sacrifice, submission to hierarchy, and loyalty to the group could be honored in a way that contributed to, rather than overshadowed, his meeting the demands of public service. On one hand, he saw some typical expectations for masculine behavior as an ethically empty means of binding politicians together to control power to serve private ends. On the other hand, he argued that, properly understood, the same notion of traditional masculine honor that justified loyalty among the participants in a venal politics could also encourage a selfless community spirit and serve as a bulwark against corruption. As he wrestled with the aspects of conservative politics he did not like, he remained self-consciously ambivalent about the public value of traditional Japanese notions of masculinity. But his ambivalence did not lead him to jettison these notions because they constituted his masculinity, and his attachment to public service, as much as they beleaguered it.

THE MAN OF *JINGI*

In his pragmatic adjustment to partisan hierarchies Takada-san demonstrated his acceptance of a politics that operates according to a brutal power logic, sometimes on behalf of interests that bring little to the community as a whole. But when he declared in one of our first meetings that a Confucian notion of duty, *jingi,* was the key to understanding the political world, he also claimed that, when it is done right, political work is more than the representation of interests. Rather, the central task of politics for a politician with *jingi* in his heart is the modeling and extension of moral well-being. Even in his most cynical moments Takada-san never completely abandoned his attachment to *jingi*. In fact it became the organizing narrative of his evolving political ambitions.

When I asked Takada-san for a fuller explanation of how he understood *jingi,* he talked to me about loyalty to others, reliability, uprightness, steadfastness. Often he added to his description of good politicians the terms *ninjō ni atsui* (to take seriously relationships with others, especially their emotional aspects) and *giri gatai* (to be punctilious about one's obligations to others). But with its long heritage in Confucian thought, the term *jingi* can mean much more. Providing a complete account of the Confucianism represented in Takada-san's use of *jingi* might be the work of a book of its own; I certainly cannot do it here. Nonetheless scholarship on Confucian texts in recent decades does offer insight into the larger ethical discourse Takada-san invokes when he speaks of good politicians as practitioners of *jingi*.

Jin, the first character of the word *jingi,* refers to the quality of humanity Confucius most praised. The character *jin* is composed of two parts; the first is the character for "person," the second the character for the number two. With a quick glance at the character, a reader of Chinese or Japanese can see that what is meant is a person with some extra element, and because, in Japanese, *jin* has exactly the same pronunciation as the simpler term meaning "person," the link between the moral and ethical concept of *jin* and any individual's personhood is clear. Contemporary translators of Confucian texts disagree about the most appropriate English rendering, but one word that contains some of its multiple connotations is "benevolence." In addition *jin* has been rendered as "authoritative personhood," "humanity," "humaneness," and "nobleness," to quote a far from inclusive list.[1] The text widely considered the most helpful for understanding what Confucius meant by *jin* is the *Analects,* a text that has evolved from a collection of aphorisms through which Confucius and his most prominent disciples offer guidance to his students. For example, the Japanese scholar Ishikawa Tadashi turns to the *Analects* when he seeks to interpret *jin* for modern readers, as do the philosophers Roger Ames, Henry Rosemont, and David Hall.[2] In many passages of the *Analects* Confucius, usually called simply "the Master," answers the questions of disciples who want to know how to cultivate the quality of *jin.*

Ishikawa explains that in the *Analects* the disciples struggle with the Master's multiple and sometimes seemingly contradictory definitions of *jin,* a quality that seems both unexpectedly simple and impossibly complex, depending on the context in which it is discussed. Ishikawa argues that the meaning of *jin* is embedded in the paradoxes of the Master's comments about it, and the first of Ishikawa's three essays on Confucius begins with these two seemingly contradictory passages from the *Analects:*

> The Master said, "How could authoritative conduct [*jin*] be at all remote? No sooner do I seek it than it has arrived. (7.30)
>
> Master Zheng said, "Scholar-apprentices cannot but be strong and resolved, for they bear a heavy charge and their way is long. Where they take authoritative conduct [*jin*] as their charge, is it not a heavy one? And where their way ends only in death, is it not indeed long?" (8.7)[3]

In some passages of the *Analects, jin* seems to be a word describing a person self-disciplined and punctilious about following social rules. For example, the Master tells his favorite disciple that a *jin* person would not "look at anything that violates the observance of ritual propriety; . . . listen to anything that violates the observance of ritual propriety; . . . [or do] anything that violates the observance of ritual propriety" (12.1). Yet in contrast to the rites-oriented individual of this passage, elsewhere the pursuit of *jin* seems to be much more complicated than "observance of ritual propriety." For example, the Master asserts that the *jin* person is "slow to speak" because *jin* is "difficult to accomplish" (12.3), whereas in another passage he insists that even a person who is capable of "refrain[ing] from intimidation, from self-importance, from ill will, and from greed" is not yet *jin* (14.1).

Then again, if in many passages *jin* seems to be a nearly unattainable state of good behavior mysteriously beyond most demanding notions of goodness, that is not the case through the whole of the *Analects*. Ishikawa points out that in other places the Master explicitly resists such a construction. In these passages *jin* seems to be an almost prosaic quality: a willingness to be helpful, a thoughtfulness about the situations of others that would not always be easy to practice but surely not an unattainable virtuosity.[4] Ishikawa claims that *jin* is neither a specific moral quality nor an abstract moral standard above and beyond the person (who is so *literally* a part of *jin*), but a way of proceeding in any kind of human sphere: self-consciously, carefully, and fully immersed in the human world. For example, *jin* is expressed in the Master's painstaking choice of clothing appropriate to season and task; the choice requires knowledge, self-awareness, and sensitivity, but it is in no way divorced from the exigencies of daily life (43).

Jin is not a specific method for prescribing or proscribing certain actions. Depending on the particulars of a situation, Ishikawa speculates, one might even commit a theft or kill another human being in a *jin* way (66–69). No action or sort of person is categorically set apart from *jin* because *jin* is about the manner in which a person approaches life from moment to moment. And though this sounds terribly permissive, Ishikawa argues that *jin* is saved from being a simple excuse for a romp by the importance placed on the social traditions and teachings contained in ritual, which the Master insists is indispensable for leading a civilized life. Ritual without the humanizing force of *jin* becomes a "civilized" excuse for oppression; *jin* without ritual lacks the necessary discipline to fortify a person. The moral challenge is to correctly balance these forces in a given situation (94–98).[5]

The term *jingi* that Takada-san uses has rich connotations of a morally developed, socially integrated human being, a modest individual who seeks to improve the welfare of others, not by holding to an abstract standard of virtue, but by working thoughtfully with his or her fellow human beings in the midst of the murk of daily life. Following Ishikawa's interpretation of *jin*, we can see why Takada-san might argue that submission to the hierarchical and sometimes ethically questionable LDP power structure is part of the task of both becoming a fully developed person and serving one's constituents with *jingi*. This reading makes even more sense when we consider the second element of *jingi*. *Gi* delivers the sense of duty in the term *jingi*, probably one reason why Takada-san first explained *jingi* to me as "duty" (*gimu*). *Gi* is a word with nearly as complex a history in Confucian thinking as *jin,* and for Confucian scholars *gi* can provoke similar debates about appropriate translations.[6] However, as used in contemporary colloquial Japanese, the word is usually more constrained in its meanings.

In fact, whereas *jin* is a word seldom if ever heard in commonplace conversation, *gi* makes its way into a surprising array of contexts quite easily. *Gi* is the first component of *giri,* a word with many uses in contemporary Japanese, and the first word of the phrase *giri gatai* (to be punctilious about one's obligations to others) that Takada-san frequently uses when describing politicians he thinks of as morally good or even sometimes those he sees as merely effective. In simplest terms *giri* is an obligation to another. In Japanese attaching *giri* to the word for sister, brother, mother, or father can signify "in-law." *Giri* is not an obligation that is simply natural but one human beings have somehow participated in devising. (Although human beings who are not capable of feeling *giri,* of responding to others in accordance with *gi,* might be seen as unnatural in some ways.) *Giri* is even commonly used to refer to a task one performs reluctantly for another, such as one's boss, who holds one to unreasonable or artificial expectations. A popular use of the term in this way is *giri choko,* the way women office workers describe chocolates they feel obliged to give irritating male coworkers on Valentine's Day.[7] As we saw in the previous chapter, at times Takada-san himself clearly uses *giri* in this somewhat sarcastic way.

Nitobe Inazō's discussion of the term in his famous *Bushido: The Soul of Japan* helps us to get a fuller sense of how Takada-san hears and uses *gi* also as a moral term. Although Nitobe's book was originally written in the early 1900s in English for English-speaking audiences, he and his *Bushido* have a new-found popularity in Japan, where his face has even been featured on the 5,000 yen note.[8] Takada-san is an acknowledged admirer of Nitobe. A government plan to replace Nitobe's likeness on the bill with that of a Japanese female writer so upset Takada-san that he spoke out against it in a meeting with his supporters. Attempting to interpret Japanese society for outsiders by speaking of the key concepts of *bushidō* (the way of the warrior) practiced in early modern Japan, Nitobe translates *giri* as "rectitude."[9]

Nitobe explains that although *giri* originally meant a sense of duty toward others that might be evident to any individual reasoning rightly, it came to mean something quite different. *Giri,* a sense of rightness compelling even onerous behaviors, was seen as a "severe taskmaster" and eventually as a *law* external to individuals who must live up to it. "Because of this very artificiality, *Giri* in time degenerated into a vague sense of propriety," bemoans Nitobe.[10] Takada-san used *giri gatai* to describe relationships between politicians that had both noble and base aspects: a selfless willingness to make extra effort to assist another who has been a good and admirable colleague, as well as the sort of crass version of loyalty useful in political horse-trading. Takada-san referred to the kind of political man who did not understand the value of these sorts of *giri* as a fool; he believed that one of the primary barriers to women's success in politics was their inability to understand and live up to the demands of *giri*.

Talking with Takada-san about the values important to political life, I came to see *jingi* and the related phrases *ninjō ni atsui* and *giri gatai* as forming a matrix of traditional notions of ethical life that guided his assessments of himself and others both within and outside of politics. Completing Takada-san's ethical matrix were his commitment to filiality and his presumption that attitudes and practices connoted in a word such as *jingi* were the particular obligations of men. Masculinism and filiality are central elements of any sort of Confucianist morality. In the *Analects*, ritual, a determinant component of the sort of life practice leading to *jin*, is first and foremost grounded in correct treatment of one's parents. In one of the earliest passages of the *Analects*, a disciple of Confucius declares, "As for filial and fraternal responsibility, it is I suspect, the root of authoritative conduct *[jin]*" (1.2).[11] The Master's emphasis on the importance of filiality in one's development as a *jin* person is such that it seems in places to trump the claims of either *jin* or *gi*. For example, the Master counsels that when one's parents are doing wrong, one ought to be gentle in suggesting they change their behavior. If one's parents refuse to listen, one should neither complain nor disobey their wishes.[12]

Takada-san lived with his parents during his first election and was running for an office his father had held before him using his father's support organization (*kōenkai*) as his own organizational base. As a result, the portrayal of filiality became a significant part of his public efforts to win election. Yet his commitment to a traditionalist notion of the filial son went beyond its usefulness to his election. Even after marrying and leaving his parents' home, Takada-san moved only around the corner, and despite his growing independence from his father's political shadow he still considered his relationship with his parents central to his life and career. "My father has the idea that we will live in an old-fashioned way as a big, extended family, and I think that's a good idea," he told me. Takada-san, like his parents, expressed concern about the failure of modern education to inculcate the virtues of filiality in Japan's young people. In fact in demonstrating his filiality by following his father into office, he acted in perfect accord with a long lineage of Japanese Confucians who argued that true filiality is best expressed through one's faithful service in public office.[13]

When Takada-san talked of *jingi* as a key notion in political life, he implied that political actors are people wholly invested in relations with others, meeting obligations to these others in a self-conscious manner that demonstrates a proper awareness of the history of social relations preserved in ritual. The sense of *jingi* a person employs in the wider political world begins with training in filial relations. But that is not all. As Takada-san understood it, a *jingi* politician is a male because the human qualities and practices described as *jingi* are male qualities and practices. In the *Analects* discussions between the Master and his disciples make almost no mention of women; this allows the contemporary commentator Ishikawa to say "he or she" whenever speaking of the *jin*-aspiring person. But Takada-san followed an older tradition of interpretation, in which women are seen as unfit for roles in public life, and men who are unable to fill public roles are viewed as somewhat less than complete men.[14]

For good and ill, Takada-san was bound by *jingi*. Because he was running as the successor to his father's political career, the idea of *jingi* fit well with the traditionalist, masculinist image he found most convenient to cultivate among constituents and supporters. *Jingi* properly describes the attributes of the sort of person he hoped voters would see him as. With its evocation of Confucian notions of human relations, the term may also have been Takada-san's attempt to render more palatable his subjection to the complicated political hierarchy in which he sought an official position: a power structure that included his father, neighbors, local interest group leaders, and fellow politicians in the Liberal Democratic Party at the local and national levels.

GOOD POLITICIANS ARE *YAKUZA*

When I returned to Tokyo in late May, after the April 1999 Unified Local Elections (in which both the Takeno town and Shirakawa Ward assemblies were up for election), I was a bit shocked by Takada-san's deep cynicism about the extent of self-effacement required to garner even a small share of the political power in his community. When I left Tokyo to go to my Takeno field site in March, I brought with me Takada-san's slip of paper with the characters for *jingi* written on it in his well-balanced hand. I asked Baba-san and his family what they thought about *jingi* as a description of the ideal politician, and they laughed. They said it sounded like a *yakuza* (gangster) word. In the early months of his first term in office, Takada-san seemed to agree with them; he actually argued that being a *jingi* politician was not terribly different from being a gangster. Yet over several years in the assembly, Takada-san's narrative shifted from his postelection "honor among thieves" notion of *jingi* to a more ethically complex vision of his work as an elected official.

Eventually Takada-san began to make self-conscious efforts to reinterpret traditional notions of honor and loyalty that, like Baba-san, he had compared to a *yakuza* ethic. Instead he argued that authentic Japanese traditions of masculine honor include the possibility of critical resistance to unethical uses of power hierarchies. The simplest conservative ideas of masculine hierarchy, what Takada-san described as like the *yakuza* ethic, provided discursive support for the social, economic, and political structures that privileged him and eased his entrance into politics. Faithfully reproducing those ideas would have continued to serve his interests, but Takada-san saw himself as an independent individual with a responsibility to act as a "good man" would. Although, he said, it would be foolhardy to simply reject an ethical system that had supported generations of admirable men before him, he was also unwilling to completely relinquish his critical sense. His reworking of his traditionalist narrative is compelling because it shows how much of his reproduction of conservative political discourse is dependent on his finding an ethically acceptable position within it. At the same time, his self-conscious search for an ethical ground in the midst of a system that simultaneously served him and dismayed him is a moment of moral opportunity in what might otherwise seem, when viewed from the outside, to be a seamless unity between structure and agent. In other words, Takada-san's attachment to the structure of his privilege is vulnerable to an argument that shows him better ways of being a good man. More important, Takada-san himself is *looking for* just such an argument.

I first heard Takada-san make the connection between conservative politics and *yakuza* ethics in the summer following his first election. Seeking answers to a number of questions I had saved up while watching his campaign, I met him for a formal interview at a coffee shop on the fifth floor of a swank department store on a sweltering July afternoon. We had met at the same shop once earlier in the summer so that he could introduce me to the shop owner, Katō-san, and another man, Tsuboi-san, both of whom were important advisors in Takada-san's assembly seat campaign. The coffee shop was just a few steps away from the department store's Chanel section, and getting to it meant a pleasantly cool walk through the hush of expensive goods and polite, perfectly dressed clerks and shoppers. On the day of the interview Katō-san was not around, but the wait staff at the café remembered us. We were ushered to a table and treated like royalty. In every way the setting seemed to offer evidence of Takada-san's inheritance of strong connections to a community structure of wealth and privilege, and Takada-san did not seek to dispel the impression.

Politics, Takada-san told me over our coffee, is simply an occupation for those who have no other talents. When I insisted that politicians could be seen as having their own skills, such as the ability to build coalitions and work with bureaucrats, he still clung to his claim: "Politics is what you do if you have no other abilities." There are those who, having gotten into politics, develop skills in building connections or in some other area, he agreed, but generally speaking politics is a world sought and inhabited by the talentless. I pushed harder. Was there nothing else?

> Takada-san: Well, after all, in becoming a politician you develop the feeling that, at least on this, I won't lose to my opponent. That's what happens for most—for the great majority of human beings—when they put on a badge. [Elected officials in Japan wear small lapel badges.]
>
> Le Blanc: Is the desire to avoid losing a kind of responsibility toward your voters?
>
> Takada-san: Rather than toward supporters, it's a responsibility toward yourself. "I don't want to be done in by that fool," and that sort of thing—"Look at this guy." That kind of thought.
>
> Le Blanc: You don't want to be embarrassed or . . .
>
> Takada-san: Well, no, I don't think that the culture of shame fits a politician. Politicians are generally "Let the laughers laugh," and in return it's "I'll be the one laughing last," you know. And even more, it's the kind of world where if you are going to laugh at something, you laugh while holding an umbrella [so that the laughs of others don't rain down upon you]. This is a *yakuza* world, you see.

I was a bit surprised that Takada-san would willingly compare his world to the world of Japan's mafia. The LDP is periodically plagued with scandals caused by the unsavory connections some of its members have had with organized crime.[15] I suggested that comparing politicians and members of the mafia implies terrible things about politicians. Takada-san decided to assume that my confusion was connected to my Americanness.

> Well, I don't know other countries but in Japan, the world of politicians is the same as the world of *yakuza*. Basically, it's the spiritual structure inside of the Japanese. If you put it in Weber's terms, it's probably "ethos." Yes, it's a thing inside of the ones we call Japanese. What the human beings living in the *yakuza* society have inside them and what the human beings living in the political world have inside them have something in common.
>
> Basically, it's ethos I'm talking about that's the common point. And the phenomena that come out of that, those are different. It's not like we [politicians] have guns like the *yakuza*. In other words, what's inside the human beings living in the *yakuza* world and the human beings living in the politician's world, they have something similar about them—they overlap a good bit.

Frustrated, I pressed further, trying to understand just how the leaders of organized crime and politics resembled each other. In both the criminal and political worlds, people tend to be *sunao*, Takada-san explained. *Sunao* can be translated as "obedient" or "docile," but there are other, more complicated senses of the term. To be *sunao* is to have a correct heart or spirit, to not be easily turned from a path, to do something without expectation of being noticed, to be easygoing rather than defiant or resistant. Takada-san went on: "These *sunao yakuza* and politicians are serious in their humanity, but they can't fit themselves within the social system. That's how things can get twisted up, go wrong. The *sunao* hurt themselves by being *sunao*. There are a lot of those kinds of people, you know, in the political world. Well, the yakuza world is the same, too, I think."

Takada-san described the people of the political and mafia worlds as *giri-gatai* (meticulous in reciprocating the favors done by others) and *ninjō ni atsui* (responsive to personal, emotional connections). In other words, obligations to others (*giri*) and connections with others (*ninjō*) dominate relations among both *yakuza* and politicians, and therefore those who are *sunao*, those who can self-effacingly, unswervingly pursue their duties to others, are valued. But being *sunao* has its costs for both *yakuza* and politicians. Responding loyally to the demands of personal connection sometimes makes it impossible to be true to oneself. Depending on what sort of master one serves, the serious straightforwardness of the *sunao* person might seem quite different when viewed from the outside—corrupt, for instance. As Takada-san explained it, "A gap appears between what society [*seken*] is looking for and the person's surface."

Takada-san was cynical enough about the submission required of junior members of a ward assembly to compare the political world to organized crime, but the obviously unsavory aspects of such comparisons did not encourage him to argue that such submission was wrong. Deferring to one's superiors was an inevitable expedient of getting political work done. Through the stories he had heard and political organizations he had experienced prior to pursuing office for himself, Takada-san had learned that displaying appropriate deference to one's superiors provides the glue that holds a political project together. He had watched his father use his long years and prominence in the local assembly to demand obedience from those who worked with him, and he told stories about his father's triumphs over resisters. Japanese citizens (even Takada-san himself) have frequently told me that the work done by local politicians is unimportant because bureaucrats in local, prefectural, and national administrative units have the upper hand when it comes to policy making, a result of advantages of access to information and prestige. However, Takada-san had also seen that his father was able to use political longevity to impress his will upon the bureaucrats who worked for the ward administration.

Takada-san told me a story of a time when his father had gone out drinking with a more junior assembly member and a bureaucrat. In recognition of both his own youth and his close relationship with Takada-san's father, the more junior assembly member referred to Takada-san's father as *jīsan*, a term that translates as "old man" or "grandfather" and can be used as a means of referring to one's own father (when he has grandchildren) or one's own grandfather or to unrelated senior men.[16] In an attempt to join in the joviality between the junior assembly member and Takada's father, the bureaucrat who had come along for a drink also began to call him *jīsan*. The bureaucrat had made an imprudent decision. *Jīsan* can have connotations of either fondness or condescension (as in "irritating old man"), depending on how the term is used, and though the term does suggest hierarchy (usually the speaker is clearly younger than the addressed), *jīsan* is not a proper acknowledgment of formal rank. Takada-san described his father's willingness to demand respect from bureaucrats who are, by law (and in this case also by age), subservient to assembly members.

> That time my father got very angry at the ward bureaucrat and threw him out of the bar. He told the other assembly person, "Throw this guy out," and made him throw him out. So then my father let it go, but the next day, the ward chief, the chief brought in the *ningen* [literally "human being," in other words, not a person known by his official rank] who had been thrown out and made him get down on his knees and made him say "I am so sorry" and such. Well, my father had that kind of weight. And another time there was a guy who was the assistant at a ward facility, in a position that's a step to becoming ward chief, but then he didn't go along with my father's will, and my father got rid of that assistant. He was thrown out, and that's why Sumitomo got to be ward chief.

The position of ward chief, a position equivalent to mayor, is an elected position, and reaching a high position in the ward's civil service is considered a means of establishing one's credentials as a viable candidate. Takada-san was unwilling to tell me much more about how the bureaucrat who was potentially on track for the ward chief's position was removed from office. The point he wanted me to get from his story was that his father could demand respect based on his seniority in the assembly and was unafraid to punish those who did not supply it to his liking. His father came across as similarly autocratic in other tales as well. For example, when a woman who was a leader in the neighborhood association was deemed obstructive to Takada-san's election campaign, his father, chair of the association, had her fired (*kubi ni saseta*), despite the fact that neighborhood association positions are, technically speaking, elected by the association members. According to Takada-san, the woman had complained a great deal, blamed others for failing to do work that was actually her responsibility, and groused about the ineffectiveness of Takada-san's campaign, even speculating that he might lose the election. Although Takada-san's father could not have kept the woman from serving in the neighborhood association if she really wanted to, she would have known that, as long as he remained chair of the association, other members would be wary of working with an officer he disliked.

Given the stories Takada-san told about his father's willingness to use his informal influence to alter the circumstance of individuals doing political or community work, it is no wonder Takada-san interpreted the political world as a place where one's fate is determined by relatively arbitrary superiors in the community power structure: the

older, more experienced men who judge supplicants for public office
on the basis of whether they are "the kind of guy they like." Self-
effacing obedience is, doubtless, indispensable in such a hierarchical
and punishing world. Takada-san's father was not the only source of
stories teaching this lesson. For example, Takada-san had learned the
importance of silent acquiescence when he worked on other politicians' campaigns for seats in the Diet and in the Tokyo Prefectural
Assembly. The candidates he worked with in these cases were aligned
with his father because they had graduated from Takada-san's alma
mater.

Takada-san explained that he had worked on the campaign of the
Diet member (the one whose luncheon was discussed in the previous
chapter) as a form of *o-reibōkō*, a kind of unremunerated service an
apprentice or vassal might gratefully provide for a master who has been
especially kind. In other words, Takada-san and his father were in supplicants' positions vis-à-vis this national official with whom they were
lucky enough to have political party and school connections. Takada-
san represented his campaign labor almost as a kind of moral obligation, born out of the superiority of the Diet member, but it was a moral
obligation with an ironic twist. Takada-san did not really admire the
man he served. In fact I heard Takada-san complain that this particular Diet member frequently made use of politicians of lower stature
without making much of an effort to return the favor. By referring to
his campaign work as a sort of vassal-lord relationship, Takada-san
highlighted the fact that he expected little from the more powerful politician, but he also put a bit of a sarcastic tone into the description of his
service. Failing to curry favor with a potential ally of such tremendous
importance would be unwise, and so Takada-san pretended to serve
him as a vassal who serves out of the sheer honor of serving, despite
feeling no such honor.

Takada-san also explained the logic of his and his father's support
for the other of these candidates, Matsui-san, the Tokyo Prefectural
Assembly member. Because Matsui-san had served with Takada-san's
father in the Shirakawa Ward Assembly, they had competed for shares
of the conservative assembly over several elections. Matsui-san was
younger than Takada-san's father, and while he remained in the local
assembly he was properly viewed by Takada's father as either a junior
or a rival. But once Matsui was competing for a seat in a different
assembly on a higher level of government, the competition for votes
with Takada's father ended, and the alumni relationship shared by

Takada and his father's former rival led to cooperation. As Takada-san explained, although the Takadas made no explicit agreements with Matsui, "there was the message" that Matsui-san would give his father the alumni votes he had received in previous ward assembly elections in return for Takada-san's assistance. "Well, naturally, helping out wasn't o-reibōkō [grateful service to a master], but helping out made sense in terms of good power politics," explained Takada-san.

In the stories he heard from his father, Takada-san was taught the importance of loyalty, obedience, and deference to getting ahead in the LDP world. Because he was hearing these stories as a son, the fact that he focused on the importance of hierarchy and submission is perhaps unsurprising. Yet he said that even in these other politicians' campaigns he learned to understand smart political practice as a matter of proper performance of one's place in hierarchical and constraining networks of masculine relations. He was also taught that political ideals would only be handicaps to overcome in getting the performances right. I asked him to share his best memories of working for these candidates, and he said he had no good memories to share. Campaign work was a matter of detaching oneself from personal emotions and ambitions.

> You just go through it disinterestedly, from your shallow side, you know. That's what elections are. If you threw yourself into it, that would be bad. That's elections. You decide you are going to work from your shallow side. You enter the election office, and you begin by asking "What is my work?" You're told, "You do this, this, and this. . . ." And you don't take up things that you can't do. It's best if you don't take up things you can't do. That's the atmosphere of an election. You know, an election is the kind of work where it's the worst trouble to take up something you can't do, you know, and clog things up.

Takada-san had joined the campaigns based on calculations about their connectedness to his father's and his own future. The candidates required competent service, and he did his best to provide it without involving his ego. The campaign work was not interesting. Becoming interested or seeking more interesting tasks would only cause trouble for those he was bound to serve. Nor were the candidates especially inspiring. Takada-san said he did not see qualities in them he wanted to emulate. In fact if anything about the candidates impressed him, it was their ability to do kudaranai (trivial or worthless) work cheerfully.

I asked Takada-san what sort of kudaranai work was required of the candidates. He explained, "It's expressing the proper courtesies to the people that your supporters bring with them—saying thank you and dealing with them in that way. Then afterward you hear they weren't anybody, you know. That's what it is—not knowing who the person is, but having to be courteous, no matter who the person is." Although he sounded as if he were complaining about everyday politeness that he might be expected to show any fellow human being, he was really pointing to something more onerous. I remembered the careful way his father had orchestrated the humble self-presentations Takada-san and I made before the neighborhood association's women's auxiliary luncheon in January prior to the election. Like our luncheon presentations, the etiquette LDP politicians are often expected to practice before potential supporters can be complicated and exhausting, laced with flowery, ritualized language seldom used in everyday life and carefully adjusted to display one's level of obligation to the person being greeted.

Liberal Democratic Party politicians who ground their claims to represent their constituency in appeals to "Japanese tradition" are not free to eschew courtesies that went out of daily use in Japan a generation ago. Years before I met Takada-san this point was impressed upon me at a dinner with an LDP Diet member's secretary and a woman who had been active in recruiting other women to join the Diet member's *kōenkai* (politician's support organization). The woman was talking with the secretary about the struggle parents go through to get their children accepted at the proper schools (she was probably suggesting that the secretary might be of use to other constituents seeking good school placements for their own children), but what I most remember was how this woman spoke about her satisfaction with the schools her own children had attended. Her children had learned to use proper, respectful language at a young age, she said, and she imitated their childhood use of very complicated politenesses. I remember the conversation so well because, in joining her for dinner, I had felt I was stretching my own capacity for Japanese respectful language to its ultimate limit. As she talked on and on about her children's etiquette education, I grew increasingly anxious about whether the woman approved of the way I spoke. Like Takada-san, I found being "simply polite" unpleasant work. My ambiguous position as a foreign researcher, coupled with my incomplete understanding of what level of politeness a native speaker of my age and position would use, made choosing words nerve-racking.

Not knowing the sort of person one is greeting means either having to act in an excessively humble manner that will turn out to be humiliating for both greeter and greeted if the supporter's status is considerably lower than the candidate's, or having to risk being seen as insensitive to another's importance. Such choices make for stressful work when one's professional reputation or career is hanging in the balance. Takada-san's appreciation for the patience shown by the candidates for whom he worked when they were greeting constituents was probably not the only reason he found the politicians' abilities to do *kudaranai* work impressive. Being able to navigate through opaque but treacherous social structures without assuming too much or too little in the way of rank was also important for much more than the chance meeting with an unknown constituent. For example, when Takada-san told me "there was the message" that his campaign work for Matsui-san could be traded for votes in his father's assembly seat election, I asked him exactly how such messages about the meaning of his campaign efforts had been delivered. I was curious about the way the terms of such cooperation were worked out, but he seemed surprised I would ask. The Takadas had not had very specific conversations with the politicians about how Takada-san's campaign service would be viewed or repaid, as Takada-san explained:

> That was an "adult's conversation," a matter of understanding from the gut [*iwazumo hara de aun no kokyū*, "to reach a sense of accord without speaking"]. In the political world, in Japanese political society, if you spell things out, people will say, "Who is this?" They'll say, "Who is this fool? I can get by without you." That's why it's a gut-level understanding [*iwazumo hara de aun no kokyū*]. It's a world where it's assumed that you understand. It's Japanese, especially so. Different from America, in Japan there are lots of things that you can't explain in words. "Agreement without words" [*aun no kokyū*], for example, or "according to your gut" [*hara de*]. You do conversations from your gut—it's *hara gei* [the art of the gut].

Two themes link all these stories Takada-san told about relationships in the political world. The first is the importance of respecting hierarchies. The second is the presumption that crucial information about these hierarchies, and the terms of relationship of the people within them, is unspoken. To enact the role of pure-hearted, self-effacing, obedient *yakuza*-politician, one must possess an instinctive understanding of what is appropriate to one's position, what is likely to be forthcoming from another, and what one owes in return. Asking for the terms of the political relationship to be made explicit is asking to be a called a fool; it is demonstrating that one cannot be trusted. The successful people in the political world Takada-san describes are *giri-gatai* (strict with regard to obligations) and *ninjō ni atsui* (committed to maintaining personal ties with others). When the terms of political relationships cannot be made explicit, long-term personal ties and a previous pattern of exchanging obligations and favors become the best guides to working through the maze of potential allies and enemies that any sort of unspoken deal making involves. A similar sort of "gut art" was practiced in the progressive politics of Baba's Referendum Association in Takeno.

REPRESENTATION AS DEFERENCE

The importance of displaying an aptitude for assessing rank and a ready obedience were familiar to me from following Takada-san's election campaign in which he had worked so hard to present himself as a filial son. As I tagged along with him as he went to the assembly hall and out to meetings with advisors and supporters in the months after his election, I observed that demonstrations of obedience to those of superior rank continued to play a conspicuous part in his political behavior. Takada-san was the lowest ranking member of the LDP delegation of the Shirakawa Ward Assembly. In the LDP meeting rooms at the assembly hall he was literally on tea duty, passing out refreshments to more senior assembly members and their guests. When I walked with him through the section of the ward headquarters devoted to the assembly, I noticed that he used only the most humble language when speaking with others, even the assembly's staff assistants. He never failed to address all of the assembly members in his party as *senpai* (senior). He made a practice of not speaking in party delegation meetings, and he said he had absolutely no expectation of speaking on the assembly floor during his first year in office.

If Takada-san had any influence on his fellow assembly members during his first session, it was because his father still played a role in his new political career. His father's words, well placed in the ears of former colleagues, landed Takada-san an assignment to the committees on which he wanted to serve and doubtless spared him the need to justify the value of his election to other members. Takada-san clearly saw his connection to his father's political career as important. He put the two extra cushions his father had long used on his own seat in the LDP conference room. He said that at first the other LDP members looked at him strangely because the two cushions lent even greater height to his already tall frame, as if he wanted to make himself more prominent in the group. But when they were told he had chosen literally to sit in his father's seat, they were indulgent—and they were also reminded of Takada-san's well-connected political father.

Nonetheless most of the indulgence was practiced by Takada-san as he worked to demonstrate his readiness to serve both his constituents and the more senior elected officials and political activists who might be of assistance to him in his career. He met with men who had assisted in his campaign or might assist him in the future, and he acted the part of dutiful young man, no matter what they said. In one case, Sano-san, a political advisor from Takada-san's campaign who had worked as a sort of election consultant for many area politicians, rambled on for over three hours about his experiences working with other politicians. He pointed out areas of Takada-san's campaign he thought had not been handled well and criticized Takada-san for being unable to pre-vent politicians from using his campaign events for their own purposes. He even chided Takada-san for his loyalty to the LDP, suggesting that his career might go further if he could distance himself from the constraining personal networks of the party. During the conversation Takada-san remained cheerful and flattered Sano-san and his friend by telling me, in their presence, how important he thought their perspec-tives would be for my research. And when Sano-san nagged him about his loyalty to the LDP, Takada-san simply said that he could never see himself with any other party. Yet after the conversation with Sano-san, Takada-san seemed exhausted and angry—and perhaps uncertain how much help he would get from Sano-san in the future.

Takada-san was caught between two competing demands for loy-alty. According to his own prescription, he should take the advice of this community leader with so many election wins to his credit. As Takada-san himself had said, election outcomes were determined by the choices that powerful community members made about whom to support. But Sano-san's advice was that Takada-san ought to think beyond his loyalty to the LDP, a party with a declining vote share and an increasingly negative image. That advice conflicted with Takada-san's vision of loyally serving his political masters, the leaders of the ward assembly's LDP delegation. After meeting with Sano-san Takada-san and I went to a restaurant for a late lunch, where he resisted my further efforts to steer the conversation toward politics. "Elections, elections," he muttered, and then turned to look out the window, occa-sionally remarking on the clothing trends modeled by passersby. He

said that he hated losing three hours to Sano-san. He complained about
the tediousness and uselessness of the conversation, and about what he
saw as Sano-san's disloyalty to the LDP.

Nevertheless Takada-san had no intention of distancing himself from
Sano-san. In fact he was planning to join the mutual friend who had
set up our meeting with Sano-san for a weekend at the friend's summer house. In all likelihood, Takada-san's ties to Sano-san would grow
tighter over time. Takada-san's own argument that a strong sense of
duty and emotional connection motivated the behavior of *sunao* young
politicians suggested that he saw a certain ethical beauty in displaying
deference and loyalty even when one did not agree with one's superior.
But his frustration with his conversation with Sano-san demonstrates
just how difficult it was for him to maintain such a positive interpretation of his own submission. In the brutal world of electoral politics
Takada-san's opinion of the ethical qualities of such advisors was far
from central to the sorts of allegiances he built. Elections require the
support of men who can move votes and presumably money; in the
case of Sano-san, Takada-san's deference was compelled by a man who
himself would not honor such deference. When, by urging Takada-san
to desert the LDP, Sano-san showed that he did not honor loyalty for
its own sake, he also spotlighted the instrumental character of Takada-
san's demonstration of loyalty to himself. Takada-san could hardly
avoid the realization that in order to win elections he was deferring to
a man who did not share his ethic. In one sense, Takada-san behaved in
the *sunao* fashion of a junior to a grand master, but because his master
was quite bald about the power calculations involved in Takada-san's
service, Takada-san himself could not escape a certain understanding
of the cynical dimensions of the political relationships on which he
relied.

In the same manner that Takada-san tried to present himself as eager
for the advice of his political elders, he also continued to work to make
himself as affable as possible in his election territory. He attended sum-
mertime community festivals. He made much of photographing garbage piled illegally on a street corner. He took me and his campaign
staffer, Satō-san, to lunch at a sushi restaurant where a supporter of
his worked. And despite the fact that he was no morning person, he
presented himself in a neighborhood park at 6:00 A.M. in order to lead
residents in the calisthenics broadcast on the public radio station during
the summer holiday. I showed up for the stretching too, and afterward
we joined a member of his *kōenkai* for breakfast. According to Takada-

san, the man was important because he had the power to influence who would be chosen for leadership positions in the youth section of the neighborhood association. (Youth sections are young in the way members of junior chambers of commerce in the United States are young. In Japan community leaders in their forties might play an important role in the youth section.) The neighborhood association provides crucial forums such as get-togethers and festivals in which Takada-san might present himself to community residents with whom he would ordinarily have little connection.

Perhaps that is why Takada-san remained pleasant as the *kōenkai* member held forth on the absence of genius in contemporary politics. The *kōenkai* member made no effort to imply that the much younger Takada-san might have the necessary spark. Not that the absence of genius mattered, the man said; politicians who are more like regular people do a better job of relating to regular people. Besides, the man offered, the real policy work is done by bureaucrats. We were all quiet for a moment, and I wondered if Takada-san was taking the conversation as an insult. In the awkward atmosphere that followed the man's remarks, his wife asserted that all politicians really need is the ability to explain what is going on in an uncomplicated manner to people like her who did not understand what they read in the newspaper. Takada-san's key supporters were comforting him with his lack of distinction and his irrelevance to the policy-making process. Nonetheless, as I had seen him do before, Takada-san absorbed the conversation good-naturedly, offering no comment of his own.

UNEARTHING A CRITIQUE FROM TRADITION

By the time he reached the last months of his first term, nearly four years later, Takada-san did have some cautious ambitions for himself that stretched beyond demonstrating loyalty to his political superiors and deference to his key supporters. He had, for example, become interested in the ward's disaster preparedness and crime prevention policies and was involved in committee work and other sorts of activities that allowed him to pursue these concerns. Another of his ambitions was to use his office to foster a renewed sense of civic engagement among young people. Takada-san believed that civic engagement required a better appreciation for the traditional values of Japan's past than he thought young people had been taught to have, but what he meant by "traditional Japanese values" was somewhat different from what he had suggested four years earlier, when he had compared his political ethos to the *yakuza* ethos. Takada-san began his first term claiming that absolute loyalty to his superiors in the party and local community power structure was his primary duty. But at the end of the term his vision of duty put a greater emphasis on serving the long-term public good than on unquestioned obedience to a superior's will. He was no longer satisfied with a notion of service like that modeled in organized crime. Still, he was no idealist about a good man's political capacity. In fact his revised narrative revealed a troubling paradox.

Masculinity, as Takada-san understands it, is both an important prerequisite for and a troubling disability in doing public work. To achieve the sort of political standing that would make it possible to use political power for good, men cultivate relationships with other men that threaten their ability to act in a way they know to be good. Takada-san sees no easy way out of this situation because he believes the relationships that bind men together in politics are essential to keeping the community strong, and that strength is, in itself, a crucial public good. Theorists of civic life often argue that communities that foster a sense of interdependence and trust among their members make for better functioning democracies.[17] But Takada-san understands the practices of masculine community that bind him to his fellow assembly members and community leaders as problematic for his community's democratic politics. The relationships built between the men in his political world are grounded in shared understandings of community. They are designed to enrich their participants' sense of trust and encourage the sharing of political resources. But as Takada-san readily admits, these relationships are the product of gender exclusion, hierarchy, and a significant degree of opacity. Moreover, high socioeconomic status, though not always determinative, certainly supports a bid to enter such a relationship. These masculinist, hierarchical, often class-related political relationships are not ideal in Takada-san's eyes, but he is dubious of the possibility of changing them for the better because he believes that the very things that make a political community function in an effective and humane manner are those that also make it sexist, exclusive, and elitist. Takada-san presents success in political life as a matter of being manfully pragmatic about the distance between the ideals and actual practices of contemporary democracy. That manful pragmatism often requires forgoing any hope for achieving good through politics.

The explicitness with which Takada-san sees his political life as a matter of navigating the hidden map of masculine relations is perhaps unusual. His narrative is the peculiar product and producer of his unique set of experiences. His rather pessimistic view of the entanglement of manhood and politics is perhaps partly sprung from his upbringing in a home with an unusual degree of reverence for the paternalistic authority structures of Japan's past. His thinking is also somewhat characteristic of the conservative political party to which he belongs; no other Japanese political party is quite as male dominated as the LDP. But the patterns of Takada-san's narrative resonate with the ways I have heard other Japanese conservative men, and even some progressives, discuss the structures of political life.

For example, in Takeno-machi Ikeda-san, a conservative town assembly member in his seventies, described his town fondly as a sort of family, bound together by trust and mutual goodwill. In his presentation of town politics as household relations and town political leaders as fathers Ikeda depicted political leaders as possessed of a paternal responsibility to act and make decisions on behalf of constituents who were implicitly likened to children. Policy understanding and agreement were not central goals of the representative relationship. Instead, those who would be representatives should cultivate "loving" relationships with constituents, presumably because these relationships engender the "trust" (a word Ikeda frequently employed) necessary to ensure that constituents will "do what the father says" by providing support for local policies. In turn, community fathers do their best to look out for the long-term welfare of their constituents' community and nation. Good community fathers can see beyond the narrow, temporary concerns of those whom they represent. In my interview with him Ikeda did not couch his political work in terms of serving the needs of Japan as much as some other conservatives did. Nonetheless when asked about the nuclear power plant proposed for Takeno, Ikeda was quick to point out the municipality's duty to accept it because nuclear power was a "national policy."

Ikeda described his understanding of Takeno-machi's obligation to "national policy" as "old-fashioned" in the same way he described his avoidance of policy explication and his preference for cultivation of personal relationships with constituents as old-fashioned. He argued that constituents should "listen to the father" leading the municipal government in much the same way he agreed to "listen to the father" of the national government, even when national policies meant enduring inconvenience locally. He described his work as district chief, then assemblyman, as doing the *iyana* (undesirable) work the community needed done. Presumably the mayor-father who submitted, as good, old-fashioned values suggested he should, to national nuclear power policy would also be taking up the undesirable work that must be done. It follows that obedient constituents would be well-disciplined children who learned the necessity of self-sacrifice through their father's example.

Like Ikeda-san, Takada-san talked about political manhood as a grim choice: a willingness to take responsibility for preserving the sense of "good" in a community while silently accepting the unvarnished truth of one's complicity with a sometimes corrupt system of power. Takada-san submitted to the sort of insulting view of his work that his *kōen-kai* member offered and demonstrated loyalty to a local politico who was admittedly ambivalent about his own loyalties. These were prices Takada-san paid in order to achieve the sort of power that would be made available to him in his role as public servant. During his postelection interview Takada-san argued that representation of his constituents was a matter of doing whatever his supporters asked of him. "Well, after all, it's the guys without any talents who enter politics, right?" he said. "Well, basically, you can't do anything yourself, so the things people say, well, you do what you're told." He described constituency service as *seou yaku,* or "taking on the role of shouldering burdens." The term that he used for constituency service, *seou,* reveals something of his understanding of politics as inherently hierarchical and duty-bound. *Seou* is also the term one might use to describe a father who would take on whatever hardship was necessary in order to support his household. Takada-san said that people who could not shoulder others' burdens should not be in politics. He assumed that American politicians must also perform *seou yaku,* the burden-carrying role, for their supporters, and I replied that they certainly did a great deal of constituency service.

But the unusual way Takada-san referred to constituency service as "shouldering a burden," as fathers shoulder the burden of being breadwinners, suggests a difference between what he sees as the proper representative role and what the more technical-sounding term "constituency service" might connote. I asked him what sorts of *seou yaku* he had performed. In the early months of his first term in office he had not yet had many requests from constituents. He had alerted administration officials about garbage left out on the streets near his neighbors and about bicycles parked where they should not be. He had passed on information to entrepreneurial constituents about requirements for licensing new businesses and pursued questions about park maintenance. He imagined he would be of help to constituents who wanted to rent ward facilities. "It's faster for us representatives to get a reservation than if regular people ask," he said. Of course members of the U.S. Congress frequently tackle constituents' problems with federal bureaucracies. They might have a staff member call the Social Security Administration to find out why Grandmother's check did not arrive last month, for example, and members of Congress sometimes get responses faster than their constituents do. And they are pleased to claim credit for their capacity to break down bureaucratic barriers.[18] Some scholars argue that such bureaucratic mazes are beneficial to members of Congress because snafus present a marvelous opportunity to demonstrate one's earnest desire to serve the voters.[19]

However, in the context of conservative Japanese politics, Takada-san's "taking on a burden" is not a simple matter of claiming credit for keeping government responsive or transparent to citizens. In fact, like many conservative politicians in both Tokyo and Takeno-machi, Takada-san does not place a high priority on responsiveness and transparency in government. For example, he does not favor the sort of freedom of information laws that enable members of the U.S. Congress to collect the information their constituents often request. He worries about whether individual privacy can be protected when government information is made available to the public, and he does not think the public will be served by having "all of the bad things" about government aired before ward voters. Moreover he does not believe that the voters are always the most responsible analysts of government policy. They want service for their narrow interests but often overlook larger concerns; that is why voters are supposed to trust their representatives to make the right decisions and guide the local administration appropriately. He argued that such trust is a basic assumption of the indirect democracy constructed by the representative system.

The paternalistic sound of Takada-san's *seou yaku* phrase for "constituency service" is reminiscent of the comments made by Takeno-machi assemblyman Ikeda-san and those I have heard in the Japanese news media when conservative politicians are called on to defend unpopular policies. By speaking of his job as bearing his constituents' burdens as a father would bear the financial burdens of a household, Takada-san, like Ikeda-san, placed himself clearly within a larger discourse that presents the political world as a paternal hierarchy. By reaching out to that discourse Takada-san at last established an independent identity for himself as a public servant. He might be required to take a submissive posture vis-à-vis his more senior political colleagues (both elected officials and community leaders), but he was a sort of gentle patriarch for most of his constituents. His *kōenkai* leaders, older than he and essential in establishing his place in the community, treated him as a sort of son who needed guidance, often gently chiding him but occasionally offering harsher criticism. And Takada-san submitted to such direction, at least to the extent that he saved his grumbling for a few friends (like me) who were not a part of the political scene. However, most of his constituents were not, as individuals, in a position to shape his political career, and they at least symbolically accepted him as a town father. For instance, once he was elected even elderly women in the community bowed to him gracefully and addressed him as *sensei*, a term of respect used for teachers, doctors, and politicians. When he talked to them he made much of how busy his assembly work kept him, and they shook their heads and tapped their tongues against their teeth in a show of concern for how his health would fare as he handled such onerous responsibilities. By winning an assembly seat Takada-san was officially transformed from a neighborhood child into a community father.

Takada-san connected himself to paternalistic traditions in many ways, including his reading at a preelection event of an old letter in which his great-grandfather was exhorted to live up to what Takada-san described as the standards pursued by all Takada men: being *seijitsu* (loyal), *chakujitsu* (surefooted), and *kakujitsu* (complete) in everything he did. Wrapping himself in the mantle of a courageous and duty-bound manhood served Takada-san's electoral needs well, but I don't think his choice to associate himself with traditionalist masculinity was merely self-serving. He admired these notions of what a man should be and believed that living up to them was his chief means of doing a significant life's work. He described himself as a person without particular talents, but he also argued that the work of an elected official was in fact perfectly suited to a person without distinctive talents, as long as that person was willing to take on the responsibility of serving his supporters.

REVISING THE TERMS OF DEFERENCE

Although Takada-san's view of the role of elected representative as a sort of community patriarch is not strictly democratic, it is not without an element of compelling moral vision. Just as Takeno-machi's Ikeda-san thought that politicians should inspire love and trust among their constituents, Takada-san seemingly wanted to believe that patriarchal politicians could help to preserve a community's cultural identity, and thus its humanity. As his time in office lengthened, Takada-san sought ways to realize this patriarchal vision of a good man doing good. He attempted this through the sorts of public speaking opportunities given to him in the assembly and through his work with young people, both in community activities and in an internship program he ran through his office. He said that if Japanese people had more pride in their history and culture, they would find the necessary strength to overcome the social and economic problems he believed they faced, everything from a decline in the quality of public education to a faltering economy. He worked to improve his own understanding of the moral resources available in Japanese history and culture by reading extensively, and he articulated what he learned in formal questions presented to the assembly, in presentations to his constituents, and in his relations with his interns. My observations of these efforts offered insight into Takada-san's persistent struggle to articulate his political work as a kind of "doing good." Yet even in his persistence he remained doubtful about the effects of his efforts on supporters and interns, and he continued to see politics as held together by unwritten masculine loyalties that undermined many efforts for better public service.

Shortly after returning to Japan to do follow-up work in the fall of 2002, I met Takada-san for lunch. As we talked about my research plans he surprised me by saying that he had recently been rethinking the demands of traditional masculine honor. When he was running for office and then beginning his service in the assembly, he had talked a great deal about the importance of loyalty to one's fellow politicians. He had not questioned the importance of obedience to his superiors, even when their demands frustrated him or seemed plainly wrong. He described his *seou yaku* as in some instances a kind of public ombudsmanship, getting the local bureaucracy to perform work when it might normally be unresponsive. He listed as examples calling on civil service officials about improperly disposed trash in the neighborhood, saving a park slated to be sold, and helping a constituent to reserve a public building for an event. However, in other ways, he saw the responsibility of the public servant as something much greater. On several occasions when we were talking one-on-one, he turned my questions about his political endeavors into more general questions of how public leaders might help to revitalize a Japanese culture he saw as enervated by a

recent decline in moral education in grade school and an endemic character weakness in political and economic leaders. He pointed to major
corporate corruption scandals, especially a couple in which unsafe or
misrepresented food products were sold to the public, and argued that
Japan faced a leadership crisis. He urged me to follow an NHK television lecture series on *bushidō* (the way of the samurai) that he had
been watching. It reminded Japanese people of a past of which they
could be proud, he said, and it remedied some dangerously incorrect
interpretations of what it meant for a man to lead and serve according
to Japanese traditions.

I took Takada-san's advice; I watched the series and read the study
guide written by Kasaya Kazuhiko, the featured lecturer.[20] (Takada-san
had rather firmly encouraged me to purchase the study guide by taking
me directly to a bookstore following our luncheon conversation about
the series.) Kasaya's lectures, as well as one of his prominent books,
are purposeful attempts to find in *bushidō* an ethic for fixing what
he sees as the ailments of contemporary Japanese society: corruption,
economic stagnation, and a general unwillingness to take the initiative
in difficult circumstances. At the center of Kasaya's interpretation of
bushidō is the claim that Japanese *bushi* (warriors or samurai) were
governed by a sense of honor that could trump the intense personal
loyalties they felt for the lords of their fiefdoms. In the NHK series and
study guide Kasaya shares a series of episodes from the Edo period
in which *bushi* imprisoned and sometimes deposed their own lords
when the lords' misdeeds seemed dangerous to the well-being of the
fiefdom.[21] "Each individual *bushi* placed great importance on behaving in a way that was loyal to his own convictions, and consequently,
even disobeying the lord's orders could be permissible," he explains in
a book-length treatment of the lessons of *bushidō*.[22] Takada-san was
especially interested in the ethical independence that Kasaya's interpretation of *bushidō* attributes to the samurai. Contemporary Japanese
have misunderstood the traditional value of loyalty, Takada-san told
me. The loyalty of an honorable man does not necessarily entail submission to a corrupt boss.

Takada-san's interest in Kasaya's lecture series is partial evidence
of his conviction that along with offering a practice that sustains one's
well-being in a hierarchical and conservative organization, one can also
find an ethic for public service in Japan's traditions of masculine honor.
I had grown comfortable with the image I had formed of Takada-san
during his campaign and early months in office as the reluctant but

inevitably filial son and obedient young man, and I was taken aback by his fascination with this revisionist history. Takada-san was self-consciously attempting a readjustment of his political philosophy. He had thought of himself as a *sunao yakuza* sort, bound by a vision of self-effacing service that he acknowledged might prohibit him from following his own will, even when he suspected his leaders were wrong. Now, as he talked about the samurai lecture series, he presented a different conception of loyal duty, one in which asserting oneself against mistaken leaders might be the best service one could offer.

For example, Takada-san explained, a common misconception about the *bushidō* idea of honor is that it required samurai to be loyal to their master regardless of what the master required of them. This misconception has led to the sort of loyalty that causes employees to cover up for the corruption of their bosses, he explained. As examples he suggested news-making corporate scandals that had long been covered up by employees, such as the mislabeling of meat products sold to consumers.[23] In the television series Kasaya had used well-known cases from historical texts to explain that instead of requiring absolute subservience to one's lord, true *bushidō* loyalty demanded that samurai conceive of loyalty as following one's internal sense of what is best for one's house (the lineage of the particular lord to whom a samurai would owe fealty) or one's *han*, the feudal domain. Sometimes this sort of samurai loyalty demanded that an honorable warrior engage in resistance against his lord; in the modern-day sense of economic warrior, he should blow the whistle on corporate corruption. Half of the series had already been broadcast by the time I heard about it from Takada-san, but it was being rerun late at night. He became so excited as he told me about the program that he offered to tape the first few episodes for me.

Takada-san said he agreed with Kasaya that a renewed understanding of Japan's past might help reinvigorate an economically and politically stagnant Japan. In fact he had taken on several college student interns in whom he hoped to inculcate a sense of civic purpose. He hoped to model his intern group on the schools of samurai-era Japan such as Yoshida Shōin's famous Shōka Juku, in which was born the philosophy that fueled Japan's move from feudalism to a modern nation-state and, ironically, ended the samurai culture. Yoshida Shōin is actually an appropriately provocative hero for Takada-san to choose. Reaching adulthood at the time of Japan's opening to the West, Yoshida saw himself as the truest of patriots. But he also left his domain without permission from his lord in order to conduct an investigation of Japan's

military and social situation in the early 1850s and was jailed for his
disobedience. After his release he built the school Takada admires.
Yoshida became convinced that a new state built around the emperor
should replace the old feudal order in which samurai reigned; he was
executed by the leaders of the sinking feudal Tokugawa government
following the failure of a plot in which his followers were to attack
a government official. Harootunian writes that Yoshida "obsessively"
pursued the problem of loyalty throughout his short life, declaring that
"he alone understood the true meaning of loyalty [in] his rejection of
that blind obedience which was standard practice in his day."[24]

With the Kasaya text and lectures and Takada-san's self-conscious
association of his internship program with Yoshida, I had exciting new
resources for exploring Takada-san's understanding of honorable manhood. Nonetheless I was also a bit surprised that he found this revisionist history of the popular image of samurai loyalty as inspiring as he did.
I remembered how, nearly four years earlier, in the coffee shop nestled
behind the Chanel section of an elegant department store, Takada-san
had shared with me a vision of the loyalty required of political men
that was far less complicated. That version had not involved measuring
one's own sense of what would be best for house and domain against
the possibly mistaken views of one's leader. Rather, a good political
man listened to his superiors and did what he was told.

Although Takada-san had admitted he was worn by the process of
enacting the filial devotion necessary for courting his father's followers
in his first election campaign, he had not entertained any alternative
path to a political career. As he described it, such obvious submission
to others was a requirement of the job. His mother had said he was
able to succeed in politics because he "had a low back" (*koshi ga hikui*,
that is, he did not mind bowing to others' needs), and he also thought
that much of his political work came down to presenting himself to
people who would decide to support him "on the basis of little things—
whether you're the kind of guy they like or not." Moreover, when I
met him for that coffee shop interview session following his election,
he spelled out an understanding of an elected official's life in which
loyalty and obedience to one's superiors were the necessary basis of the
sort of human relations that made governance possible. Watching him
as he settled into the new routines of his life as a ward assembly member, I could see that submission to older, more experienced men was a
conspicuous component of his behavior. It seemed to me then that he
would continue throughout his career as he had during that first elec-

tion, always obedient, occasionally miserable, generally unwilling to articulate a clear personal vision.

Yet at this luncheon in fall 2002, nearing the end of his first four-year term, Takada-san was talking about a different understanding of masculine loyalty, a more complex notion of traditional obedience. He has continued to run an intern program in his office; whenever I return to Tokyo he invites me to lunch with his current interns, men and women from a range of top Tokyo universities. They ply me with questions about American politics and prod me for my view on the most current international relations crises. Sometimes Takada-san joins in, and the interns seem to relish it when he and I hash out the terms of our political disagreements.

Some of the interns are simply looking for experiences to list on their résumés, but others are searching, a bit like Takada-san, for ways to reinvigorate and "preserve" what they see as the real Japan. On my last visit a very conservative male intern from Waseda University gave me a business card with a photo showing him garbed as a student from the late nineteenth or early twentieth century. He spoke of a tradition of ideal-driven and intellectual men from this earlier period of Waseda's past. These men were of a better quality than those at Waseda today, he insisted. He claimed that these men had been proud of Japan and had served the nation well. He said he was working to shape himself into this earlier man of quality. As I shared a bus ride with him from our luncheon spot to a train station, he admitted that he wanted to devote himself, at least for a time, to the study of great ethical texts. He wondered if I had any advice to offer him in his pursuits. I had only the vaguest of comments for him. In our luncheon conversation he had presented himself as the sort of nationalist I frankly fear, arguing that it is time for Japan to stand on its own in foreign affairs and suggesting that it might be time for Japan to have its own nuclear weapons. (Importantly, the conversation was only a day or two after North Korea's test launching of several Taepodong missiles.) Whatever my disagreements with the intern's particular foreign policy ethic, however, he serves as evidence that Takada-san's project of spreading a notion of ethical civic engagement through his small ward assembly member's office is working.

Takada-san still understands political life as demanding many compromises with a power structure he sees as prone to corruption. In fact he interprets women's failure to win power in the LDP as predicated, at least in part, on the fact that they are unwilling to cultivate the sorts of interested relationships that make it easier to win supporters and thus elections. Although he is explicit about the fact that some of those male relationships of mutual interest can easily develop into a trading of favors that is often a bad way to make policy and at times simply illegal, he also argues that it is immensely difficult and perhaps even dangerous to the fabric of the community to change the male way of doing politics.

Nonetheless I was pressed to do some revisionist work of my own. In the end (which is, of course, no sort of conclusion for Takada-san himself) I came to see Takada-san as a provocative example of the way individuals may weave and reweave their own narratives, a case study in why merely understanding the patterns of larger social structures is insufficient for depicting the intertwining of moral and political life. In asking why and how Takada-san wrestles with the traditionalist ethical system that comes with his claim to powerful manhood, I was forced to look not only at gendered power structures but also at how a somewhat self-conscious individual manages within the constraints of these structures.

Why does this matter? Structures such as social expectations for what a man should be are resilient but elusive. Sometimes we can find in laws or institutional practices the means of maintaining these structures. For example, we find structures that maintain the masculinity of politics in institutions such as Japan's local assembly electoral rules that make the informal assigning of territories through backroom deal making and the inheritance of constituency organizations an elective benefit that privileges men such as Takada-san over middle-class salarymen and most women. Nonetheless in many ways structures such as the masculinity of the political world persist because countless individuals reproduce them quite faithfully through small, consistent daily actions, even when those individuals see the structures they reproduce as oppressive to themselves.[25]

With his revisions of his political narrative, Takada-san was seeking a readjustment in the nature of his political existence. His revisions were perhaps not very radical, and I don't think they sufficed to erase his deep cynicism about political power, at least not during the time I was conducting research. And yet he did change his political narrative and some of his corresponding political behavior in ways noticeable not just to me but to his supporters as well. His new rhetoric about masculinity and politics also highlighted aspects of his narrative, such as his attachment to a view of human relations as inevitably hierarchical and gendered, that seem to be especially resistant to alteration. Examining both the shifts and spaces of persistence in Takada-san's rhetoric about political men allows us to see how hard he works to make ethical sense of his own political behavior. An appreciation of that effort may in turn help to refocus us on the role of an individual's ethical commitments and the power of storytelling practices in political life.

CHAPTER 4

Cheating as a Democratic Practice

Throughout the evening Baba-san and I have been talking about Takeno politics. Now it's so late we have given up making more tea. Instead Baba pours a little hot water into my cup, *sayu,* he calls it, a fancy word for "hot water for making tea." He sucks on his cigarette; his body has crumpled below the level of the table. His legs have slid far under the blanket tacked around the table edges to hold in the warmth from the *kotatsu* heater attached to the bottom of the tabletop.[1]

"In high school my sister and I sat under the *kotatsu* like this, smoking," Baba says. "We studied just enough to pass. She would get tired and give up and go to sleep, and seeing her I would fall asleep, too."

> She was very, very gentle [the Japanese word here is *yasashii,* meaning careful, considerate, gentle or nice], but her spirit was strong inside that gentleness. I remember when she died, she said "Aah, it's gotten dark." [And] I can never forget what she told me about doing business.
>
> When I went to Tokyo to be an apprentice in another shop, she was living in Kokubunji [a Tokyo suburb] and going to art school. She had no money. All she ever had in her little refrigerator was cabbage and carrots and rice. But she would always make me dinner in her little kitchen. It was a fun time, and then after a year my mother came to get me. [Mother] was tired of running the shop herself.

Baba told me more than once how ambivalent he had been about returning from Tokyo and about taking over the store that had been in his family for three generations. His mother had pulled it out of debt when his father died in World War II and saved it for Baba, but he hadn't really wanted it. He said his sister was special to him in part because she had always understood that ambivalence; he could be honest with her about it. Just before dying in her early twenties, she told him, "You can do business only with those who accept you as you are. Don't follow the ones who leave you; don't turn away the ones who come." In his Japanese, it's a tidy, rhyming phrase: *Saru mono owazu; yoru mono kobamazu.* Baba told me these words more than once too.

Somehow his discussion of leading the nuclear power plant referendum revolt against the Takeno community leaders and of related political battles frequently brought him back to stories of this sister. In fact, I was in town less than twenty-four hours when he came to me with a small paperback book. "This is for you," he said. It was a collection of his sister's paintings, poetry, and diary entries. Later he brought out his own copy of the book and pointed out to me the poems and paintings that most intrigued him. "I don't know what she meant," he would say. His sister had obviously read a lot of literature; her writing included allusions to Proust, among others. Baba had read almost none. But this did not stop him from puzzling over her words or from asking if my many years of education could help me better understand them. She seemed to live in his mind on a daily basis, and she haunted his house.

In the late 1980s Baba rebuilt his house on the same shopping street plot his family had owned for generations. The new house was tall and narrow, in the spare style of Japanese modernism. The furniture and other details were so bland, so common to Japanese middle-class homes, that his sister's sizable and colorful abstract paintings arrested me when I found them hanging in the steep staircase and in the traditional tatami-mat room, in the alcove beside the Buddhist altar honoring Baba's sister and mother, where a more typical Japanese brush painting of pines or bamboo should have been.

On this particular late evening Baba tells me another tale about his sister.

> It wasn't that we were really poor, but I always got my sister's textbooks the year after she used them. My books were always missing pages, but most of the time I spent so little time reading them that I didn't notice they were missing pages. Once I remember being called upon to read a section from my book, and it wasn't there. I had to ask the guy next to me for a book. It turns out my sister had been cheating the whole time. When she didn't have time to get ready, she had to occasionally remove a page from the book and use it as a crib sheet. I didn't know this until she graduated. When she graduated she wrote a poem in the school newspaper. It said

that she had never flown in an airplane, but by cheating her way through
school she had known a greater exhilaration than taking off from land.

When Baba tells me this story he laughs delightedly, the kind of laugh
that pulls him sideways, sucks the breath out of him in hoarse, smoker's
gasps. He loves this story of his cheating sister.

Of all the many hours I spent listening to Baba-san talk about politics
and life in Takeno, this story stands out in my mind most clearly. I have
been puzzling over the meaning of his sister's cheating ever since. Why
does Baba find this example of cheating so thrilling? After all, in obvious ways Baba-san did not like cheaters. His referendum movement was
grounded in the belief that corruption had short-circuited democracy
in Takeno-machi. Because he has spent his life selling sake, Baba can
talk in rich detail about political cheating: how politicians bought beer
gift certificates from him to distribute to constituents, and how many
bottles of sake he and his children delivered to campaign offices. I never
met anyone in Takeno who would challenge Baba's accounts of corruption. Instead they just added to his list, like the taxi driver who told
me about the year that most of the town's children received bookstore
gift certificates (mailed from a Tokyo postal code) that bore the name
of a mayor who was seeking reelection. On one occasion I had a conservative assembly member open his ledgers for me and describe—on
tape!—how much he had spent on constituents' funerals in the previous
week, despite the fact that funeral gifts from politicians are explicitly
barred by Japanese law. Baba is hugely passionate when he explains
how money from outside interests, such as the company hoping to build
the nuclear power plant, have distorted local politics. I have seen him
tense with suppressed anger when he suspected lavish entertainment of
constituents was going on among members of his own movement.

Moreover Baba was fully committed to eschewing traditional patron-
client relations in his own political work. He often insisted that the real
reason he wanted to form the Referendum Association was not to stop
the nuclear power plant but to finally give citizens a direct means of
voicing their opinions. In fact he and the other leaders of the Association
officially took a neutral posture about the plant prior to both the
self-administered and official referenda results.[2] Baba-san was especially proud of the fact that, for the self-administered referendum, the
Association had contracted with an independent accounting firm that
kept the ballots locked away from even Association members and that

tallied the results without the Association's interference. All meetings of the Referendum Association were open to the public and the media; funds for the organization were managed scrupulously and openly accounted for. I sat in on several discussions about funding the campaigns for the 1999 assembly elections, something I would never expect to be allowed to do when following a typical conservative campaign. Baba's friends described him as honest to a fault; his grown children have been known to complain about his inability to hide his true feelings. Baba himself told me he cannot stand being dishonest. Even Iida-san, a very cynical young journalist friend of mine who was dispatched to Takeno about the time I moved there, became a Baba convert after spending nearly three years following Baba's Referendum Association. The best word for Baba, Iida-san said, is *seihin*, "a beautiful or clean poverty." Iida was making a direct complimentary reference both to Baba's insistence on a politics that does not involve the traditional Takeno practice of cementing relationships with the distribution of patronage goodies and to Baba's willingness to endanger his own financial well-being in order to press for a more participatory political community.

I have finally come to see Baba-san's attachment to his memory of his artist-cheater sister as part of his attempt to renegotiate his notion of who a good man is and what a good man does. We might think it easy for Baba-san to see himself as a good man. After all, at substantial risk to himself he challenged a political power structure so corrupt that clearly illegal behavior is regarded as commonplace. In the process of building the Referendum Association movement he helped to change the demographics of the town assembly and mayor's office. He gave women (several of whom he personally recruited) a new political role. He was instrumental in stopping a nuclear power plant from being built in his hometown, and even those of us who believe nuclear power is a necessary choice can accept that a man seeking to stop the building of a nuclear power plant in his town is operating with the safety of his fellow townspeople at heart. Baba-san was no hypocrite about energy either; with the exception of the small *kotatsu* and about five space heaters (two of which I used in *my* office and bedroom), he did not heat his house in the winter or cool it in the summer. While I was living there in late winter and early spring, the kitchen was cold enough for us to safely leave fish on the counters overnight! Even Baba-san's store office had only a portable kerosene burner for heat.

We might think Baba-san need do nothing other than recall the referendum movement achievements to see himself as a good, community-minded man, but we would be wrong. Baba-san lived in a masculine world in which the rules for who a good man is, rules Baba was often instrumental in enforcing against his peers in the referendum movement, exclude the kind of man who, in midlife, deserts his networks of friends, walks away from the men who run the town, and endangers the business that had supported his family for more than 100 years so that "the townspeople could finally say what had always been in their hearts to say." Although he might have relished a view of himself as the leader of a movement with unprecedented successes under its belt, Baba-san frequently mused on the ways he was as much a misfit in his community as a leader of it. On more than one occasion he told me that he failed to fit into the breadwinner model, how weak his commitment to being a businessman was, and how few real friends he had.

When Baba-san challenged the men who had long dominated Takeno politics, he was automatically drawn into conflict with expectations about masculine behavior he had helped establish. That is why, despite the many ways we, from the outside, might seek to see him as a good (or successful) man, he ended up resisting that simple definition of himself. Instead he saw himself as a kind of inspired cheater. The referendum movement was a direct challenge to the authority of town fathers toward whom Baba had once shown deference. Perhaps there is no clearer evidence of that challenge to masculine power in Takeno politics than the five women from the allied pro-referendum groups who ended up commanding seats in the Takeno Assembly; before the beginning of the referendum movement those seats had belonged to conservative men. But as a Referendum Association leader, Baba-san also relied on a range of masculinist strategies he learned in the circles of male conservatives whose power he had challenged. He used notions of masculine self-control to manage movement participants' behavior and reinforced his own authority by playing up his image as a benevolent patriarch.

Baba-san's challenge to the network of conservative men who had controlled Takeno politics prior to the referendum movement was seen by many as a betrayal of his former friends. We might think that because Baba-san eventually led a revolt against a corrupt political system, he would tend to see himself as a better man than the old friends from whom his political activism had separated him. Yet at times Baba-san seemed to find his choices almost as discomfiting as his old friends had found them, as if the shift he had made from his former life as a small businessman, savvy in the intertwining networks of conservative political leaders and other businessmen, to the leader of a movement with a powerfully antipaternalist thrust did not rest easily in his conscience. To do what he thought was right, Baba-san had betrayed the ethic of manhood according to which he believed he should live.

Baba-san was caught in a bind. He never really abandoned the masculinist notions his conservative friends had shared with him: an aversion to idealism and a tendency to judge himself and others by their willingness to do "what men are supposed to do," whether as family providers or as trustworthy and loyal friends. But those notions of traditional and pragmatic manhood had helped justify his former friends' deference both to the nuclear power plan brought to Takeno by a large company and national-level government officials and to the exclusive and corrupt public decision making that had come along with the plant proposal. Although he had profited from it when he was younger, Baba-san eventually came to despise the corruption, and by building the Referendum Association he sought to root corruption out of Takeno politics. He had decided to reject conservative dominance in Takeno politics, but he had not rejected the notions of manhood dominant among conservatives.

The commitment and deference he required of the referendum movement men Baba himself had not displayed toward the men with whom he had come of age and worked for the first fifty years of his life. Instead he had betrayed them, and he did not find it easy to justify that betrayal by referencing higher principles. Actually he often expressed suspicion of principled justifications for the "sacrifice" of others' well-being. So Baba-san needed a means of speaking about the way his leadership of the Referendum Association challenged his vision of himself as a member of the community of town fathers. I think that is why he found the memory of his sister's high school cheating so compelling: as a cheater who joyfully turned her cheating into poetry, she offered an image of betrayal that had its own integrity. In evoking his memories of her as he struggled with the seemingly endless political conflicts engendered by the Referendum Association's challenge to the Takeno status quo, Baba-san connected his own betrayal of Takeno's conservative town fathers to his sister's creativity and joyful confession. When his discussion of Takeno politics led immediately into memories of his sister, I heard a parallel between what he recounted of her poetic assertion of independence from the expectations placed on her to be a "good student," expectations she never denied were fairly placed, and his own assertion of independence from the expectations placed on him to be a good man.

Baba became what his fellow townspeople saw as a revolutionary leader precisely because he was a sort of cheater, embracing neither the system he opposed nor the preexisting groups that challenged it. And although his greatest political achievement might have been in increasing the transparency of community politics, the challenge he faced as he transformed himself from a supporter of the conservative establishment to the leader of its undoing was not in coming to understand the value of transparent community politics, or in fact anything about politics at all. His challenge came in adjusting himself to the uncomfortable position of being a man who seemed (sometimes even in his own eyes) not to act like one. Followed carefully, Baba-san's development from beneficiary of the local power structure to an agent of resistance to it draws our focus to the incompleteness of his conversion to resistance. Balancing himself uncomfortably between his attachment to pragmatic masculinity and what he saw as his not entirely defensible rejection of Takeno's male leaders, Baba-san forged an unexpected position for himself as an agent of change in Takeno politics.

In examining Baba-san's persistent struggle to understand himself we can see how gender expectations are arrayed against any man's potential challenge to his community's status quo. But we can also see that a man need not be a committed gender-role revolutionary to force a break in the link between gender expectations and the community power structure. What he must be able to do is find a means of justifying a partial defection from the patriarchal identity that also, paradoxically, has nurtured his willingness to sacrifice himself for others. The image of Baba-san's cheater-artist sister helped him manage that paradox. If he could be a cheater with integrity, then he need neither reject nor fully submit to the demands of Takeno manhood. Embedded as it was in a political movement, this half-measures, cheater posture of Baba's became a means of asserting moral agency against otherwise pervasive power structures such as the LDP domination of Japanese politics and the relentless breadwinner expectations that shape men's identities.

MASCULINE IDENTITY
IN THE REFERENDUM ASSOCIATION

At the end of the previous chapter I pointed out that Shirakawa Ward assemblyman Takada-san had a sometimes difficult relationship with the image of traditional Japanese masculinity, a vaguely defined but nonetheless important structure that shaped both the political community in which he worked and his own choices about how to work within and for that structure. I talked about Takada-san's own sense of the importance of working to gently reshape elements of his and others' understandings of masculine duty and masculine loyalty. In the end Takada-san's reinterpretation of traditional masculinity did not present a fundamental challenge to the gendered power structure of conservative dominance in his community's politics. However, as we followed his narrative we could begin to grasp the role that complicated ethical choices play even in the reproduction of preexisting power structures, such as the dominant discourse about how a good man behaves. Viewed against Takada-san's eventual deference to masculine hierarchies he saw as deeply problematic, both the radical dimension of the ethical stance Baba takes in eventually scorning those same hierarchies (in his cheating of their rules) and the potentially great personal costs of that stance become clearer. Indeed Baba-san's decision to resist masculine hierarchies to which he had been loyal most of his life is intriguing because, in many ways, he and his fellow Referendum Association members did not think about the requirements of manhood much differently from Takada-san.

For Takada-san, being a good man and being a good political leader in his community were both contingent on negotiating his relationships with other male leaders in a pragmatic way. Takada-san presented himself as inheriting his father's special role in the community, as working to uphold the Takada male tradition of public service marked by self-effacing sincerity, loyalty, sure-footedness, and commitment to duty. He described the requirements of this work, both in its most negative and most desirable senses, as marked by deference to traditional values greater than his own interests *and* to ruthless political power hierarchies. He admitted the dangers of commitment to a world in which the ethic of loyal obedience to men more powerful than himself threatened to squash other values—a world in which the ethics of public service became, in some ways, like the ethics of men in organized crime. Takada-san also worked to reinterpret his traditionalist ethic of service to incorporate a notion of community and national needs that would justify small forms of self-assertion against the conservative political hierarchy; nonetheless he did not plan any major assault on the way things were done in the LDP-dominated political world. First, as a conservative thinker he did not quibble in any basic way with LDP dominance, even though he admitted that the party was often ineffective and sometimes downright corrupt. Second, he saw most forms of resistance to the existing power establishment as imprudent and, worse, a shirking of one's fundamental manly duty to bear discomfort of all sorts for the sake of serving others in a practical way.

Takada-san once explained to me that men control political colleagues whose behavior seems foolish by reminding them of their obligation to be men. For example, a politician might say to a troublesome junior member of his party, "What are you doing? You're a man, aren't you?" Failing to be seen as a man by those above oneself in the power hierarchy means political disaster. Takada-san was quick to remind me that it was women's inability to understand or enact that very sort of deference of one man to another that constrained female advancement in Japan's conservative political mainstream. He also told me a story of a much more senior man in the local LDP organization who found himself marginalized in the party hierarchy after making ill-advised attempts to distinguish himself from the rank and file by expressing his opinions more confidently than his position allowed and by unilaterally pursuing election strategies viewed as "eccentric" and "idealistic." That man was eventually forced to separate from the LDP and to compete for office as an independent.[3] Takada-san was thoughtful about power, ethics, and masculinity. But, in his own words, he was also simply "realistic." He argued that the kind of man who deserved political power also had to be capable of a man's burden, which, among other things, meant upholding masculine relationships of mutual trust, even when doing so meant suppressing his own ideals.

In most ways Baba-san's vision of a good man was not very different from Takada-san's. When Baba-san and his fellow Referendum Association men spoke about their political engagement, it was often clear that, like Takada-san, they believed that a good man does not have the luxury of taking a purist stance. Accepting without complaint the messiness of the power structure within which one must work to do good was often presented as the mark of a man who can carry a man's burden, just as accepting the toil and constraint of being a breadwinner was also a mark of a good man. Baba-san could have chosen to reject the pragmatic, self-effacing notion of manhood that characterized expectations for behavior in Takeno's dominant masculine networks, much as it did in Takada-san's Tokyo political world. But Baba-san did not reject that notion.

Even if Baba had been inclined to reject traditions of masculine pragmatism and deference to masculine hierarchy, it is doubtful he could have done so and still have succeeded in leading the referendum movement. Masculine pragmatism in the service of others was both an immensely useful organizing ideology of the Referendum Association and a shared language with which Baba and other leaders could manage Association members. In contrast to anti–nuclear power plant activists with ties to local Socialist and Communist Party organizations, environmental movements, or nationwide networks fighting the spread of nuclear power, most of the Referendum Association men had come to political activism in their midlife years. (Baba-san's cousin was the one noteworthy exception among the top leaders.) Prior to joining the referendum movement, the bulk of movement members had participated in community networks that had indirectly supported a masculinist, conservative hegemony. The farmers had belonged to the local farming cooperatives, which traditionally have been an organizational resource for the LDP.[4] Small businessmen had belonged to the Takeno Jaycees, also a supporter of LDP politics in the town. Those who were salarymen had generally tried to stay out of politics.

Most of the men at the center of the Referendum Association worked to portray themselves as "regular men," in contrast to those they looked on as "political activists." This partly came out of their founding agreement. As Baba and others explained to me, many groups of anti–nuclear power activists had protested the plant from the fringes of Takeno politics in the decades before the referendum movement got started. But they were consistently branded as left-wing ideologues more interested in opposing the conservative establishment than the exigencies of town government. For that reason leaders of the Referendum Association focused not on pressing voters to stand against the plant but on giving voters a chance to express an opinion without the cost of having to associate themselves with the larger aims of fringe leftists. The Referendum Association leaders publicly declared that they would not take a position on whether the nuclear power plant should be built until after the referendum was concluded. Of course many Association leaders secretly opposed the nuclear power plant, and they suspected that given a chance to vote specifically on the plant, the majority of Takeno voters would also oppose it. Still, in their founding ideology the leaders agreed that forwarding the true voice of Takeno-machi citizens was their most important objective. Even several years later, in 1999, the only requirement for all Referendum Association candidates was that they put prominently on their campaign literature the declaration that they were committed to upholding the referendum results in local policy.

The Referendum Association men were thus committed to presenting themselves as the voice not of antiplant activists but of "regular" Takeno people. Their regular people image served the Association's needs as the group sought to build a new coalition to fight the nuclear power plant. But the Association's leaders did not draw their image on a blank slate; it suited them well because it dovetailed with their pre-existing commitment to viewing themselves as typical men: pragmatic and loyal, well used to sacrificing their own needs while meeting the responsibility of providing for others.

The easy fit between the Referendum Association leaders' presentation of their movement and their attachment to a notion of the good man as a pragmatic, loyal provider was obvious in the judgments they made about other political activists. For example, one of the local groups that supported the referendum and opposed the nuclear power plant was the Japanese Communist Party. The Referendum Association men worked with the single Communist elected to the Takeno assembly. They were courteous to him; they kept him abreast of the general direction of their election strategy; and when the assembly was in session they shared their thoughts about upcoming controversies and votes with him. But in private the men were very critical of the Communist Party. They saw it as unyielding and idealistic. "If there's one thing I'm not, it's a Communist," Baba-san would say with great emphasis, despite the fact that he confessed to occasionally voting for Communist candidates for offices such as the prefectural assembly.

Moreover it was not simply communism from which the men worked to distance themselves, but idealism generally. Once, when I returned to Baba-san's home after spending the evening observing a meeting of the Green Association, another group allied with the Referendum Association against the nuclear power plant, I was treated to a particularly intense display of the Association leaders' antipathy toward idealist activism. Two of the Association's key men had been chatting with Baba-san. One was Takahashi-san, the farmer who served a term in the local assembly as a representative of the Association; he was a man Baba-san repeatedly described as a "good man." When I told the men where I had gone for the evening, Takahashi-san began to complain about the difficulty of working with the assemblywoman from the Green Association in assembly work and in preparation for the upcoming elections. She was too focused on "social welfare," he said. She did not see the importance of getting enough anti–nuclear plant candidates to stand to enable voters to elect an antinuclear majority.

He insisted that the Green Association members were proud of being in the minority because they thought it made them special; in other words, the Greens did not seem to understand the fundamental reality of assembly politics: that numbers are power.

Baba-san added that the Greens were probably actually Communists. "I'm so sick of their talking about 'welfare' and 'volunteer activities.' I hate the 'volunteer' thing! Most people who say they want to volunteer or say they want to make a 'welfare society' are just trying to cover up their real motives with pretty words." I'm not sure what he thought their real motives might be in this instance, but he offered frequent praise of hardworking men and clearly despised what he saw as rent seeking by some local businessmen. For example, he criticized local developers who, he said, pushed for the nuclear power plant because they were hungry for public works contracts that would be associated with the site development. He might have thought the Greens were also, in a way, rent seekers when they demanded more government support for social welfare services, such as child and elder care, in which many of them worked.

Takahashi-san agreed and pushed the critique further: "I hate those words. You can't make a society that is a 'welfare society.' That's *amae* [childish or naïve]." Being naïve seemed to be an unacceptable form of self-indulgence in the eyes of Referendum Association men. Most of the time they were expected to feel in their guts a sense of what was in the wind, of how to behave so as to be seen as real men, and of what the proper hierarchy of the Referendum Association really was (although it did not correspond to any organizational chart, as Baba-san made nearly all final decisions and had absolutely no official organizational position). It was just as Takada-san was expected to do in Tokyo's Shirakawa Ward.

On my last night staying with the Baba family, I joined the Babas, Takahashi-san, and a few others for dinner at a restaurant. It had been only a few weeks since the conclusion of the assembly election, and everyone at the table was still trying to interpret the results. Two of the Referendum Association's five candidates had lost their bid for election. The incumbent Takahashi-san was one of them. How was it that the same electorate that had provided a large antinuclear majority in the referendum a few years earlier had failed to return a majority of antinuclear candidates to the local assembly? "Maybe it's just that most voters do not want to choose an antiestablishment candidate," Baba-san suggested. Takahashi-san was outraged. "I am not an antiestablishment person," he insisted. Given that he had devoted much of the past six years to fighting the town's conservative majority, Takahashi-san's claim that he was not antiestablishment was in many ways ridiculous, and everyone at the table burst into laughter. Still, Takahashi-san's frustration made some sense. He always portrayed himself as a practical farmer, a rational man's man. When he was in the assembly he had been the one most likely to demand more detailed information about budgets; he appealed to common sense: "Why pay more than we have to for facilities upgrades? We should get more bids." He did not describe himself as a partisan of any sort, and perhaps he resisted the tinge of "naïve idealist" he heard in the term "antiestablishment." Couldn't he stand against a corrupt and wrongheaded local government without being antiestablishment?

If the notion of pragmatic manhood was presented as the ideology of the Referendum Association, it also provided a sort of tool box for managing the inevitably difficult decisions and tense human relations during the campaign season. In the months leading into the 1999 elections, conversations in gatherings of Referendum Association members, both at formal meetings and in more informal settings, often focused on conflicts, both within the Association and with the other groups in the referendum alliance. The conflicts were provoked by the strategic challenges of running an election in an at-large district, where all candidates, even those who shared common political goals, were conceivably in contest with all others. For example, when men in the Referendum Association and other referendum alliance camps talked about whether they could support prospective candidates for election to the local assembly, they peppered their explanations with the term "responsibility" (sekinin). I had not heard the term used quite that way when I studied female candidates for local assemblies. Instead women, even in Takeno, tended to talk about running for office as a means of overcoming their previous, "irresponsible" (musekinin) disengagement from politics.

When I asked specific questions about the responsibilities of men in the referendum alliance, I got answers that revealed their paternalistic thinking about politics. Men who were working or considering working for male candidates had the responsibility of making sure that a candidate did not risk his livelihood by running. This was partially motivated by mutual appreciation for the male breadwinner obligations I explored in chapter 1. In fact some men whom Referendum Association leaders discussed as potential candidates were never invited to consider running because the leaders decided it would be irresponsible to urge a man to engage in a campaign he likely could not afford.

But even when the prospective candidates were women and were not assumed to be risking a better, more secure salary by running for office, the Referendum Association men still debated their responsibilities toward the candidate. As it became clear that if the Association wanted to expand its slate of candidates it was going to have to seek out women, one of Baba-san's friends commented that his wife insisted that a young, single woman who "could wear a miniskirt" would be the best choice for a candidate. Baba-san initially voiced worries that young women would injure their reputations as future wives and mothers by running for office. He did not want to be responsible for making a young woman's life "crazy," he told me. When I suggested that perhaps women should be allowed to decide the risks for themselves, he disagreed. If he asked a young woman to run for office, he would be responsible for her. Shortly after Baba-san, his friend, and I had this conversation, the Referendum Association agreed to allow Miura Yukiko, a young, unmarried woman, to run for the assembly under the Association banner. Baba-san took responsibility for her election campaign in a way he did not for the campaigns of either of the men or the two middle-aged women.

Prescriptions for behavior in a conflict, often delivered by Baba-san as he acted the part of candidate counselor in his shop office or in individual meetings with candidates and their volunteer campaign staff, frequently included advice that boiled down to "just being a man" and emphasized the importance of a kind of emotional continence. Of course Baba-san was arguably echoing a view widespread in the Referendum Association. I was told by other Association men that no real man ever breaks promises and that real men don't express worry. Men who changed their mind about alliances (and thus broke promises) were sissies or *yowa mushi*, literally "weak bugs."

Still, Baba-san seemed to be the leading advocate of stoic acceptance in the referendum movement's participants. One man told me that although campaign conflicts were making him angry, he was working to keep the anger stuffed inside (he pointed to his stomach) because his anger would just make things harder for Baba-san, presumably by embarrassing him. Confronted with a wide range of stories—from tales of frustrated candidate spouses lashing out at other candidates to foolish comments or downright unethical behavior—Baba-san seldom expressed his own feelings. Instead he would gently tell men and women worried about campaign conflicts to keep their emotions under control. When a rumor broke that a bribe had been paid to a voter by a supporter of a Referendum Association candidate, Baba-san made a few very sharp-toned phone calls. When it seemed possible (although not certain) that the bribery incident was a misunderstood and perfectly legal business transaction in which a candidate's uncle had given his own business card and a discount certificate to a legitimate client, Baba-san urged that everyone concerned about the incident "shut it away in their chest."

Although he counseled both men and women to stow their feelings inside, Baba expected more composure from men than women. When his wife got furious at comments a man from one of the allied camps made about a female Referendum Association candidate, Baba-san laughed. "You've got to say my wife's clear about her opinion, and that's good, isn't it?" he said. He never spoken indulgently about male anger and often insisted that he himself felt no anger, even while his wife protested that she knew him to be as frustrated as she was. Perhaps Baba was more generous with outspoken women than he was with men because he expected women to play a distinct role in politics, just as his wife played roles at work, at home, and among their movement friends that differed from his.

Baba and his wife divided their household, business, and political work, despite the fact that they shared their days more fully than would be expected for many couples in Japan's gender-divided society. In marriages where the husband is an employee in a firm he does not own, husband and wife spend much of their day, and often the evening, apart. However, in their small business Baba-san's wife worked as a partner, something she said she had expected to do when her parents, also small business owners, helped to arrange her marriage to Baba in her early twenties. She was constantly at the shop, and he consulted her in any decision that might affect its well-being.

Baba had asked for his wife's support before endangering customer relationships by starting the Referendum Association movement, and she was a party to many of the impromptu evening political discussions at their home. She frequently expressed strong opinions about Takeno politics, and Baba-san made no obvious efforts to calm her. She attended all of the general Referendum Association meetings, and her connections with women in the area allowed her to contribute regularly to discussions in which Baba-san and other Association leaders tried to hash out the best campaign strategies. Like most of the Association women, however, Baba-san's wife did not herself attend many of the important strategy meetings. Moreover she claimed to heartily dislike politics, shaking her head at Baba's apparent enthusiasm for it. Of course she also seemed proud of his political work, often saying he had no other choice but to lead the movement. "Who else could do it?" she would ask.

Still, Baba-san and his wife divided political work in their home much as they divided work in their store, with Baba as the deal maker and delivery man and his wife as the gatherer of information and the keeper of books. I think they divided the emotional labor of politics as well. His wife expressed strong opinions and intense frustration that Baba calmly admitted he shared. His views were voiced, but he was allowed to play the role of bemused patriarch. I doubt either of them was conscious of it, but her outbursts gave him a convenient backdrop against which to highlight his own manly reserve.

On rare occasions Baba did approve of emotional expression by men, but this was a different sort of exposure than that he indulged in his wife. Yanagi-san, the mechanic who finally agreed to serve as one of the Referendum Association candidates in the assembly election, initially faced great resistance from his extended family. The sitting mayor, a Referendum Association member, was asked to visit Yanagi's family to plead for their support of Yanagi-san's candidacy. According to the story I was told by a group of Association members who had joined the mayor in the visit to the family, the mayor bowed from his knees and cried a bit as he begged the family to support Yanagi-san's candidacy. "If Yanagi-san hadn't decided to run [*fumikitta*], if he hadn't just made up his mind to break through family resistance [*koshi o kitta*] after the mayor let tears flow [*namida o nagashita*], he [Yanagi] would have been in a very bad position," Baba-san explained to me. In other words, if Yanagi-san had turned the mayor down, then the mayor would have seemed a weepy and ineffectual man, and Yanagi-san's movement colleagues would have seen him as churlish for putting the mayor through such humiliation. Because Yanagi-san decided to run the mayor's image was bolstered by the crying scene; the Yanagi family's capitulation showed the mayor to be a powerfully persuasive leader whose tears demonstrated an admirable sensitivity to the sacrifices the family was making for the town's welfare.[5]

Yanagi-san's campaign provided ample opportunities for me to observe how Baba-san and the other Association leaders impressed the rules of manhood on one of their peers. They repeatedly described Yanagi-san's candidacy as a great test of his ability to maintain his composure. When he gave an emotional announcement of his decision to run for office at a meeting of the full Referendum Association, the verdict among the leading men was that he was a risky candidate because he was not a "good talker." Throughout the campaign they chided him for seeming out of control. One time, while discussing his voter outreach strategy in the back office of Baba's store, Yanagi-san mistakenly grabbed my tea from the little shelf built around the kerosene heater where we all habitually placed our tea. "Oi! Omae ha Robin no ocha o nonda zo! Ochitsuke zo!" Baba-san shouted. This is a patronizing, highly masculinized way of saying "Hey, you, you drank Robin's tea! Settle down!" It seemed to suggest that Yanagi-san was on the verge of becoming hysterical. Yanagi-san failed to win election, but to hear Baba-san and the others tell it, he won the real battle, the one with his emotions. When the election results came out Baba-san visited the losing candidates at their homes, and he proudly recounted how, when it was announced that her husband had lost, Yanagi-san's wife bawled but the candidate "acted in the right way," telling his wife to calm down and shrugging off the loss.

As when he chastised Yanagi-san for drinking my tea, Baba-san's way of speaking was often that of a wise or bemused patriarch. He frequently mobilized the distinctly masculine vocabulary available in the highly gendered Japanese language when he talked with other Referendum Association members, even if they were women and even at times when he was speaking quite gently or sympathetically to his listener.[6] And he never failed to mark his age when he talked with those younger than he. In his late fifties at the time I met him, Baba-san was perhaps five to ten years older than the average Referendum Association member, though he was certainly not the oldest. Yet his persistent use of informal, masculine vocabulary seemed to press his age and sex advantages through language even further than they might have stretched based simply on objective criteria. Even men who were ostensibly his equals tended to speak a bit more formally to him than he did toward them. His language habits were so distinctively assertive that Iida-san, the same journalist friend who eventually came to praise Baba-san's ethic of "beautiful poverty," once complained that I was easier to talk to than Baba-san. My nonnative speaker's stiff use of Tokyo-style Japanese was more formal than Baba-san's, and thus it provided a certain comfortable restraint in the conversation, Iida-san explained. Baba-san's informal way of talking distressed Iida because, since he was younger than Baba-san, he did not feel comfortable matching it. Baba-san's rollicking use of regionally inflected informal language positioned Iida as a son or a sort of young apprentice, making it hard for Iida to present himself as a media professional maintaining an appropriate distance from the subject of his reporting.

Baba-san's presentation of himself as the Referendum Association's wise patriarch extended beyond his use of language. He told me that being involved in community politics meant being willing to "drink the dirty water with the clean [*seidaku o issho ni nomu*]." He made the comment to me as he tried to explain why the year before the Referendum Association had formed he had backed the conservative challenger for the mayor's office, who only promised to poll the citizens on the plant, when he could have backed the clearly antinuclear candidate put forth by the principled (but naïve) Green Association. He told me that he had worked to teach his cousin, Ota, an acceptance of the truth that some dirty must come with the clean. I did hear him saying similar things to Ota-san when Ota got worried about the damage that might be done to the Referendum Association as Baba-san sought community men who had never belonged to the Association as potential candidates. As he pressed upon his fellow movement members the importance of suppressing some portion of the niceties of their ideals in the service of the Association's larger goals, Baba-san also presented himself as the leader of a masculinist hierarchy that commanded deference and loyalty from its members in much the same way that Takada-san had described LDP hierarchies as doing. Therefore, although Baba had ridiculed Takada-san's self-conscious use of Confucian terms such as *jingi* as a *yakuza* way to think, I could not always tell if Baba-san's understanding of a good man's political ethic was truly distinct from Takada-san's.

When Baba-san became one of the Referendum Association's founding members his long-standing and lucrative ties to the network of conservative politicians in Takeno were severed. But, after all, Baba-san had come of age as an insider to the conservative male networks that dominated Takeno, and therefore it should not be surprising that he approached his role as a leader of a political movement with some of the same masculinist conceptions and strategies in hand as LDP politicians in a Tokyo ward. We might wonder why, given the chance to profit simply by going along with men who were in most ways little different from himself, Baba-san chose to risk his reputation as well as his business by becoming a founder of the Referendum Association. Perhaps there is nothing to say other than that he believed a nuclear power plant was not the sort of thing that the people of his town should have thrust upon them by men demonstrably more interested in rent seeking than in their town's welfare. Even Takada-san, who was nearly twenty years younger and whose locality faced nothing as divisive as a nuclear power plant or "let them eat, let them drink" corruption, sometimes felt resistant to the masculinist hierarchies of LDP politics in Tokyo; he succumbed to them because he knew he was unable to pursue the public work he valued without them. Takada-san knew he could not afford to be a naïve idealist; for that matter, Baba-san did not like the idea of being a naïve idealist either. So the most important question might not be *why* Baba-san wanted to be free of the conservative networks that dominated Takeno, but *how* he managed to achieve that freedom when so few ever had.

THE CHEATER AS AN ETHICAL STANDARD

Even before the Referendum Association was formed men in Takeno who did not approve of the nuclear power plant project or who were offended by the culture of money-power politics it had spawned had some political alternatives to chumming up to the dominant conservatives. They could join the Social Democratic Party, they could join the Communist Party, they could join one of a small handful of officially nonpartisan antinuclear groups (which were all led by people with ties to the established left parties), or they could keep their heads down and try to stay out of politics altogether. For men like Baba-san who tended to see the Left as either dangerously or childishly ideological, the established alternatives to conservative politics seemed almost unmanly, and the strategy of keeping one's head down was hard to practice. As Baba-san explained, when conservative town leaders came by urging his attendance at an event, he found it quite awkward and potentially bad for business to refuse. Taking a stance against friendly pressure to turn out for a rally or a drink might be seen as precisely the kind of purist, ideologue's display that pragmatic men avoided. Most of the men I met through the Referendum Association confessed to having been in some way mobilized by conservatives in the past; we might see that as an effect of the pressure on them to present themselves as pragmatic, loyal community men.

When at last Baba-san decided to gather his friends to form the Referendum Association, he might have tried to throw off the pressures embedded in the conservative notion of masculine relations along with conservative dominance of the local assembly and mayor's office. However, he did not relinquish his attachment to a notion of the good man as a self-effacing pragmatist who serves his fellow men loyally because that is part of his duty as provider for his family and community. Instead he struggled to defend his desertion of the masculine networks of his youth for the new ones he constructed as he built the Referendum Association. In that struggle to see himself as a good man when he sometimes seemed, in both others' and his own eyes, to have become simply a self-indulgent man, Baba-san built a narrative about himself that highlighted rather than resolved the contradictions built into his stance with and against manhood traditions in Takeno. His temporal linking of his ideas about Takeno politics with his memories of his artist-cheater sister in the same long conversations provides a window into how he embraced the contradictions of his community position.

As we follow the different narrative threads connecting his sister's high school cheating to his own engagement with Takeno politics, we will see that Baba-san's narrative offers us multiple possibilities for interpretation. For example, talking about his sister's rebellious youth served as a means of drawing attention to his own youth, a time in which he argued he had shown the kind of instinct for freedom that energized his completely unexpected midlife turn to political activism. But more important, retelling his memories of his artist-poet-cheater sister allowed Baba-san to present his uneasy relationship with the rules of traditional, pragmatic Takeno manhood and with traditional, pragmatic Takeno *men* as a creative undertaking instead of as an unresolved problem with his way of being.

Baba-san's recollections about his sister's incorrigibility (How else can one describe the attitude of the student who cheats and then publicly declares her dishonor as exhilarating?) appear to be clearly associated with his sense that masculine duty had constrained his life. Even on its surface his story associates her with his year in Tokyo, briefly free of the family business to which, as the only son of a war widow, he would be yoked his whole life. As a young woman and an artist, Baba's sister had not had to face the long and repetitive days in a small-town shop, but somehow she had still understood his plight. She knew he did not want to be a sake shop owner; she knew he did not have a personality suited to cultivating relationships simply for the sake of business, and so she advised him to do business only with those who could "accept him the way he was." In fact when she told him to neither chase those who left him nor turn away those who came to him, his sister counseled Baba against both the deference and the encumbrance that would ordinarily be expected from a small businessman who must cultivate his customer base in a small town, selling a product traditionally central to the cementing of masculine networks in Japan. We could say that, in a way, his dead sister had given Baba-san a sort of handicap for the manhood game. He could not be expected to cultivate the sort of interpersonal obligations other men might cultivate because his character had never been properly formed for doing so. His wise sister had seen that.

Baba-san further emphasized the connection he made between his sister and his frustration with masculine constraints by shifting from talking about her advice to him into complaining more generally about the expectations placed on men as workers. First he would recall how his sister had told him, "You can do business only with the ones who will accept you the way you are." Then, on the heels of that memory, he would launch into an energetic critique of the self-sacrificing work ethic that the Japanese are in the habit of associating with Baba's generation, Japan's first postwar generation. "I hate diligence [*kinbensa*]," he would say. "I hate effort [*dōryoku*]. I hate working for a goal. I am not a responsible type [I'm *iikagen na hito*]. But what I am is a person who doesn't quit." Sometimes, almost on the verge of losing control of his emotions, Baba-san would recount how, when they finished middle school, many of his fellow classmates boarded red-eye trains bound for cities such as Osaka and Tokyo to take jobs in factories that were growing with the booming manufacturing sector in the late 1950s. He would tell me about waving and crying as his friends departed and about friends who had "given their whole lives" to those factories, fueling Japan's meteoric postwar economic rise and ending up with nothing but exhaustion in return.

Baba-san's emotional story of the migration of his middle school friends reflects a demographic reality. During the 1950s and 1960s the young men of rural Japan (or the "back" of Japan, in a direct translation of the term *ura nihon* then widely used and now considered impolite) did migrate in massive numbers to the leading cities, where their cheap and compliant labor fueled economic growth.[7] Moreover the words Baba used for diligence (*kinbensa*) and effort (*dōryoku*) are highly popularized descriptors of the salaryman workers to whom Japan's postwar economic growth is typically attributed.[8] *Kinbensa* and *dōryoku* are words viewed as so central to modern Japanese culture that they appeared early in my Japanese-language training. The words are even a regular part of the formalized conversation about work presented in television dramas.

If Baba-san had simply criticized the self-sacrifice demanded of men in the years of high economic growth, he would be offering a fairly standard left-wing critique of the human costs of an untrammeled national appetite for economic advancement. Significantly, however, he includes himself as an object of his critique in an oddly ambiguous manner. To call oneself an *iikagen na hito* is to say literally that one is a person satisfied with getting things correct in only a general way, or to say that one pays little attention to detail, or that one is irresponsible. Baba-san *could* say that he despised the human costs of the postwar years and that both his own career choices and his later political engagement were motivated by those feelings. In fact, he often did say that he thought the mentality that justified the sacrifice of hardworking people to greater national goals was unacceptable. As examples he sometimes used the loss of young men in World War II, men like his father, who was reputed to have said just before being shipped out to the front after his final leave that he did not want to fight. Baba-san also pointed out that as engines of economic growth, power companies had long been allowed to exploit the poor. He would urge me to consider the countless lives lost in coal mines prior to the war. However, when he insists that he is an *iikagen na hito,* in contrast to the diligent men who slaved on the factory floors of booming Japan, he is not attributing the difference in his life choices to his principled stance against the high-growth agenda. Instead he is asserting that he was simply never good enough, obedient enough, or hardworking enough to get caught up in the sorts of things that men his age were generally consumed by.

The narrative is actually more complicated yet, because although Baba-san hated diligence and asserted that he was lazy and irresponsible, he constantly lionized the hardworking men of his town who worked *isshō ken mei* (literally, put their whole life into it) in order to support their families. Even of himself he regularly said, "One thing I can do is work *isshō ken mei*." And the truth is he did. Even though he never griped about it, his job at the shop was physically punishing. He made more than ten delivery rounds a day, sometimes serving as many as fifty customers in the ten trips, hauling beer kegs and crates of sake bottles in and out of tiny, dark corners of bars, carrying restaurant-size crates of beer and tonic bottles into awkward kitchen entrances, and even making stop after stop at the homes of residential consumers to drop off a week's supply of beer or sake and pick up old bottles for recycling. He had taken only a few vacations in more than fifty years; even in the midst of the most demanding part of his political work, he did not close the shop, which was open all day long, six days a week. In the evenings after work, he did the books with his wife.

When I asked Baba-san why he had continued to run the shop if he did not feel oriented toward sales, he simply said that it was his duty to do so. His widowed mother had spent her adult life struggling to keep the shop for him. He expressed the same sort of uncomplaining acceptance of the trying aspects of running the shop that he urged on the younger men and women in the Referendum Association when they confronted difficulties. In some ways I found it hard to see how Baba-san's willingness to give himself over to the family business, despite the fact that he felt ill-suited for sales, was very different from the choices of his middle school classmates who had moved to big cities and spent their lives on factory floors.

One possibility is that Baba wanted to draw a line between the kind of hard work that good men do uncomplainingly because it is their duty and the way that image of the hardworking man was cultivated as a means of constraining men. In other words, Baba was distinguishing between the honorable qualities of a man who willingly takes up manly duties and the dishonorable qualities of the man who uses other men's submission to duty as a means of controlling them for personal gain. In fact one of Baba's oft-repeated criticisms of the conservative leaders was that they pursued their own enrichment at the expense of the long-term welfare of the townspeople, even as the hardworking regular people of Takeno were too consumed by making a living to do anything about the abuse. Baba-san admired (and actually obeyed) the rules of manhood that commanded a man to self-sacrifice as provider and bearer of a family's legacy, but he also distrusted the popular evocation of masculinist notions of self-sacrifice, just as he distrusted the "pretty words" of the social welfare leftists in the Green Party.

But this still leaves us in a problematic place with regard to understanding Baba-san's enjoyment of his sister's cheating, for if he despised some men's self-serving manipulation of honest men's devotion to duty, how could it be that he admired his sister's cheating? To understand this we have to come back to the fact that Baba-san saw his own stance vis-à-vis the cult of the diligent man of effort as that of the irresponsible *iikagen na hito,* and this despite the fact that he daily demonstrated and even attested to his own capacity for unrelenting work. How could Baba-san possibly be an *iikagen na hito?* For the answer to that question we have to return to the essence of what cheating is. Baba-san did not misrepresent himself (at least not once he joined the referendum movement), and although he was seeking a political advantage over his opponents he was not seeking that advantage illegally or for personal gain. In those ways, then, Baba-san was not a cheater.

But another way of understanding cheating is as a form of disrespect: disrespect for the rules by which a test should be taken, a game should be played, a marriage or friendship should be honored. If we put it a bit more abstractly, cheating is disrespect for terms by which a relationship operates, whether the agreement is about who is allowed to touch the game ball with his hands, or a teacher's decision that students may not reference notes as they answer quiz questions, or to whom one owes faithfulness. If cheating is failure to treat a relationship with the care others give it, then a very hardworking man who has nothing but disrespect for the popular terms by which hard work is generally categorized and assigned a value (diligence, effort in the service of national economic growth) is, in a way, cheating. He insists on doing the hard work *and* conspicuously refusing the social approbation with which he should be rewarded. That refusal actually undermines the larger social game of men's hard work because it says that social expectations about why he does the work are not what motivates him to do it. The man who works very hard but says he hates diligence (when it is roundly praised as a proper masculine virtue) is highlighting his perception of (self-indulgent) independence from those who are in a position to praise or punish individual men for their modeling of the behaviors collectively demanded of all men.

To make this clear, recall that Takada-san explained that men in groups such as political party organizations could rein in their subordinates by saying something like "What are you doing? You're a man, aren't you?" An oblique reference to the duties of masculinity will work to constrain the behavior of the reprimanded man only if he generally agrees with his seniors on the rules of manhood. If the man disregards *most* of the rules of manhood, he would likely be so marginalized in a conservative political party or a local citizens' movement that he would have little power, and constraining him would be less of a concern for other group members. However, if the man objects to *some* of the manhood rules while being a model representative for most of them—for example, if he hates the notion of diligent men even though he values hard work and self-sacrifice—then the men with power in a group will want or even need to control him. But given the objector's incomplete attachment to the rules, a mere reference to his manhood is not necessarily a reliable means of constraining his behavior.

If Baba-san had thought it generally wrong for men to shape their behavior to fit expectations for masculine pragmatism and duty, he would not have felt like a cheater. But the fact is he did not encourage other men to pick and choose from the list of widely expected masculine behaviors. I think that he saw his exempting himself from some versions of diligent manhood as demonstrating a painful degree of disrespect to other men who were daily effacing themselves in an effort to accomplish their manly duties. I think that is why Baba continued to describe a number of men who supported the nuclear power plant as good men and why he emphasized the extent to which his Referendum Association colleagues were hard workers. We might view Baba-san's nonconformity as evidence of his admirable willingness to stand with his convictions, but he was less certain of the goodness of his choices. His own philosophy of manhood ridiculed men who placed too much importance on "naïve" or pure-hearted convictions as self-serving idealists.

That is the reason Baba-san's approach to the masculinist discourse and practices that shaped the behavior of men engaged in Takeno politics seemed to him to be a form of cheating. He did not reject most aspects of masculinist discourse; he was a vigorous practitioner of many kinds of masculinist means for managing relationships with others. He did not offer a coherent alternative to Takeno's traditionalist, pragmatic masculinity that could become a target of the conservatives' critique. He simply refused to meet some of the expectations placed on him even while doing his best to access the benefits of his status as an established community patriarch. He was not loyal to the men among whom he had originally risen as a businessman and community member to the sort of stature that allowed him to play the role of town father, and when those men attempted to sanction his betrayal by withdrawing business and social approval, he remembered his sister and laughed at his old friends.

There is still one more part of the "cheating" puzzle: if Baba-san's cheating could be recognized only in his late-night self-narratives it would not be an especially significant part of his political being. Certainly his own recognition of his position as a cheater of Takeno's manhood rule is important; it allows us to see that he was not simply confused about what was expected of men but was self-consciously engaging in resistance. Yet to see his cheating as a practice of agency in a democratic system we need to know not only that Baba-san resisted a complete submission to the expectations of manhood but also that his resistance to the manhood rules was actually part of the political work he did, rather than a simple expression of feelings he happened to have at the time in his life when he also chose to become politically active. In other words, if the men in the masculine networks he had deserted to start the Referendum Association did not recognize his behavior as a betrayal that ought to have been controllable with reference to his manhood, then we might say that Baba-san had simply failed so fully under their manhood rules that he had become a complete convert to some alternative way of being—an enemy as opposed to a treacherous friend. But if he had been a simple enemy (an outright opponent) of the conservative regime that dominated Takeno-machi politics, his association with the referendum movement would probably not have been quite as useful as it actually was in placing the movement squarely within the realm of something in which "regular people," especially "regular," breadwinning men, could be safely engaged, as distinct from the left parties and long-term nuclear power opposition groups that had never been supported by a majority of townspeople.

In fact Baba-san's incomplete conversion from the conservative paternalism with which Takeno had been managed to the side of the nuclear plant opponents was mentioned as a prime reason for his effectiveness by leaders in the various camps of both plant supporters and opponents. In other words, his "cheating" of Takeno's masculine networks was integral to his political identity not only in his eyes but also in the eyes of other community leaders. Before the referendum Baba had supported the conservative town fathers, had joined the local chamber of commerce and the Lions Club. Whenever elections came around he had plied his connections and benefited from the purchases made by competing conservative politicians who wanted goodies to distribute among their constituents. He had not flinched at their illegal practices. When the police came around asking questions about those purchases, he had not refused to cooperate, but he wasn't overly helpful either. "I couldn't be known as the store owner who snitched on the politicians," he explained.

Before the referendum Baba literally marched with the supporters of the power plant project, donning one of the vests the organizers had given marchers to wear as symbols of their solidarity. His old Lions Club friends remembered this; one of them, who was a leader among the pro-nuclear businessmen, shared this with me when I interviewed him prior to meeting Baba. When Baba finally took his plan for a referendum to the small group of leftists who had opposed the plant from the first announcements in the late 1960s, they were hesitant to trust him. "We had seen him marching on the other side," more than one told me. Even though they supposed Baba had joined the pro-plant group only out of consideration for his business, they still wondered if he was reliable now that he had decided to change sides.

The men on the pro-nuclear side who had been Baba-san's friends remained puzzled about his new identity. Some of them were still friends, coming by his office periodically and generally maintaining cordiality. Two of the interviews I conducted with assembly members who supported the nuclear power plant happened only because Baba-san prevailed upon the men to meet with me as a favor to him. Others, of course, refused to speak to Baba-san. His consciousness of their break with him was still so raw four years after the Referendum Association had begun that he sometimes described himself as a man without friends, despite the fact that, with the occasional exception of Sunday afternoons, his home and office were crowded with visitors from before breakfast until late in the evening. His wife also sometimes talked bitterly about other couples with whom they had been friends since youth but who no longer spoke to them. She blamed the other couples for deserting them when Baba's political inclinations became public. As I interviewed both the pro-nuclear men with whom Baba-san remained friendly and those with whom he either had broken or had not had ties, I was struck by the extent to which conservative men seemed to associate Baba-san's troubling position as a leader of the referendum movement with a weakness, not in his ideology, but in his manhood. And when Baba-san rued lost business or his and his wife's lost friendships, he also sometimes seemed to blame his personality more than the political divisions in the town.

Sometimes the links between Baba-san's movement position and his problematic manhood were made indirectly. One conservative friend of his, Hirose-san, described his own engagement with the nuclear power plant as the result of his slipping into a campaign for an assembly seat in the "natural flow" of things after having been involved in the local youth group of his neighborhood association. Then, when he was a new assembly member, his seniors in the assembly "allowed" him to (or "made" him; the Japanese verbs would be exactly the same in this case) present a resolution before the assembly calling for the support of a nuclear power plant. It was the late 1970s when this resolution was passed, so Baba-san had been Hirose-san's friend for decades after this public declaration of support for the plant. Hirose-san told me that he had never really considered whether he was for or against nuclear power in and of itself; he said accepting the plant had appeared to be a way of providing economic growth and jobs for the town's young fathers. He explained that, at any rate, the Takeno town government had little control over nuclear power policy, which must be fought out at the National Diet level. Moreover, although people might worry that nuclear power is dangerous, without it Japan could not expect to compete in a global economy, and Takeno might face great difficulties even competing with nearby towns.

Hirose-san claimed he never fundamentally opposed holding some sort of referendum (though he did not vote for the Takeno referendum ordinance), but he pointed out that when asked to decide on the nuclear power plant question in a referendum, citizens, women especially, made ill-informed decisions because they had been preyed upon by outsiders: "All those people who came in from all over the country and ran [nuclear plant] opposition movements [said] 'It's dangerous, [think of] the children.' Human beings, we all have strong emotions. Schoolteachers were saying to the children, 'You know, nuclear power is dangerous. Tell your mother and father.' Caught up in that, the young mothers said, 'Well, it's better not to have such a dangerous thing.'" Hirose-san implied that if the referendum advocates had been responsible patriarchs, the town would have been safe from the hysteria of young mothers who had been the victims of emotional manipulation by outsiders. Instead the referendum had been held; an important and complicated issue had been overly simplified and left in the hands of impressionable young women. Economic opportunities for Takeno were at risk and, Hirose-san said, "the husbands who are the pillars of their homes are meeting with restructuring [layoffs and demotions as companies reorganize to cut costs]. Jobs are being lost. Their children or grandchildren are graduating from universities, but even if they try to go to work, there's no place to work."

Whether they highlighted the referendum as a naïve means of solving public policy dilemmas, as Hirose-san did, or described Baba-san as a carousing publicity-seeker, as another conservative assembly member did when I interviewed him, the conservatives with whom I spoke directed their critique of Baba-san to the ways he failed to meet the criteria of a pragmatic town father by being either naïve or, ironically, the very *iikagen na hito* (irresponsible person) that Baba-san himself claimed to be. The pro-nuclear conservatives further intensified their focus on Baba's failings as a man as opposed to political differences by emphasizing their own ambivalence about the nuclear power plant. They had supported the plant not because they believed in nuclear power but because they doubted their town could survive economically without an industry of some sort; they had made tough choices as responsible fathers.

In his public pronouncements on his role in the Referendum Association, Baba-san repeated his claim that whatever happened, the citizens deserved a chance to have their say unobstructed by the combined practices of intimidation and bribery that had long shaped voter response to Takeno political controversies. Thus his formal complaint with the conservatives was actually with their political practices. Even so, the conservatives ignored his political critique and drew attention to his manhood. The conservatives never addressed the fact that the referendum movement also sharply criticized the exclusivity and corruption of decision making under conservative power. They might have tried defending themselves against Baba-san's political complaint by insisting that the townspeople must want the nuclear plant because there had been a long period of voter support before the referendum for assembly candidates who were open about supporting the plant. Perhaps the conservatives suspected such a defense would be unpersuasive; after all, the tradition of bribery was so well known that no one tried to deny its effect on politics. However, to the extent that conservatives really believed accepting the nuclear plant was the only smart economic choice for their town, they might have argued that a bit of bribery was simply a realist's approach to doing a man's duty, finding a way of helping the young mothers make peace with the tough decision involved in accepting the plant. Even Baba-san, who despised the politicians' corruption, did not fault the voters who received the bribes: Why shouldn't the townspeople take whatever was on offer from their political leaders when otherwise they were given so few real choices and could expect so few real benefits from their community's political system?

Although Baba-san did raise a clear protest against Takeno's decision-making processes, his way of talking about his break from the conservatives to form the Referendum Association showed that, with the conservatives, he saw his movement identity as also tied, in significant ways, to his choice to step outside of some elements of Takeno's manhood tradition—his decision to cheat on the manhood rules while playing the manhood game. Baba-san distanced himself from the Left of the antinuclear movement by using some of the same strategies that the pro-nuclear politicians employed to criticize him: shaking his head at naïve ideology and emphasizing his commitment to Takeno's hardworking fathers. In managing the complexities of the Referendum Association's electoral battles, Baba-san also resorted to masculinist strategies practiced in conservative camps. When Hirose-san explained that as a young assembly member, his seniors made him or allowed him to present a resolution in support of the nuclear power plant, we can imagine him learning to "drink the dirty water with the clean" in a way parallel to that Baba-san insisted would be necessary by Referendum Association members if they wanted to do important work for their community. When Baba-san mused that he had no friends, that he was an *iikagen na hito,* his words could have highlighted not only his sense of the rift between him and the conservatives who had shaped the world in which he had grown up but also a bit of the conservative's own frustration in trying to make sense of who Baba-san had become.

We should not forget that despite the ways Baba-san's use of masculinist discourse paralleled uses found among conservatives, he eventually became a leader of a movement that directly challenged the conservative way of doing things. The Referendum Association put in place practices that prevented their "dirty water" from ever becoming as dirty as the conservative political water was widely acknowledged to be. As I mentioned earlier, finances in the Referendum Association were openly and carefully accounted for. Unlike conservatives who admitted to bringing candy boxes to constituents' homes or cash remembrances to supporters' families' funerals, the Referendum Association spent its money on producing leaflets describing their movement's activities, printing business cards for their candidates, and providing basic campaign assistance such as signs for campaign offices, and even these were hand-painted in the prefabricated building the Association used as an office. Membership in the Association was open, most meetings were open to the public, and the Association was willing to run previously marginalized people for office, including women, as long as they would agree to represent the townspeople's views as expressed in a public referendum. When questions arose about whether a strategy was legally acceptable, the Association leaders consulted the law. I know this because one time they used *my* handbook on Japanese election laws to settle a question about appropriate candidate behavior during the official campaign period.

Baba-san was a cheater of manhood, but not a political cheater—and maybe that's the most striking part of his story. His political ethics forced him into a confrontation with his duties as a man and to other men. But he did not give up on either his strong attachment to traditionalist masculinity or his strong attachment to a vision of a political world much more transparent and egalitarian than that managed by the dominant masculine network of his town. Baba-san chose to straddle the contradictions and to soothe the sense of loneliness and failure he sometimes expressed by reminding himself of how his sister had always known that he would never quite fit in and by sharing vicariously in the airplane-ride joy she got from her own defiance of rules. Because he was willing to take the cheater's posture Baba-san was able to position himself in a unique space in Takeno politics. Other men who felt uncomfortably sandwiched between the unrepresentative and corrupt Right and the ideologically aggressive Left could associate themselves with Baba-san's almost traditional manhood. And he honored these men's commitment to their breadwinner duties, even though that commitment sometimes kept them from becoming a political force. In fact, aided and abetted by Baba-san's incomplete attachment to traditional manhood, men whose own political participation was curtailed by breadwinner obligations might have felt freer to ask their wives and daughters to run for office on their behalf. Following Baba into an accidental feminism that he himself seemed to pursue quite reluctantly might have seemed nothing more than manly pragmatism. Baba-san's half-measures, cheater's posture toward Takeno's manhood discourse helped create a new space in which new people could practice politics after decades of stalemate.

Eventually the referendum alliance stopped the nuclear power plant. At Baba-san's urging the alliance representative who had become mayor used the power of his office to sell a very small piece of municipal land inside the proposed plant site to a group of twenty purchasers (mostly referendum alliance members) who formed a legal covenant preventing any landholder from selling his portion of the collective holding to any person or entity that might sell it to the nuclear power plant. The mayor argued that the sale was consonant with the wording of the official referendum ordinance urging the mayor to "respect" the wishes of the townspeople as expressed in the referendum results. The mayor was challenged in court by conservatives who said he had abused his authority, but in the midst of the challenges he was reelected by a majority of Takeno voters. Following his reelection he survived two court challenges, and when the Japanese Supreme Court refused to hear an appeal the power plant company, at long last, withdrew its proposal to build a plant in Takeno-machi.

CHAPTER 5

The Art of the Gut

In December 2002 I scheduled an interview with Katō Susumu, a leader in the little talked of but growing world of Japanese political consulting. In the fall I had added another man's election campaign to the list of those I observed in my attempt to understand the link between masculinity and the use of power in local politics. Katō and a volunteer staff were instrumental in developing that candidate's campaign strategy, and I was meeting with him to get a more complete sense of how power was distributed in the campaign office.[1] Generally Katō works with progressive candidates from what are called the "citizen" (*shiminha*) ranks: candidates who disavow affiliation with established political parties of either the Right or the Left. In the past decade he has been a force in campaigns for a number of important offices for such citizen candidates of the independent center who have won governorships, seats in the National Diet, and mayoral races.

Ochi Ichirō, the candidate I had added to my study, was a true political independent running a "homemade" citizens' campaign for the mayoralty of the regional city, Fukuzawa, population 240,000.[2] In terms of his ideological orientation and the sorts of supporters his campaign attracted, Ochi's campaign was much like the campaigns run by members of the Referendum Association seeking elected office in Takeno-machi. Takeno actually provides some suburban housing for people employed in Fukuzawa. But the scope of the Ochi campaign was much larger than the assembly seat campaigns run by the Referendum

Association. Ochi sought office in an electorate more than ten times Takeno's. To best the highly organized campaign of his chief opponent, who was supported by all of the major established parties, Ochi needed professional help. He got that from Katō and his followers.

In mid-November 2002 Ochi surprised local journalists by winning the mayor's office with his new campaign style. In other ways Ochi-san was not surprising. When he described his run for office as something he felt he owed his community, he sometimes echoed the notions of masculine duty I heard from both Takada-san and Baba-san. From what I heard in conversations with members of Ochi's campaign office, his stature among his supporters was connected to his reputation as a self-effacing "good man" who had worked hard at his first career as a journalist and was a "good son" to his parents, who owned a well-known local business. Ochi-san's narrative did not present significant challenges to the ideas I had begun to form about the place of masculinity in men's political engagement. Nonetheless my experience interviewing his consultant was responsible for, at long last, drawing my attention to the importance of unspoken, "gut" politics among the men I studied in Takeno and Tokyo.

When I met with Katō in Tokyo in December 2002, following Ochi's November victory, I hoped to gain a better understanding of the decision-making hierarchy in Ochi's campaign office. I did not expect masculinity to be a central part of our conversation, but early in our long discussion Katō-san offered a characterization of his relationship with Ochi that immediately recalled for me the subtleties of masculinist hierarchies I had heard about in my months working with Takada-san and his LDP campaign for the Shirakawa Ward Assembly. I asked Katō-san how he, a Tokyo-based political consultant, and Ochi, a new politician in a rural city, got connected and how Katō and his staff came to be important forces in Ochi's campaign. Katō talked around the question a bit, mentioning some overlapping acquaintances, describing the circumstances in various partisan camps at the time the previous mayor announced his retirement, and then he said, "It was *aun no kokyū*." As he tried to recollect more details of his early meetings with Ochi, Katō returned to the phrase. "Really, this was a perfect case of *aun no kokyū*."

Aun no kokyū describes the sounds one makes when opening and closing one's mouth (or when one's mouth is fully open or nearly closed): "aaa" and "uhhn." The phrase also recalls the two fierce-looking statues often found guarding the entry gates of Buddhist temples. The mouth of one is opened to signify the "aaa" sound; the mouth of the other is closed to signify the "uhhn" sound. The Buddhist term originates in Sanskrit, but in everyday, contemporary Japanese the term has its own life. Japanese–English dictionaries translate the term as "perfect timing." But in Japanese dictionaries the sense of a perfect harmony of feelings is included as well. At other times one might say, idiomatically, "Iwazumo [without a word], aun no kokyū." This was a phrase Takada-san used when he tried to explain how arrangements for campaign assistance had been worked out between his father and other politicians, and when I pressed him for clarification he offered *hara de* (through the gut) and *hara gei* (art of the gut). In other words, a connection that is fixed by *aun no kokyū* is one that is grounded on a moment of perfect, wordless harmony between two or more people.

With that description of the term *aun no kokyū* one might conclude that Katō and Ochi had an extraordinary sort of bond, the kind few men in politics ever have. But the fact is that they had not met before working out the deal marked by this wordless accord. Moreover the term *aun no kokyū* or terms like it are used to describe bonds between men in politics far more frequently than one would imagine possible if deep, personal connections were always a requirement for an appropriate application. For example, the deals that Takada-san described using the term *aun no kokyū* were not deals involving men with whom he or his father felt at all close; they were exchanges based on mutual interest that outside observers might recognize as such. The men were of the same party; they sought office at different levels of government, but their districts overlapped geographically. Cultivating constituents for each other's campaigns was only slightly less self-serving than cultivating constituents for their own campaign.

Takada-san used notions of gut connections to explain a number of other instances of political deal making. *Aun no kokyū* is such a commonly used term that neither Takada-san's use of it nor Katō's would have been likely to draw notice in the ear of a native Japanese speaker. When I Googled the Japanese for *aun no kokyū* I found more than 104,000 Web citations.[3] These led me to a curious combination of sites that offered lengthy Japanese-language explanations of the origin and meaning of the term and sites that used the term as if it needed no explanation. One site used the term to describe the way political leaders in Japan and other Asian countries might similarly calculate symbolic political gains from the visit of a Japanese prime minister to the Yasukuni Shrine honoring Japan's war dead, as an unspoken, indeed unspeakable mutual recognition of the benefits even World

War II enemies could share in having the shrine visits as a point around which to rally nationalist sentiment.[4] By the time I heard Katō describe the cementing of a new and complicated political relationship, one that included deals on finances, endorsements from higher level elected officials, and the dispatch of staff to Ochi's office for more than a month of intensive election work, I had become fascinated by the fact that, not infrequently, important power relationships among political men were fixed with wordless accords.

When Takada-san explained *aun no kokyū* as "the art of the gut" he also claimed that there are times when seeking to render arrangements more explicit through verbal exchanges will make one seem stupid or untrustworthy. This is more than having the sense to keep one's mouth shut; silence held the center at precisely the sort of moments that explicit discussion would appear to be called for, such as the dispatch of sizable financial or personnel resources. We might assume the existence of informal or less than explicit agreements about power sharing in any political system characterized by patron-client relationships and backroom deals, as is Japan's. But my informants shared a shortcut vocabulary to describe moments when silence was the distinctive mode of power. The fact that such a specific vocabulary exists highlights the special value assumed to inhere in political deal making that is not simply informal but is actually *wordless*. That is, both explicit and informal deals might be useful to their makers, but they would never rank as high as those deals in which the agreement between the deal makers was already so nearly perfect that the deal *need never be viewed as a deal at all*.

The gut-based, wordless *aun no kokyū* accord is also deeply masculinist. That is why I have chosen to come back to it toward the end of the book. In Japanese politics masculinity and power seem inseparable. I have sought to see into the complexity behind that appearance of unity. Following Baba and Takada through months of electoral activity and listening to them and to their friends as they sought to describe, justify, and—often for their own purposes—make sense of their behavior, I was able to map a range of ways in which what is expected of men because they are men actually constrains their engagement with political life. In many of the situations in which I observed masculinity as a force at work on (or on behalf of) the men in Tokyo and Takeno, my informants acknowledged a persistent gap between what they wanted or hoped to do and what, as men, they thought they must do. Describing how they bridged the gap between the demands of being men and their own understandings of what constitutes community-minded political work was an important part of the narratives of their political careers. Takada-san sought to manage that gap by asserting a more authentic interpretation of the basic values of traditional Japanese manhood, whereas Baba-san managed similar frustrations by asserting that he failed to meet his community's traditional expectations for manly behavior because he took an independent moral posture, engaging in a kind of honorable cheating. Still, serviceable as they are, Takada's and Baba's tactics for creatively reusing the materials of masculine gender expectations do not encompass all of the important ways that masculinity influenced their political engagement.

In truth, although social scientists have not yet made a great effort to trace how notions of masculinity shape the behavior of men in politics, much of what masculinity does in politics is not very hard to see once we look for it. With only a small amount of prompting Baba-san and Takada-san are able to describe the connections between what they hope to do in politics and what they believe is required of them if they are to function as good men. Both men are also able to clearly articulate why the requirements of manhood present them with troubling dilemmas as they pursue what they think is the good of their communities. Perhaps Baba-san and Takada-san are extraordinarily self-aware, but I did not choose them as research subjects for that reason. More likely, men who willingly and successfully present themselves as leaders of their peers in a democratic system are forced into some degree of self-consciousness about the potential conflicts between their self-presentation as men and their true ambitions. What is problematic, however, is that the parts of the manhood-politics equation that community leaders such as Baba-san and Takada-san can articulate do not fully explain the power of masculinity in politics. In fact to the extent that the discursive power of masculinity is most apparent to Baba-san and Takada-san when they find it *constraining,* we would be hard-pressed to explain why they remain loyal to a masculinist worldview.

Having articulated for themselves just how delimiting manhood can be for a good man, why don't Baba-san, Takada-san, and others like them work to dismantle gendering discourse structures? Of course the men do make productive reinterpretations of gendered discourse structures; they make masculinity more inhabitable for people with their political ambitions. Being a cheater on dominant manhood practices in Takeno gives Baba-san a useful and unusual position on his community's ideological horizon: he is neither an impractical leftist nor a bought-and-paid-for old boy. By declaring himself a follower of a new vision of a more correctly understood samurai ethic, Takada-san is able to find some peace with his own position in a political system about which he has quite complicated feelings. By sharing this renewed sense of ethical tradition with students in his intern program, Takada-san is also able to see his work in elected office as meaningful over the longer term, even when it requires immediate compromises with power structures he dislikes. Both Takada-san and Baba-san *can* manage to act as ethical agents despite these gendered constraints on their efforts, but we might wonder why they *must* do so. Rather than engage in such elaborate renovations of the discourse structures they inhabit, wouldn't it be easier for both men (and presumably many others) to simply reject the gendered terms of their political engagements and construct newer, freer political identities?

The answer to this question lies in the politics of the gut accord. Despite the extent to which men like Takada-san and Baba-san are willing to acknowledge many of the frustrating demands embedded in social understandings of manhood, one area of manhood practice remains outside the reaches of easy articulation. Persistent male dominance has led to the popular assumption that political power is by nature manly, and it encourages the corollary assumption that powerful men are made so by a kind of mystical, natural force: the wordless persuasion skill described by Takada-san as *hara gei* (the art of the gut). Real men have power by virtue of being men not only in their adherence to obvious manhood rules (such as Baba-san's teaching of emotional continence) but also by grasping, in their gut, the nuances of complicated masculine power relationships. Those who have to speak explicitly about gut politics in order to follow their operations are possibly not real men because they do not have a natural instinct for men's relationships.

Just as a capacity for gut politics is the test of a real man and thus a means of access to realms of power largely controlled by men, gut politics provide men who care about doing good (as men, or even as human beings) their best resource for achieving that good. But gut politics would lose its mystical and self-reifying force if fully articulated; once a gut politics move is overtly described, the men involved have lost their claim to the *natural* sources of masculine power, ending up instead with a mere strategy of self-presentation that might be mimicked, even renovated by others who are not natural men. As Takada-san explained, anyone who needs to have things explained too fully is either a woman or a fool. (And, of course, in saying as much to me he highlighted, however inadvertently, that *I* am a woman—and perhaps a fool about Japanese politics!) Men who would access the power of gut politics must act in ways that reinforce larger silences about masculine power.

When I return to Takada-san's stories of gut politics in the section below, we will be reminded that the persistent use of gut politics by men who dominate the political arena can lead to bad policy, or something worse: actual corruption of the democratic process. Takada-san is clear-sighted about the dangers of gut politics, and he argues they will persist as long as what he calls a "men's culture" dominates Japanese political life. Nonetheless Takada-san is also quite reluctant to surrender man's dominant role in politics; he does not believe his community can be well served without recourse to the resources of men's culture. He is an avowed conservative and neotraditionalist; perhaps he is simply wrong about what would serve his community.

Yet although we can dismiss conservatives such as Takada-san, the power of gut politics will endure because even men who are committed to working against other forms of masculine dominance are still likely to work in ways that reinforce the masculinist power of the gut. This is because their best tool for doing good is the art of the gut, and the art of the gut cannot be used by men who will not respect its silences. In gender studies we often operate on the assumption that working to reduce the constraints and differential privileges produced by gender discourse structures is in itself a fundamentally ethical intervention into power's operations.[5] As a woman in a male-dominated academic discipline, I am a persistent activist against gender constraint myself. The art of the gut is a bulwark of the mystique of masculine superiority in Japanese politics, and so we might assume that an inclusive and egalitarian ethics of power would require that gut politics be dismantled.[6] But as we trace the art of the gut through the stories below, we will see how much more complex the ethical realities are. Baba-san's use of gut politics helps us to see why that aspect of men's political culture has such strong roots, even among men who are critical of Takada-san's traditionalist worldview. Even Baba-san, who is critical of most exclusive and unequal social structures, mobilizes the most exclusive of masculine privilege structures, and does so for the express purpose of combating exclusion and inequality. The unsettling truth is that pursuing masculine gender privilege and using power ethically may be, at least sometimes, the same thing.

THE ART OF THE GUT AS A MAN'S ART

In a sense, I take a very small risk in asserting that *hara gei* is a vessel of masculinism in Japanese political life. For one thing, women speaking polite women's Japanese are not as likely as men to use the term *hara* to talk about their stomach; they usually use the term *o-naka* (literally, "the insides," with the attachment of an honorific *o*). *Hara gei,* therefore, simply sounds masculine. Just as "gut" is not a common term in feminine usages of Japanese, the practice of describing political relationships as grounded in a wordless accord also seems to be uncommon among women in politics. The female politicians I studied in earlier projects and in Takeno and Tokyo in 1999 made the details of their recruitment to politics and the formation of their support organizations an explicit, and sometimes central, part of their political career narratives; this was true even for LDP women.[7] None of the female activists or candidates I followed explained her campaign endeavors to me as the result of gut accords in the way that the consultant Katō explained his relationship with Fukuzawa City mayoral candidate Ochi.

Silence certainly has its place in the organizations of female politicians with whom I've worked. Some questions can't be asked, even in women's campaigns. For example, I have found it difficult to get details about finances in female LDP campaigns. Progressive women candidates usually claim to value transparency in campaign affairs, and that does mean more researcher access to campaign finance information and other aspects of the organization. But even in those campaigns some aspects of the candidate's personal life (such as a divorce) might be off-limits for discussion. Campaign staff may also gloss over conflicts among themselves. Nonetheless when I have asked women politicians about how the connections and allegiances necessary to their political success were forged, they have always given me detailed accounts, usually full of emotional and specific stories about the moment when important relationships began. We might debate the accuracy of such narratives. Pressed, I would argue that women's stories place a suspiciously heavy emphasis on the transparency of motives and the clarity of relationships, but the place of the narratives in political women's self-understanding and self-presentation is indisputable.[8] Women politicians frequently claim that improved communication with constituents is one of their goals.[9] Moreover, even if I did not have women's political narratives as evidence, men's insistence that women are incapable of using the art of the gut helps underline the masculine character of gut politics. In fact Takada was not the only man who described women as unfit for politics because of their inability to grasp the terms of their political position without a clear explanation. A male staffer whom Katō brought into Ochi's mayoral campaign argued that women are less powerful in politics because they simply don't understand some of the unspoken realities of political relationships. Takada-san echoed this view. In his story the art of gut becomes the distinction between men and women that explains masculine dominance of political life.

Over the years since I followed his first campaign for office, Takada-san has told me a number of stories about political relationships grounded in the wordless *aun no kokyū* accord. Most of the time he did not draw an overt link between masculinity and the skill at gut politics that makes wordless accord possible, but one time he did. He explained the connection as he told me a story about how a wordless gut politics shaped the atmosphere of a meeting between the LDP members of the Shirakawa Ward Assembly and representatives of various constituency groups that supported the LDP. The ward government was entering the season for drawing up its annual budget, and the LDP assembly delegation called the meeting to give the group representatives a chance to share with the officials they had helped to elect their hopes for budget allocations relevant to their groups. I told part of the story at the end of chapter 1, and I want to finish it here.

Earlier I described Takada-san's frustration when confronted by male constituents' requests for special consideration for their interest groups in the ward budget negotiations. I pointed out that, even though he thought of himself as a fiscal conservative, Takada-san expressed some sympathy for men whose requests boiled down to demands for government subsidies for a failing line of work. He understood why, in their role as breadwinners, men might seek government help to keep going in a business that is no longer economically viable. But here, as we look more carefully at gut politics, I would add that Takada-san said he felt so acutely the pressure to sympathize with men as bread-winners even when their budget requests were bad policy because of the nearly silent gut politics atmosphere that pervaded the meetings of LDP assembly members and interest group representatives. Takada-san said that everyone involved looked at each other as if to say "Understand my gut. See it [my request] from your gut."

Takada-san claimed that this was exactly the sort of situation in which the fact that most elected officials are male affected the way politics is done. Once the atmosphere of gut understanding was established,

assembly members felt unable to say they could not fulfill a constituent's request. Instead, said Takada-san, assembly members would look
at the interest group representatives "*zuruzuru* [as if afraid to take a
stand, as if retreating], watching the color of their faces." The assembly
members hoped that the interest group representatives would understand the difficult budget situation the assembly confronted, he said.
But the groups' representatives didn't seem to make a great effort at
extending their understanding to those responsible for the entirety of
the budget. When they made their case and were greeted with a silent
room, they could "dig out" some meaning from that. In other words, if
they wanted to, the constituent group leaders could feel in their gut that
their requests would be hard for the LDP leaders to pursue while also
seeking a responsible ward budget.

Still, given the assembly members' dependence on their supporters,
the interest group leaders had an advantage. Silence might reveal the
discomfort of the pressured assembly members, but it also allowed the
preexisting assumption that the members were indebted to the group
leaders for their electoral support to stand unchallenged. The representatives of the interest groups could thus work the art of the gut
to their advantage. The assembly members felt bound to say "We'll
see what we can do," even when they viewed a budget request as
financially unsound. Takada-san explained that the whole atmosphere
was held together by preexisting notions of how things are "between
men" (*otoko dōshi*) that were shared by the assembly members and
their constituents. To illustrate these preexisting notions, he threw out
a few stock phrases for me: "Otoko dōshi no yakusoku darō" (It's a
promise between men, right?) and "Otoko dōshi no chikara darō" (It's
the power between men, right?). Takada-san thought that the gut sym-
pathies also worked on the side of the interest group representatives
because the budget requests tended to be tied to support of the line
of business in which the group members worked. Thus their requests
for consideration in the budget deliberations were also appeals based
on the group leaders' obligations as breadwinners, obligations that the
male assembly members felt bound to understand and honor.

Takada-san explained that female assembly members are unlikely
to respond in the same generous way to interest group requests, for
several reasons. First, female assembly members are less likely to fall
for the breadwinner appeal. Second, they are less likely to draw on the
resources of industry-connected support groups in order to get elected,

and so they are less likely than men to feel obligated to consider those groups' desires. Finally, and most important in Takada-san's estimation, women simply do not hear the gut messages that are delivered among men.

In fact, Takada-san said, an inability to read guts is why women are less likely than men to be in elected office, especially as representatives of the LDP. Women's lack of gut instinct works into a sort of cycle of exclusion. Women are not obligated to most of the interest groups that dominate conservative politics because women do not have the instincts necessary to cultivate the sorts of relationships with interest group leaders that are necessary for getting elected. Women are more likely to win office as representatives of minor parties such as the Japan Communist Party, where the process for earning the party's endorsement and the practices of divvying up campaign territories and other resources are explicit and fixed. He pointed out that in his ward, the LDP delegation included only a single woman, and he argued that in parties such as the LDP, where obtaining party endorsement, financial support for electoral activities, and the division of electoral territories is often managed through informal, personal networks, female candidates are bound to struggle. A decade earlier I had heard almost exactly the same analysis of the challenges for LDP women from a male manager of an LDP female candidate's campaign for a seat in the Diet.[10] Takada-san added that the chief advisors of the one female LDP member of the Shirakawa Ward Assembly are men who are well known for their ability to cultivate interest groups and to "read votes," a skill Takada-san claimed is related to the art of the gut.

Women do not have gut instincts for the development of the "thick" relationships political men develop, and they are therefore not bound by any corresponding sense of deference and obligation that bind men to each other, even before a word is spoken. Because women cannot feel their way through political relationships from the gut, they do not display the qualities that Takada-san values in male politicians he admires. At least in politics, women are not *ninjō ni atsui* (committed to human relationships) or *giri gatai* (punctilious with regard to obligations to others). Yet Takada-san had used these terms with me years earlier when he described the ethic of conservative politicians as, in some ways, similar to the ethic of Japan's mafia, the *yakuza*. When he explained how gut politics compels male assembly members to take a more positive line toward interest groups' budget requests than they would have if they felt free to pursue the most responsible financial policy for the ward, I thought he might be subtly suggesting that the masculinization of politics was, overall, a negative thing. When he described female politicians as free from male networks of obligation and deference, I was temporarily convinced that he was making an argument for a differently gendered future politics. But that is not at all what he meant.

Takada-san did think that female politicians would be likely to be refreshingly frank about the limits of the ward budget, but frankness was not on the top of his list for a politics that serves its community well. He seemed to firmly believe that women could, in some ways, do a better job at this kind of politics than men. But this insight did not lead him to jettison his attachment to the very masculinist norms that trapped him in deference to the gut's art. First of all, as I said earlier, he argued that women find it hard to enter political life precisely because they lack an instinctive knowledge of the ties of hierarchy and obedience that bind men. Supposing electoral practices could be changed so that the number of women in elected office increased, women might bring with them a way of "cutting cleanly" through the pressures of the men's interconnections, but in that very cutting they would be dangerous. Takada-san claimed that men's art of the gut and *giri-gatai, ninjō ni atsui* ethic knit the human relationships of the community together and protect the community from breaking: "So *giri, ninjō* is what knits you and me and [my friend] Nagoya [over here] and maybe four or five [others], and without it we'd be *bara bara* [atomized], isolated, maybe not Riesman's lonely crowd but like that—and in that there is something to lose, I think."[11]

PLYING THE ART OF THE GUT AGAINST INSIDER POLITICS

For Takada-san, the art of the gut that interest group leaders used to press for special advantages in the ward budgeting process is worth preserving despite its link to rent seeking because it is part of a larger culture of informal but thick relationships that bind men to each other, and those relationships are the force that make a community something better than a crowd of strangers. Of course Takada-san is a traditionalist, and his vision of what constitutes a healthy community includes gender-differentiated social and economic roles and emphasizes loyalty, filiality, and other senses of hierarchy, obligation, and deference much more strongly than qualities many democrats might cherish in community politics, such as equality, transparency, accountability, and individual choice. If it were only traditionalists who value the art of the gut, we might simply say that true democracy requires a sacrifice of masculinist gut politics.

However, as I emphasized by opening this chapter with a progressive's use of the gut politics rhetoric of *aun no kokyū*, the art of the gut is also important to men for whom Takada-san's conservative values are unacceptable. Perhaps the best evidence of this reality is Baba-san's use of gut politics to pursue his political goals for Takeno. As a founder of Takeno's referendum movement, Baba was a vigorous advocate of direct democracy. As a supporter of assembly candidates who were women and middle-aged, middle-class men, Baba set himself at odds with Takada-san's vision of men who take on political leadership as a special family legacy. And in his leadership of the Referendum Association Baba-san was a vocal supporter of transparent and accountable political organization. Nonetheless Baba-san practiced gut politics; in fact, if anything, his strongly articulated democratic values drove him to do so. By examining Baba-san's use of gut politics we can see how gender discourse structures and community power structures are interwoven in very complicated patterns. Even men who want to assert ethical independence against the masculine-dominant power hierarchies that prevail in their communities may find that playing up their gendered privilege is one of the most effective tactics available to them.

During the campaign season in which I lived in Baba-san's home I often thought his great political skill was his capacity for narrative. As his group's unofficial spokesperson, Baba shaped group identity, debates, and press coverage and arguably won campaigns with his ability to present the Referendum Association's undertakings as hearkening back to the true democratic spirit of the plain, hardworking citizens of Takeno.

But narrative was not Baba's only skill. On many occasions I saw him use strategic silence, a sudden cold silence in response to the joviality of a business contact he found unreliable, a quiet raised eyebrow at a journalist or community leader with whom he disagreed, a taciturnity with an acquaintance he confessed to finding excruciatingly boring.[12] One use of silence that left an indelible mark on my memory was his intervention into the conflict about Miura-san's 1999 run for the Takeno Assembly as a Referendum Association representative.

As I explained in earlier chapters, in the 1999 assembly elections the Referendum Association was working in a loose alliance with several

other groups that opposed the nuclear power plant to elect candidates
to the town assembly who would agree, in accordance with the referendum results, to ban construction of the plant. The challenge for
the antiplant alliance was that Japanese local assembly elections are
run in an at-large district. This means that all candidates run in the
same district, each voter chooses his or her favorite candidate, and in
the case of this town, the top twenty-two win seats. Each candidate
is technically forced to run against every other. Candidates who are
working together tend to appeal to the same group of voters and thus
may find themselves competing for shares of the same votes. When a
group like the antiplant alliance wants to field a large number of candidates, it runs the danger that its candidates will, in the terms the strate-
gists used, "eat each other," splitting the vote in such a way that fewer
candidates are elected from the slate than the slate's overall popularity
with the voters would indicate should be elected. This is because the
most popular candidates may win too great a share of the total votes
in support of the slate, and the less popular candidates will be left with
too few votes to win seats. If the votes were more evenly distributed
both the more and less popular candidates might win, but when votes
are very unevenly distributed among candidates with shared ideology
and goals some votes end up being "wasted" on the most popular candidate. Therefore candidates representing parties or groups that are
overall much less popular with the electorate may win more votes than
the weaker candidate of the leading group.

Tensions developed between the various groups opposed to the
nuclear power plant as the assembly election neared. Each group worried that its own candidates would lose crucial votes to candidates from
allied groups. Because the at-large district and the single, nontransfer-
able vote in local assemblies make this a common problem in Japanese
local politics, it is traditional in many localities for campaign leaders
to do a little market fixing, arranging with other like-minded activists
to prevent unnecessary losses. Campaign leaders from the same party
or from allied groups agree to limit the total number of candidates representing their common interests. Thus it is not surprising that many
of the *aun no kokyū,* art of the gut agreements Takada-san described
are agreements of precisely this sort: controlling candidate numbers
or assigning like candidates unofficial campaign territory boundaries
within the district. In fact the leaders of the Green Association, the
Communist Party, and the Social Democratic Party all told me they felt
it would be dangerous to try to increase the number of candidates they

supported over the number they had elected in the previous assembly elections. This meant that each group was still supporting only one candidate, with the exception of the Social Democratic Party, which supported both an officially endorsed candidate and the independent wife of one of the local party leaders.

However, despite worries in the allied groups and the Communist and Social Democratic Parties that the number of antiplant candidates was already too high, Baba's Referendum Association was committed to fielding at least five candidates, two more than the three they had fielded in the election four years earlier and three more than they had previously been able to elect. As I have said before, the Referendum Association wanted to run five candidates because Baba and others in the group who were close to him believed the election would offer a truly meaningful choice only if voters had the opportunity to replace the old assembly majority, which had ignored the referendum, with a new one that would support it. If the Referendum Association could field five candidates, then, with the help of candidates from other allied groups, referendum groups could give voters the possibility of electing an antiplant majority to the local assembly. It would also be the first time in the history of Takeno-machi that voters would be given an opportunity to elect a majority not connected to conservative LDP politics.

The Association struggled to find five candidates, and only at the last minute, just a few weeks from the election, did they find their fifth, Miura, a woman in her midthirties and the daughter of a member of their group. As even members of the Referendum Association acknowledged, Miura was a problematic candidate because she had a less than spotless image. She was a single mother; she had borne her two children while living in Tokyo for a decade, and when she returned to her hometown with her children in tow she did not offer a very full explanation for the absence of her children's father. It seemed possible she had never been married. Miura's father too had experienced his share of friction in small-town relations when one of his businesses failed. Members of one of the allied groups called Miura a "fringe" candidate. Even many in Baba's group expressed doubt that she could win the election. Yet though many of the antiplant alliance leaders pointed out her weaknesses as a candidate, they also feared that her candidacy would still be attractive enough to eat up votes other alliance candidates needed. She was pretty and had strong friendships from her high school days. She was active on the PTA at her children's school, and she had an organizational advantage with which we in the United States are quite familiar but that is relatively unknown in Japan: she belonged to an active Christian church.

With Miura's entry into the campaign a series of talks began between the leaders of the different groups in the antinuclear alliance. Members of the former Socialist Party who were backing another female candidate, Kagawa Miyuki, whose husband, Kagawa Akira, led the Socialist wing of the alliance, were concerned that she would lose votes to Miura. They wanted to strike the sort of deal that has typically been struck among candidates of the same party in Japanese assembly elections. Kagawa Miyuki, Miura, and the other alliance candidates would agree to divide the municipality into informal constituencies based on both geographic and organizational lines. So, for example, Kagawa would agree to contain most of her vote-seeking activities to certain neighborhoods and groups, such as a local women's club to which she belonged, and Miura would campaign in different residential areas and stick to the PTA connected to her children's school.[13]

For several days after word of Miura's decision to run got around, the antinuclear alliance, delegates of the leaders of the Kagawa faction, and other alliance groups came in and out of Baba's house. Conversations among Baba, his wife, other Referendum Association members, and Kagawa's delegates were long and loud. Almost nothing else but frustration with Kagawa was talked of in the Baba household for more than a week. Miura's extended family even prevailed upon her father to keep his daughter from running. Baba-san had originally been reluctant to run a young woman for the Referendum Association, but once Miura-san successfully persuaded him to accept her candidacy, Baba told me that he thought it unreasonable for people to complain about the "questionable" background of Miura's children. Whatever her relationship with their father might have been, Baba said, it was certainly both a private matter and Miura's right as an adult to make decisions about such relationships as she desired. Moreover, he said, it was Miura's father's duty "as a man" to resist pressure from the extended family.

Baba-san claimed that once Miura decided to run, the leaders of the various antinuclear groups and parties (all of them men) did not have the right to keep her from doing so. Nonetheless the behind-the-scenes deal Kagawa's group sought is so standard in Japanese elections that I thought surely Baba would be willing to consent. I'm afraid I even said something of the kind to him. But Baba, a rather radical democrat, would have none of it. This kind of dividing of the votes before the voters themselves were given a chance to consider the choices between them was a great rudeness toward voters, he insisted. All of the candidates should campaign vigorously in any place or organization they found welcoming. The voters would decide who wins. Baba became irritated with the resistance to Miura's candidacy, and eventually his irritation turned to anger. He refused any suggestion of brokering an agreement over constituencies and griped at length about the arrogance of the old Socialist Party with which Kagawa had long been associated, about how it had always thought it knew what was best for the people, about how it always commanded its constituencies as if they could not think for themselves. In a bitter joke Baba-san, for whom money-power politics were usually referred to as a great evil, said he preferred the conservatives' little bribes to the Socialists' commands from on high. The bribes at least showed some sense of respect for the right of voters to choose for themselves. The nasty insinuations made about Miura's personal reputation only added fuel to the fire at Baba's house.

The war between Kagawa and Baba broke out into the open when Kagawa Akira tried to secure for his wife exclusive campaign assistance from Wada-sensei, a former high school science teacher active in the anti–nuclear plant cause for decades and highly regarded by all alliance members in part because he had long remained above partisan divisions. Wada-sensei lived in a small village within the municipality of Takeno. Miura's high school friends were especially active on her behalf in that village, and either she or her friends had approached Wada-sensei for help in the election. In the previous election he had done what he could to swing his village toward Kagawa Miyuki's candidacy. Now Kagawa Akira feared his wife would lose the votes this respected figure might command. Importantly, Akira kept a firm hand on his wife's political endeavors. Kagawa Miyuki ran in Akira's place because he could not forgo his regular salary for the salary of an assembly person, and Miyuki's campaign organization was entirely dominated by Akira's male Socialist colleagues. At the opening party for her campaign neither she nor her women supporters sat in the main room. They waited in the kitchen with the celebratory red rice.

Kagawa Miyuki's losing votes to Miura was not a simple matter of one woman being preferred over another; it also meant an ebb in Akira's power in the already embattled local Social Democratic Party and in the local antinuclear movement with which he had maintained ties for decades longer than Baba-san. Kagawa Akira seemed to believe that, if

Wada-sensei backed the notion of a behind-the-scenes division of the antiplant vote, Baba would have to do so as well. Among other things, Wada-sensei had been an important mentor of Baba's righthand man, his cousin Ota, who had worked alongside Wada-sensei in the antiplant movement for nearly thirty years. Kagawa Akira and his intermediary went to Wada-sensei and proposed a constituency deal that might be worked out for Miura. Wada-sensei would continue to lend his support to Kagawa Miyuki, but in return Miura would be given sole access to the votes in the residential district where she had grown up.

Kagawa Akira called for a meeting, and Baba agreed to hold one at his home during a lunch break from his duties at his sake shop. Wada-sensei, Kagawa Akira, Kagawa's intermediary, a man named Shinoda, Baba, Ota, and Miura's father gathered at Baba's living-room table. Baba reserved a cushion near the table for me, and as an excuse for my presence in an otherwise all-male group I served tea, silently and nervously (partly because Baba-san had cheerfully pointed out to me on a number of occasions that I didn't make very good tea). Wada-sensei explained that the various discussions about who should work for which of the alliance candidates had become terribly confusing. He pulled out a set of copies of a written agreement in which were detailed his role in Kagawa's election and Miura's special rights to particular residential neighborhoods. In consideration of Wada-sensei's exclusive commitment to Kagawa's campaign, one of the operatives from the Kagawa campaign would be dispatched to aid Miura's campaign. Baba looked at the agreement for some time in complete silence. "This is not the sort of election our group conducts," he said quite softly. Then, with a very gentle smile and stiff, raised eyebrows, he said only, "Please take this away," the way one might politely ask a waiter to remove an unacceptable dish from the table.

Ota made a few remarks, offering a short version of Baba's philosophy about the ways leaders' behind-the-scenes agreements to divvy up their supporters' votes were rude to voters. But even Ota, usually full of things to say, offered only the most minimal explanation. He leaned across the table toward Wada-sensei and said, "All we ask is that you think about the purpose of this election, the purpose of electing these people, and that you act in the way that is best for that purpose."

"I understand [*wakarimashita*]," Wada-sensei said. He gathered the copies of the agreement from the tabletop, and the meeting was over. Later, talking with Ota, Miura's father, and me, Baba argued that Wada-sensei had been manipulated by Kagawa Akira because he had helped

Kagawa Miyuki in the past and felt it too awkward to say he might help Miura this time around. Baba thought that because the effort to build an agreement constraining Wada-sensei's mobilization efforts to the Kagawa camp had failed, Wada-sensei would probably feel free to do what he might to help Miura after all. In the end, Miura took the greatest number of votes of *any* of the candidates running for the assembly, whereas in terms of received votes Kagawa Miyuki was near the bottom of the list of candidates who still managed to win a seat. There is no way of knowing how much the failure of her husband to get an agreement affected her outcome, but given the difference between her finishing position in her first election (near the top) and that in the election in which Miura ran, it is quite possible that Miura did eat away some of Kagawa's votes with the help, or at least the neutrality, of Wada-sensei.

At any rate, significantly for Baba's position within his own group, his quiet way of sending Wada-sensei packing was considered a triumph, and I judged Ota relieved at having bested his mentor without having to render their disagreement very explicit. Finally, the real losers on the overloaded referendum slate were the two male candidates backed by Baba, the incumbent Takahashi-san and the newcomer Yanagi-san. Both had accepted Baba's claim that a behind-the-scenes division of the vote was unacceptably constraining on voters' choices and candidates' campaigns, Takahashi-san with real enthusiasm and Yanagi-san after some urging. The Referendum Association's female candidates were obviously more popular with voters, and that probably had much to do with their gender. However, had Baba's group practiced old-fashioned, behind-the-scenes vote division, at least one of the two men, if not both, might have been elected. The three Association women who won seats had the votes to spare.

Whether one judges Baba's silencing of the constituency deal making as wise depends on whether one agrees with his assertion that true democrats show a courtesy to voters by giving them a meaningful choice and avoiding backroom politicking designed to improve the electoral chances for a given ideological group. Even if politically unwise, Baba's silencing was successful, and successful among men with longer histories of political action and a predilection for backroom deals. Just as in other political deals that were nailed together with silent accord, the import of the occasion was marked by what *was not* or *did not have to be* said. In the meeting with Wada-sensei Baba never said explicitly what kind of election his group wanted to have, and even Ota's explanation of how the group conceived of proper courtesy to the voters was obscure. It was not at all a direct address to the text of the agreement proposed by Kagawa Akira and Wada-sensei. By the end of the meeting Ota, as Baba's surrogate, had said only that Wada-sensei ought to consider the true purpose of the election; he never specified what that purpose was. Nor did he explain why the proposed agreement would undermine that purpose. As in the case of the other political agreements, such as the deal between Katō and Ochi over the Fukuzawa City mayoral election, lots of prior, explicit negotiating among surrogates had taken place, but when it came to fixing the final outcome, the most important people in the room said the least. Members of the groups involved read the power of the agreement into the space of silence created by the leaders' constraint.

Baba's assertion of silence is intriguing for several reasons. First, in many ways Baba's great political gift was the gift of gab. Most of the time he persuaded those around him with moving narratives about community life and the essence of democratic politics. Therefore his assertion of silence at key moments during a contentious electoral season suggests that the art of the gut is a practice with some structural power. In other words, the strategy of silence existed in the social milieu Baba inhabited and could be readily understood by his interlocutors, even though Baba seldom made use of it himself. Second, expressions of antipathy between the parties prior to the mobilization of silence had been voluble. Baba's effective use of silence was somewhat surprising given the tensions going into the situation, but the quieting effect of gut politics in this situation may be a key to its power. Much that was difficult was quickly and cleanly disposed of. Given that the issues were never debated again in any of the camps involved, participants seemed to accept the gut ruling as conclusive, something they probably had learned in prior experiences with gut politics. Participants in the conflict might have learned to value gut politics for future contentions as well.

Significantly, Baba's mobilization of silence in this case had the effect of forcing the end of a common electoral tradition that is arguably one of the chief reasons most women and many men are discouraged from seeking political office. Baba greatly constrained the power of the local progressive elites to use market fixing to keep newcomers out of electoral politics. Moreover the effect of ending the market fixing was the election of two new progressive women, two women more than the previous assembly had held. In fact only five years prior to the election I observed, only one woman, a conservative, had ever held a seat in the Takeno Assembly. By the end of the election six women held seats: one conservative, two antiplant progressives from outside Baba's group, and the three from the Referendum Association. Baba was a powerful leader in both election cycles. By protecting Miura from campaign constraints, he opened the field of leadership in voter mobilization to Miura's friends, men and women in their thirties who had never been involved in electoral politics before. Given that three of the Referendum Association's five candidates were women and that other male candidates seemed unavailable, one might see Baba-san as simply having pursued his political interest in resisting an election strategy that would have constrained Miura-san's (or any candidate's) electorate outreach options. Yet if it served his interests, the effect of his use of gut politics was also the erosion of a masculinist practice of candidate control that typically works to the disadvantage of women and others new to politics.

Baba used a strategy that settled conflict in part by relying on the very masculinist, insiders' politics it helped to dismantle. How did it work? One answer is that silence gives the upper hand to preexisting assumptions. For example, Wada-sensei's reputation for remaining above partisan bickering meant that his attempt to broker a deal between different electoral camps could be derailed by his peers' and mentee's refusal to acknowledge a change in his approach. In confronting their nonacknowledgment Wada-sensei would have to disavow the basis of his own reputation. Another reason silence is powerful might be that it suggests that what the reasonable man would do is follow the lead of the silent man. The very fact that men play a situation as if nothing needs to be said suggests the awkwardness, perhaps naïveté of speech. Silence may also be more effective when used among men who are already engaged in a common undertaking and would prefer to agree anyway. As with the "aaa" and "uhhn" gods who guard the gates of Japanese temples, silence guards certain harmonies within a gentleman's agreement. To render a piece of the agreement explicit is thus, by definition, to challenge that agreement and the power structure it helps hold in place. To the extent that the participants in a negotiation want to maintain much of the preexisting power structure, they are forced to submit to the power play inherent in an exercise of silence.

Silence is the insider's strategy.[14] The man who would be an explicit speaker is compelled, before ever addressing the point at hand, to show how much he is not an insider by having to spell things out that others can know just by gut. Kagawa Akira and his surrogate found themselves in the unseemly position of having to explain too much. And the very fact that they talked a lot about the potential for deals made them

laughable. During one heated discussion prior to the meeting with
Wada-sensei, Baba's wife (who, of course, was not invited to the Wada-
sensei meeting) even called Kagawa a male geisha. So Baba's mobilization of silence may have worked in part because he called the bluff of
the other movement leaders. They were afraid to risk looking as if they
did not naturally belong to the movement center by appearing unclear
about what its men were supposed to be doing. Silent agreements may
also be valuable because they do not make explicit what one man wins
and another loses. If we think about Takada-san's phrases describing
promises and power "between men,".we can see that when one man is
connected to another through the gut, they are aligned not for a specific purpose but as *men*. In other words, silence used to thwart explicit
agreements seems to say that explicit agreements threaten the visceral,
uncontainable bond one good man may have with another. Explicit
agreements may have their uses, but they do not require that one be a
man, nor do they work to reproduce one's manliness before others. An
exercise of silence is an exercise of manhood that helps to preserve the
"natural" mystique of a masculine power structure.

The paradox of Baba's manipulation of silence is that he pushed the
Wada-sensei agreement off the table by implying that the men around
the table shared a notion about their responsibility for the treatment of
the voters in electoral politics that, in fact, undercut the responsibilities
leading activists had traditionally undertaken on behalf of the voters.
Baba's version of implied responsibility had a chance in part because
it worked with the notion that the antiplant movement was bringing
about a change in politics, one in which democracy would work differently and better than it had under long years of corrupt, conservative
town politics. Those had been years in which the very men at Baba's
table had struggled for a meaningful role. To put the paradox another
way, Baba's use of masculinist tactics simultaneously appealed to a
paternalist sense of the men's responsibility for the well-being of the
community and used that appeal to insist on the removal of some of
the structural barriers that made Takeno's citizen movement politics a
bastion of paternalist power in the first place.

GENDER AND POWER STUDIES AND THE ART OF THE GUT

By focusing on how and why Japanese political men apply silence to
manage power we can better understand why the structures of male
dominance are both difficult to delineate and hard to change. In many

different fields gender studies have demonstrated how the dominance of some men has effected the silencing of other men and women. Gender scholars now commonly accept that members of dominant subcultures obtain power in part because certain silences are sustained about their privileges. The American political theorist Iris Marion Young has shown that dominant men have an advantage over women (and other men) in discourse about justice because men begin as the normal, the unmarked case, whereas women's claims for justice must begin by first laying the ground for legitimacy in the terms of justice recognized as normal in the male-dominant world.[15] Dominant men's positions are often perceived as representative of the "general," "objective," or "reasonable" positions in contradistinction to the "specialized" or "self-interested" claims of marginal groups.[16] Gender scholars also now broadly agree that male dominance is complicated by the fact that not all men are equally able to work the levers of privilege; distinctions such as class, race, and even occupational category force some men to subject themselves to the example of other men who represent a "hegemonic" or "normal" man.[17] The operation of maleness norms against women and some men is also difficult to critique because, though being male is often essential to participation in dominant social or political groups, "maleness" may not, in and of itself, be considered an expressible quality; men who ask what the rules of maleness are may be automatically considered by their peers to be less than men, unable, in other words, to feel their manhood in their gut.[18]

The problem of what is unspeakable or must be known in the gut limits critical analyses of power. We can know that those outside the dominant groups are marginalized and often silenced simply by tracing lines of exclusion. For instance, we can quite easily see if women are not present in sizable numbers in a local assembly or not included in strategy discussions among the leaders of political organizations. To some extent we can also measure the exclusion of people along other variables, such as class. When groups are explicitly exclusive, such as some groups of conservative Japanese male politicians who proudly hew to the notion that women's proper duties are in the home, not the public sphere, we can easily account for marginality and silencing. However, tracing the process of silencing is much more difficult when dominant men both *claim and believe* that they are and should be inclusive of others unlike themselves yet fail to be. As Young has pointed out, structures of dominance can become especially hard to see, and thus combat, in contemporary discourse situations in which most participants believe that "explicit and discursively focused . . . sexism [has] lost considerable legitimacy."[19]

Takada-san's experience of art of the gut politics occurs in a political arena in which most men assume that men are better suited than women for politics. In fact I'm sure my readers will have noticed that in my work with Takada-san I was not actually in the audience for gut negotiations. I was lucky enough to have Takada-san share them with me, but he would probably have thought it inappropriate to bring me to the sensitive meetings where gut politics was in play. Fortunately, seeing gut politics at work is not essential to tracking masculinism in the LDP. The fact that in such a traditionalist environment the art of the gut limits the power of marginalized groups is not a major concern for its users; the gut is just part of an arsenal of strategies that are already explicitly exclusive. Even if we find it hard to capture gut politics at work in traditionalist groups of men, we can use other forms of exclusion as a proxy measure. But Baba-san's case is more complicated, and for that reason more revealing of the tenacity of unarticulated masculinism in political life.

In Baba-san's mobilization of silence we can trace how and why silencing might be effected against women and nondominant men even when explicit structures of male hegemony have been explicitly rejected by participants, such as the conviction men and women might hold that women, and some kinds of men, are not suited for political life. After all, the gut negotiations I witnessed were over the assembly campaigns of *two women*. In Baba-san's case, silence is used as a power tool by one political man who is silencing others with the goal of expanding the margins of who counts as a political person. Ironically Baba-san is forcing silence upon his fellow men to give a greater voice to both nondominant men and women. His use of the art of the gut is instructive in part because it allows us to document a form of complicity with the power status quo, to demonstrate how people who might in some ways be considered allies in struggles for greater equality make use of power structures that undercut some of their aims. Nonetheless the more significant lesson of this case may not be in how complicity takes place but in why. Like the art of the gut deals Takada-san describes as exclusive of women, Baba-san's gut tactics also effect exclusion, but I think he employs them quite self-consciously in order to forward an ethical accord that has as one of its effects the suppression of the very political practices that helped to manage previous exclusions. In other words, silence is used in this case to change the ethical rules of the political game. The art of the gut, and the masculine dominance it supports, are hard to root out of public life in part because this art offers a very effective means for producing constraint in a situation in which masculinist behaviors are the norm, especially when the constraint sought is a constraint on masculinism itself.

At the heart of much gender study is the hope that gender structures will be reformed when men and women become more fully aware of how their gendered behaviors reinforce power relations that constrain themselves and others in troubling ways.[20] Gendered power strategies are assumed to be the problem, and insight into them the solution. If we paid attention only to Takada-san's description of the art of the gut we might still be able to cling to this assumption. His acceptance of art of the gut politics corresponds with his acceptance of a highly gendered division of labor. We might imagine that if we change his and his fellow conservatives' attachment to the gender divide in politics, their attachment to the art of the gut would eventually shrivel away. But Baba-san's use of gut politics offers clues to why the gender liberation formula often fails to work the way we think it should. Despite the fact that he is both philosophically attached to ending the insider game of politics and perfectly willing to share a new politics with women and with hardworking men who previously could not make it into the local elite,[21] one of Baba's most significant efforts toward undoing the gendered nature of the political realm was his enacting of a paternalist understanding of male responsibility.

Baba-san views himself as a cheater of traditional manhood. He uses its resources, but he openly laments the costs men must pay in order to fulfill their masculine duties. He mocks terms such as "diligence" and "effort"; he scorns the image of the salaryman's sacrifice for a richer Japan that justified his generation's intensely gendered social order. Nonetheless Baba is unlikely to disavow his masculinist tactics precisely because he both wants to bring about social change and believes it is his duty, as a *man*, to do so. The challenge Baba poses for the student of gendered power structures is that his masculinist identity and behaviors persist as part of an ethical matrix in which he seeks a world many gender scholars could admire. In the end, Baba's sense of paternalist responsibility coupled with his inclusive philosophy benefits women at least as much as, if not more than, it benefits nondominant men. In his masculinist relationships with community leaders he has valuable resources for toppling certain kinds of structural barriers to the participation of new people in politics. Yet in managing relationships through the art of the gut he reinforces the participants' attachment to paternalist responsibility, despite the fact that he also presents himself as an "irresponsible cheater" of his community's expectations for masculine behavior. And if the art of the gut silences those who would stand in the way of structural changes, it also erases the evidence of the original conflict, making the structures that remain somewhat harder to perceive and perhaps harder to fight as well.

The paradoxes of Baba's case remind us why gendered notions persist even among those who are quite aware of how burdensome they are. Men who think of themselves as good people want also to do good things. Showing them how notions of masculinity constrain them won't be enough to change their allegiance to those masculine notions. Even clearly seeing that social notions of manhood are deeply problematic for themselves and others, some men will accept the added burdens associated with mobilizing masculinist strategies. They are not thinking primarily of themselves; they are being men for other people.

We might be tempted to say that power grounded in the mystified, gendered gut is illegitimate. Good men should eschew such opaque arenas for more transparent and eventually inclusive operations. Of course a persistent thrust of politics in modern democracies is to open previously opaque arenas. The corruption in Japanese political affairs presents a good justification for attacks on decision-making processes that allow the gut to triumph. The freedom of information ordinances being enacted by local governments across Japan are evidence that men and women are already working to reduce the space in which the politics of the gut can effectively operate.[22] The Takeno-machi referendum is clearly another. Moreover, as I am sure many of my readers also do, I disagree with Takada-san's traditionalist notion of politics. I can imagine a world of political leaders who act as he claims women do, seeking transparency in their relationships with each other and with those whom they represent. The arrival of women in Takeno-machi's assembly had some clear effects on assembly politics: most of the women focused more on issues such as child care and recycling than the men before them had, and most of them cultivated a new method of reaching out to their constituency. The female representatives sent out newsletters to voters, wrote accessible explanations of the town budget, sought to build networks of knowledgeable supporters from whom they might draw new policy ideas. The men who previously dominated Takeno politics had never done these things. Democracy was broadened in Takeno when the masculine lock on politics was undone.

Given the fact that Baba-san's objective in the gut politics session I witnessed was stalling the market fixing that had helped to keep electoral politics the exclusive province of town fathers, we might say that Baba himself has contributed to an eventual decline of gut politics as a way of managing Takeno. To the extent that we think politics should not be an insider's game, we should applaud that decline. But even as we cheer, we should pause for another look at Takada-san's and Baba-san's positions. If we dismiss gut politics altogether as just a bad way of doing things, we may miss an important connection between manhood and ethics. A new gender discourse in which gut politics is viewed as illegitimate would mean new opportunities for women and for those men who lack some of the resources (in terms of socioeconomic status or even personality) to manage others with their gut. But that new gender discourse would not, in itself, make its users into ethically minded individuals. In a new gender discourse power would be structured differently, but the challenge of finding and using the remainder of ethical autonomy available within those new structures would not go away.

What makes Baba-san's choice to use a highly masculinized strategy to open the electoral field to a "fringe" newcomer compelling is that it is an ethically minded (mis)use of the power structure in which he finds himself. It is the ultimate sort of cheating. Baba gets what he wants from the men around him by doing two things. First, despite his sometimes radical critique of modern Japanese manhood, he holds on to enough of his status as a town patriarch to call a traditional closed-door meeting with the other male leaders of his political alliance. Second, he relies on the expectation that men will not reveal themselves as unsubtle players of gut politics (the expectation, in other words, that men will value looking manly more than they value many other goals) in order to manipulate the meeting. Baba can do this because he is willing to live with the gap between his structural identity as a town father and his behavior. What makes him powerful as a leader of the Takeno resistance is not his ideological commitment to democracy, nor his opposition to nuclear power, nor his resources as a well-established local businessman. These are significant parts of who he is, but many others share these qualities. In the end what makes Baba powerful is that he is willing, even when he describes it as a painful experience, to live askew of social expectations. He neither is welcomed by the left activists he bests in his quiet living-room meeting nor is he any longer a member of the Lions Club networks of his youth. He has supporters, a family, close friends, and his convictions, but socially speaking, Baba-san no longer has a *place*.

When we look back at Takada-san's story of the gut politics at the budget planning meeting, we can see that he actually tells us why Baba-san ends up displaced. In the uncomfortable silences that develop as constituents press their budget requests upon the LDP assembly members, Takada-san says, everyone looks at everyone else as if to say "Understand my gut." The winners are the men who do not give in to that discomfort. Usually, Takada-san says, the assembly members will feel compelled to give in, at least a bit. They feel obligated to men who helped them get elected, and they feel obligated simply as fellow men, fellow breadwinners, to support their constituents' endeavors (even if political scientists might describe it as problematic rent seeking). But we can imagine—Takada-san helps us do so by spelling out the pressures for us—the assembly member who would resist that pressure. Takada-san imagines that assembly member to be a woman (although he's dubious about how she gets elected). Yet given his careful elaboration of his frustrations with the policy results of such practices, we might imagine it could someday also be Takada-san.

What stops Takada-san from resisting another's use of the art of the gut against him is not his unwillingness to see the gut accord as problematic but his attachment to a world in which his fellow men and women are more than members of a "lonely crowd." Takada-san values manly sacrifices for the sake of *ninjō*, thick human connections. He does not see how *ninjō* can be preserved in what he calls the "dry" political world we would have if the art of the gut were no longer practiced. If I put Takada-san's case to Baba-san in this way, I doubt he would dispute Takada-san's concern for *ninjō*. Baba-san is lonely; he says himself he has no *nakama*, no group of insiders to which he belongs. I think about Steve Gough, his unauthorized question sparking the revelations of decades of pollutant leaks in my friendly hometown of Oak Ridge; he does not live there anymore.

Salad and Cigarettes for Breakfast, or How to Find Democracy by Losing Your Sense of Perspective

By the time Iida, my journalist friend from Takeno, confesses he has completely lost his objectivity, our shared beef tongue soup pot has boiled down to a scummy mass. The remaining pieces of tongue, which Iida keeps popping into his mouth with the compulsive rhythm of the young and thorough eater, are thick knobs that hardly bear gnawing, let alone chewing. Tucked in this warm restaurant, one floor below the rainy streets of the Ginza and beyond the reach of cell phone signals, we are lost to Tokyo.

Iida's startlingly good mimicry and journalist's capacity for recalling detail have transported us right out of the bright hum and stomp of a busy Tokyo district to a small town on the cold Japanese coast. His current engrossment in covering the return of the Japanese hostages from North Korea, the biggest news story to hit Japan in decades, has been forgotten. All of my responsible researcher's questions about how Supreme Court appeals work have been packed away. We are talking about events from three years ago, the mayor's bid for reelection in Takeno, and Iida isn't Iida anymore, but the mayor's friend Baba. And Baba is talking to a group of citizens, urging them to put this mayor back in office for a second term so that he can complete the project he and Baba and the Referendum Association started more than five years ago: the project to put the citizens' wishes as expressed in a referendum into effect by stopping the building of a nuclear power plant within the town's boundaries. Iida, playing Baba, is re-creating the scene for me because I wasn't able to be in Takeno for the mayor's reelection and because Iida wants me to understand how he was changed that year from a determinedly objective young reporter to one of Baba's devotees, from the twenty-something cynic he had been when I met him during my fieldwork to a true believer in the power of one good man.

I remember when I realized I myself had crossed the line. It was during the city assembly elections held in the spring prior to the mayor's election. I was riding in the backseat of one of the election cars announcing the pro-referendum candidates of Baba's group. We were cruising the villages and beaches of the township, with one person in the car shouting out names and slogans over loudspeakers whenever we passed a cluster of residences or businesses. We would pass by a field and see an old woman bent over a row. "Hello, Grandmother, we are supporting Toda." We would wave fervently. She'd straighten her back as much as she could, push her wide-brimmed hat back just a bit, check left and right, squint our way, and often wave. "Thank you, Grandmother! Thank you so much for your support!" Then off we'd go, looking for more people scattered around the edges of what would be rice patties again before the month was out.

My cell phone rang. It was Takada-san, calling from the midst of his own campaigning for the Shirakawa Ward Assembly in Tokyo. Takada-san's booming voice and formal Japanese startled me, even though only a month or so earlier I had commiserated with Iida when, still newly assigned to the small Takeno town office of the prefectural paper he worked for, he had complained that he did not know how to talk to these country people who could not (or was it *would not,* he had wondered) use proper formal Japanese. With Tokyo people it was easier to know one's place in the treacherous exchange of words, Iida and I had agreed. But now Takada-san's elegant phrases and polished urban accent pushed out of my phone at me like a blast of ice water in my ear. He wondered if I was coming back to Tokyo to see more of his campaign. "I don't have time," I responded, a silly response because, as an independent researcher on a generous grant, I had nothing but time. "I can't get there just now. It's, ah, a little difficult, you could say." I was hoping he'd fall into the Japanese way of accepting the unfinished and hesitant statement as a fairly firm gesture toward "No." He didn't.

Then Takada-san's father grabbed the phone. "We need you to come up here and come to my son's platform presentation." He was less courteous than his son. "I can't," I said. "The bullet train will only take a couple of hours, why don't you . . ." We rounded a corner to a more

remote location along the cliff-lined coast, and my mobile connection
cut out. I breathed a sigh of relief and turned off the phone. I didn't
want to go back to Tokyo, to the candidate I suddenly saw as a conservative rich boy, and to his imperious father, and the doting, silk-clad
women of the neighborhood association, and the antiquated formality
(showing how very aristocratic they were), and his tired mother, and
the all but certain victory. Takada-san's case mattered for my research,
would balance it beautifully, but at that moment I didn't care.

Instead I joined the others in the car for lunch at the Referendum
Association campaign headquarters. The hikers in the group had collected wild shiitake and an assortment of mountain vegetables, and the
farmers had dropped off the freshest potatoes and rice. The miso soup
was as good as it can only be in the countryside where people still have
it for two or three meals a day and each wife has her own special way
of, as they say, "taking the flavor." Baba-san was there, on a break
from his shop, eyes aglow as he collected the stories of the various car
crews, nodding and smiling indulgently, encouragingly, and a little bit
wryly, as different campaigners recalled the waving grandmothers, the
men who turned away, and the children who followed on bicycles. Baba
ate well as he listened, and the women running the kitchen served him
with the attentiveness due his status as the group's uncrowned king.
He praised the food and went for a second helping of the salty miso.
"Stop that. That's bad, you shouldn't do that," I scolded loudly, and
sheepishly he put the bowl down. "His blood pressure," I explained to
the watching women. And then I knew: I was in too far.

It hadn't started out this way. In fact the start was not auspicious at
all. I had begged his family to rent me a room in their house because no
one I knew could come up with any other idea of how to house me in
such a small town for two and a half months. My arrival was awkward.
The family was busy with its business and the upcoming wedding of
Baba's son. The Babas' house was interesting enough, a long, narrow
modernist thing built on the site of the old row house and store that had
been in the family for more than 100 years. There were spare furnish-
ings, unexpectedly high ceilings, and bold abstract art. But the place
was frigidly cold because, like the oldest farmhouses in the region, it
lacked central heat. But that wasn't the worst part of it.

Baba was a chain smoker. When he rebuilt the house, he put special
ventilation fans in the ceiling of every room, but all around the edges
were troubling brown-black stains, the way the tar stains the filter of
a cigarette as one smokes it. And it wasn't just Baba who smoked non-

stop; almost all of his political and business associates smoked too. Because they were in the house whenever the shop was closed, it seemed the air never cleared. On my first night there, Baba's wife showed me around. They had a beautiful Japanese bath, with a separate shower in which to scrub down before sinking into the deep tub of hot water. A cupboard in the adjoining room was invitingly full of towels. "Just help yourself," she said. I was tired from the move from Tokyo and from struggling to keep conversation going with complete strangers, and so I took her up on her offer to take an early bath. But the air was so cold in the bathroom that I was nearly frozen before I dove from the shower into the tub, and I had to keep adjusting the thermostat upward, trying to sink some warmth into my bones. Finally, beet red and steamed into placidity, I stepped out and reached for a towel. I knew I'd need to dry myself quickly or I'd get cold again. But as I began rubbing my wet head I realized that even the towels were rank with the smell of tobacco. I coughed and gagged and somehow managed to dry myself. Huddled in bed under an electric blanket turned up to 9 out of 10 and a pile of comforters, sweatshirts, hiking socks, and the like, I typed into my laptop. "Why do I get myself into these things?" I wrote. "I could be at home in Virginia now, comfortable in bed with my husband." I felt profoundly stupid—and alone.

My first morning I woke to my sinuses pounding from the constant nicotine buzz when one of Baba's business associates, accustomed to stopping by for a prework coffee, began pounding on the front door and screaming "Good morning! Good morning!" Eventually I dragged myself into the living room. The family table was surrounded by Baba's friends, the man who ran the *yakitori* (grilled chicken) restaurant a few houses over, the man who ran the take-out noodle shop, and the guy who had banged the door open, who worked for a brewery owned by a movement supporter's family. They were all smoking; a huge ashtray a good four inches deep and six across was overflowing with butts. I would have run, but I was too cold and too desperate for coffee (which I could see was nice and thick in the carafe in the middle of the table), and the only heat came from the *kotatsu* heater under the table. I gave up on breathing and tucked myself in under the blanket that was tacked around the table to keep the heat in. Cheerfully Baba-san's wife served me a breakfast salad of greens, daikon sprouts, corn kernels, and seaweed. She placed it by the ashtray and urged me to eat up. I ate the salad I would normally never countenance before noon but put my foot down at milk. Yes, I knew it was good for me, but I couldn't actually drink it. Not in the morning. Not ever, really. (Especially not with salad and cigarettes, I might have added.) And like all my Japanese friends, the Babas clucked in soft concern. I was weak at mornings, they could see.

It was more than a week before Baba would waste any time talking to me. In our first conversation he declared that I obviously didn't know very much about the history of the citizens' movement, and he assigned others—his children, ages twenty-five and thirty-one, and the man from the brewery—to bring me up to speed. He was oppressive in other ways as well. I went out one night to observe a strategy meeting held for Miura-san, the woman whose run for the town assembly as a Referendum Association candidate had caused such controversy in the Takeno anti–nuclear power camp. The people at the meeting were young, mostly my age, and boisterous, and it was nearly midnight before I was home. Baba was sitting up, and he was mad. "Do you know the word *mongen?*" he asked. "Curfew?" "Yes, and we have one here, and you have broken it." "A curfew?!" We both ignored the fact that no one had ever breathed a word to me about a curfew. "I can't have a curfew. I'm married. I'm in my thirties. I'm a college professor. I own a home!" I protested. "Owning a home is not such a big thing," he replied. A week or two later, when a friend from a nearby town, also a college professor, stopped by to take me to dinner with him and his wife, Baba caught him before I could get out to the car and explained my curfew. My friend laughed at me as we drove to his house, but he knew better than to challenge Baba. I was home before eleven.

As I'm sure my readers have guessed by now, somewhere along the way Baba and I became fast friends. In the end we both cared a great deal about small-town politics, even if for different reasons. Baba spent hours explaining to me how he and others had startled cynical pundits by resisting the corrupt conservative establishment that had run their town for decades. He would defend the rural little guy's right to resist the unsafe and unsavory public projects dumped on them to serve the needs of an urban society bent on incessant economic growth. He understood all the reasons his town was blamed for what is called "regional ego," the Japanese version of the not-in-my-backyard syndrome. But, he said, the local people must have the right to say no to projects like the nuclear power plant because he did not trust the national government or leaders of corporations such as the one that wanted to build the plant to have the people's welfare in mind.

Years later, in that Tokyo restaurant, Iida told me the story of a speech Baba gave during the mayoral campaign I missed, re-creating Baba over our dinner table better than I will ever be able to.

> The supporters of the plant had these gatherings with a thousand or so people in big public halls. And the plant opposition [the incumbent mayor's supporters] had these little gatherings in small facilities with just a few cushions on the floor. And it was winter, so it was really cold. And only a few people would have come in, and Baba would be sitting there on the floor, and he would say "I'm Baba the sake seller." At first there were only a few people there, and Baba just sat cross-legged on the floor and started talking, and then little by little more and more people gathered.

This is when Iida asks me if I know the word *seihin,* which means to be a person who worries, not about wealth but about doing things properly, or "to be satisfied with poverty in a cleanly lived life." Iida thinks *seihin* is the core of Baba's way of being. He actually bends his own stout form to look like Baba's skinny, pretzel-flexible one, stretches his own roundish face to make it seem just like Baba's gaunter one, with its wide smile, simultaneously teasing and gentling. Then, Iida says, Baba would say that he wanted to talk a little bit about his feelings about the plant project, not about the usual question of whether the plant would be unsafe for the environment, but his thoughts about the plant's proponents, who frequently pointed to the economic benefits the plant might bring the town.

Iida scrunches himself up to look positively folded, as Baba can look when speaking earnestly, and as Baba habitually does Iida holds his head off to the side, twists his mouth around, begins to look as if his body is apologizing for its very presence. Iida speaks in Baba's cigarette-raspy voice:

> What it is in the case of this nuclear power plant is that those who are already rich want to be richer. But I think we have enough here, I think this is good enough. If we just keep saying we want more wealth, there is no end. The plant won't make everyone better. It will make things better for those who are already doing well enough, and after they have gotten that, what will they want next in order to be richer? Things will go back to way they used be in the old days.

I am familiar with the story because I have heard Baba talk about the many ways the poor suffered during World War II and in the early years after the war ended. I have also more than once heard Baba say with characteristic cheerfulness that all one needs is a single tatami mat at night for sleeping on and half a mat in the day for sitting on. He has said this to me in his cold house, warming his feet under the single heated table.[1]

Iida repeats the story of the election speech, tells me how moved he was to see people gathering in the hall, listening to the unprepossessing words of the sake seller. The tale ends with the mayor's reelection and the mayor's sale of land on the plant site to an antiplant group covenanted against reselling it to anyone who will allow the plant to be built on it. Iida tells me how the sale withstood the court challenges brought against it by the well-funded pro-plant faction. Then he tells me that he himself cried on the day the Tokyo High Court decision was announced. "I was just overcome by how overwhelmed Baba was," he says. Baba reminds him of the heroic Japanese men of the past, Iida explains, and confesses to having spent time digging out information about Baba's past from Baba's friends and relatives. Iida says he wants to solve the mystery of Baba's quality, but he doesn't know how, and although Iida says he now thinks Baba is largely responsible for a history-making small-town rebellion against the "let them eat, let them drink" corrupt patronage relationships of postwar politics, he also knows he can't tell his colleagues how he really feels. "They'll laugh at me," he says. "They'll say, 'Iida, you've lost all of your objectivity.'" But at least I can remember how hard, how much harder than I, Iida tried to resist the idea that there is something special about Baba.

Iida's story in the Ginza restaurant that night was one of victory, but as I explained in earlier chapters, the election in which I was a participant observer did not go quite as well. The Association's two male candidates lost their bids for assembly seats. One of the losers, Yanagi-san, was inexperienced and awkward as a candidate, and few were surprised at his failure to win a seat, but the other, Takahashi-san, was an incumbent, perhaps one of the best liked men in the whole referendum group. He had refused to campaign very hard for himself because he wanted the young woman, Miura-san, to have a chance to win supporters to her side. She won too many, Takahashi too few. Baba and his friends always described Takahashi as serious and hardworking, honest and good. He was a farmer who got up at 4 A.M. to tend his greenhouses before the assembly sessions started so that he could be at the town hall on time. Moreover Takahashi-san had been among the group leaders who pushed hardest to get a full slate of candidates out and running. More than one person, his wife included, had urged him to consider that he might lose his own seat in the process of backing other candidates, but he said that he had learned in the assembly that

democracy is numbers, that numbers are power, and that he couldn't
see his lone service as a benefit for his constituents if he didn't have
allies to help make his constituents' preferences into policy realities.
Nonetheless those who had warned Takahashi-san were right. In devoting efforts to building a full alternative slate with which to challenge
conservative hegemony, he had endangered himself. Takahashi, a good
man, acting as an unselfish supporter of a fellow candidate, had lost his
own chance to do good work.

And there was more bitter irony. On the night the votes were counted
most of us sat in the prefabricated building that was campaign headquarters, waiting nervously for a call from group representatives who
waited for results at the high school gym, where the election officials
counted ballots. Finally the phone rang. The top two candidates were
clearly in the seat-winning group. Then the caller said it looked like all
five were getting in. "All five?" asked the woman who answered the
phone. When we heard this we started celebrating, passing around cans
of beer, thanking each other, shaking each other, laughing and crying.

Then the phone rang again, and the same woman picked it up.
"What? Some mistake? Takahashi and Yanagi actually lost? They lost?"
Everyone stopped moving, and the only sounds that could be heard were
a few stifled sobs. Baba, shoulders looking too heavy to bear, stood up
and left, off to the houses of Takahashi and Yanagi and the painful job
of thanking them for their efforts.

Baba told me he felt bad about Takahashi's loss and worried about
what would happen to the town as long as the divide continued between
the pro-referendum mayor and the pro–nuclear power conservative
assembly. He sat up late, talking to me long into the night. Between us
we had a hand-scrawled sheet with the vote tallies for each candidate.
Baba's group and the candidates from allied groups had suffered in
part because the conservatives had done an eerily good job of dividing
the votes among themselves, in spite of the fact that several of the more
prominent conservatives from the previous assembly had retired to be
replaced by men with more questionable reputations who had been in
and out of the assembly many times over the years. The vote tallies for
the pro–nuclear power candidates were simply too perfectly even. It
seemed likely that some powerful organizational forces had been working behind the scenes, probably mostly in a perfectly legal fashion but
still not in an especially democratic manner. Baba shook his head over
the list. We wouldn't talk about it with many others; most in the group
were uninterested in what the complicated evidence of voting numbers

might indicate. Baba began to ponder what the group members would say about this dissatisfying end to their hard work. And then he offered me what I would later hear him tell the whole group.

> The way I look at it, we ran a *subarashii* [outstanding] election. If we had not insisted, if *shitsukoi* [aggressive] Takahashi had not insisted, unrelenting, that I go out and find yet another candidate, he would not have lost his seat. But then the voters, who get only one small chance in four years, one brief moment in which to participate, would have faced a no-contest election. In their one chance in four years, the townspeople would have had no choice. This election was *subarashii*.
>
> It was not a bad thing that, because of the mistake, we were all wildly happy for a few minutes. We got to know what it would feel like, and that will help us through the mayoral election.

A day or two after the assembly election an editor from Iida's paper came to Baba's house to interview me, to get the perspective of a political scientist who had spent months watching the campaigns and election in this lately contentious little place. I had no perspective to offer him. I complained that the members of the pro–nuclear power plant camp misrepresented themselves in their campaigns as being for economic development. With only one exception they had failed to reveal in interviews or pamphlets that they were still firmly supportive of the plant that citizens had voted down in a referendum three years earlier. I did not mince words. "From a democratic perspective, this is sleazy," I said. I insisted the editor look with me at the odd uniformity in conservative vote totals. He shook his head, humoring me, feeling perhaps a little sorry for me. Hadn't I known things would work out this way?

The pro-referendum group went on to win the mayoral election and eventually to see the end of the nuclear power plant project. But we didn't know that would happen as the April town assembly election season gave way to early May and to Japan's string of national holidays known as Golden Week. People in Takeno-machi aren't given to taking real holidays during Golden Week, in the way city dwellers are. The townspeople come home on leave from factory jobs or service jobs in nearby towns, and they plant their rice seedlings. In fact the town temperatures actually drop for a week or two as the rice paddies are flooded and the wind ripples across the cold water, creating a refrigerator effect. But Baba decided that, for the first time, he would close his shop for the three days of Golden Week.

Because he made nearly daily deliveries to the small restaurants in the area, three days' worth of deliveries had to go out at once. His son took leave from his regular job to join the family, and I threw myself into the job too. Baba's wife ran the retail shop. Their daughter and son prepared each new truckload for delivery, and Baba and I drove the small pickup through the narrow streets and unloaded beer kegs, sake, and soda water into the tiny kitchens of tiny bars, the bigger kitchens of inns, and even the back storage room of a friend's booming new-style crab restaurant. We bounced along the hills under the clear spring sun, with the colors of cherries and peaches, forsythia and wisteria bursting forth among the acid green and heartbreaking early red of Japanese maples. We loaded and unloaded, and I shocked cooks and restaurant owners who had their backs turned by singing out the sake salesman's "Mai do domo!" (Thank you every time!) in a convincing imitation of Baba. They would turn around to say a word or two and jump when they saw me.

"This is how Takahashi bears [the election loss]," Baba said as we drove around one corner. "He just works hard. That's what I do. I just work as hard as I can."

On the first day of Golden Week Baba, his wife, his cousin, the cousin's wife, and I climbed the mountain that dominates the landscape of the town. At the top, even though Baba is slightly allergic to the alcohol he sells and seldom drinks, we all shared little sake cups of a strong liqueur the local winery was trying to market. We all got just a bit hazy sitting in the sun sipping, and then, unreasonably happy after the long winter and disappointing election, we all tripped down the back side of the mountain, down the cliff on the sea's edge, right by the area where the nuclear plant was supposed to be built and to the water over which the setting sun shone red and gold. Baba's daughter picked us up in her car and we all went out to eat at the crab restaurant, where we talked about crabs and not about elections. After the meal Baba leaned back and pulled out his cigarettes. He nudged me and, grinning, offered me one. I took it. I took some long, deep breaths and exhaled a cloud of that terrible stuff.

In a few days I would go back to Tokyo and to the smoke-free and victorious Takada-san. My husband would come to join me for his summer vacation, and I would begin a long struggle to get Baba out of the way of the Great Political Truths my research was supposed to tell. Then, in a little restaurant in the Ginza some years later, I would admit to Iida that I would not win that struggle, that like Iida, I had come to see Baba, the individual, as the key Political Truth about which I wanted to speak. I had come to see Baba's quirky capacity to see wonder and a sustaining beauty in a moment of misunderstanding about an election loss as a phenomenon that my discipline ought to record, to seek to understand, to debate in our scholarly papers, to present in our classrooms. I had come to see Baba's all-you-need-is-half-a-mat pleasure at the world as an ethic I ought somehow to teach myself and then my students.

Captured by Baba-san's stories, I listened more carefully to Takada-san's. I realized that, like Baba, Takada viewed his political life as a matter of cultivating his character as a man. Even while he was mindful of the practical realities of elected office, Takada did not let go of the belief that politics is finally about the ethics of the individual men who wield power.

Social scientists are often at great pains to distinguish themselves from journalists, but in at least one particular they are quite similar: their attachment to the value of objective distance from the subjects of their study. Work like mine, dependent on the details in stories from chance conversations and the peculiarities of the flow of events in particular places at specific moments, always runs the danger of being labeled "mere journalism" by social scientists who place a higher value on generalizable findings about large groups of people who represent a clearly distinguishable subset of a given society. To the extent that, like Iida, I have come to nurse the notion that some of the events I studied were brought about by the admirable force of character of a single man, I suppose I might lose even my qualification as a "mere journalist." Of course in some bodies of theory related to the work I do here, especially gender theory and discourse theory, groups of scholars have long insisted that we retain a critical doubt that any observer's position—whether the position of the journalist, social scientist, teacher, or some other—is ever truly objective. Yet there is quite a long step between a scholar's humble acknowledgment of the many social blinders, such as race, class, nationality, and gender, that may occlude a pure view of her subject, and her assertion that the person she has made into a research subject is deserving of study simply because he seems *to her* to be more compelling than other people, simply because, in a few ways, he seems *to her* to be better than other people. Even when scholars use a tight focus on a single individual's experience as a means of revealing to their readers the social world they study, social science etiquette commonly demands that the subject of such individual attention be defensible as a *representative* of others who are like him or her; this is especially true in political science.

In scholarly custom a book's preface is the place we may properly acknowledge our personal attachment to our research subjects, as we explain how impossible it is for us to thank them for their many gifts to us, how much they have taught us about how to live life, how much they have come to be like our mother, father, or siblings. I must confess that I love to read a good preface precisely because that is often where a scholarly book's writer is most alive, most willing to take risks, most disarming. Nonetheless, to a great extent I celebrate the courteous restraint involved in the practice of keeping our lists of personal relationships within the early few pages of a book. After all, unless we ourselves are the subjects of our studies, we are unfair (to our readers, at least) when we crowd out what could be said about the people we are studying with an excess of fascination with ourselves. When we aspire to an objective rendering of the social world, we correctly (in my view) emphasize the value of seeing, for what they are, ways of being that are not our own. Although it is surely a kind of arrogance to assume one has actually achieved objectivity, to strive for the objective perspective is, on the contrary, a practice of humility, a thoughtful expression of self-doubt.

So when Iida-san rued his loss of objectivity about Baba-san, and in hearing Iida I was reminded of my own loss of perspective, I knew in my own skin Iida's dismay at himself and felt the danger of our positions. But in that meeting with Iida-san several years after my fieldwork in Takeno-machi I was also fascinated by the way his loss of a journalist's distance had changed the way he thought about politics. I remembered meeting Iida for the first time, at a dinner with a group of journalists about two months before I took up residence in Baba-san's house. At that dinner Iida and his colleagues filled me in on much of the political background of Takeno—how the conservatives had dominated politics for so long, how famous Takeno election corruption was, and so on. They spoke with distance, telling the interesting and sometimes ridiculous affairs of people in a town to which they expressed no connection. My political science colleagues will easily imagine the tone of the conversation, cynical and knowing. It's the same one we adopt when talking over the latest elections or the failed strategies of famous political leaders. I'm sure my students have heard it from me when I laugh at the latest scandal in Japanese politics and tell them, "It's too bad for the voters, but it's fun for political science!" Iida's original cynicism was so familiar to me that his conversion to an out-and-out Baba fan was initially a shock.

As I listened to Iida-san talking about Baba-san what struck me even more than his uncanny portrayal of Baba-san was how contemplating the question of what made Baba-san such an unusual town leader encouraged Iida-san to speculate on the qualities of leaders in general, on the nature of men in contemporary Japan, and on what it would take to get more people like Baba into politics. In social science-y words, Iida-san's attachment to Baba had the effect of attaching him more personally to the problem of citizenship in a modern democratic regime. When Iida compared Baba to political leaders from Japan's past, he did so in part as a criticism of contemporary political leaders. But by admitting that Baba-san had so moved him that he had lost his objectivity, Iida-san also confessed his belief in the possibility of an admirable politics for his own day. I think that in learning the fine details of Baba's way of moving and talking so well that he could credibly reproduce him for me, and in coming to share Baba's aspirations so fully that he cried on the day Baba's referendum group survived a major court challenge, Iida-san came to love Baba-san, and to love Baba-san's notion of "enough is enough," or in Iida's words, *seihin*, politics.

When I compare the cynical Iida I remember from our first meeting with the Iida who performed Baba-san's campaign speech over our pot of beef tongue, I think that Iida's (perhaps only momentary) loss of his journalistic objectivity allowed him to commit himself more than he had been able in earlier years to the possibility of building a better world through politics. In other words, by becoming a true believer in the power of Baba-san, Iida-san, who as a political reporter for a midsize Japanese daily newspaper is very much a man of medium privilege himself, came to believe in the importance of the choices made by power's middle managers. I may be wrong, but I think it will never be easy again for Iida-san to dismiss what seems questionable in the world around him as the inexorable "way things get done." I think he will always wonder who is responsible (and whether that "who" is himself). Listening to Iida muse over what it might have been in Baba-san's upbringing that allowed him to become such a remarkable man, I can also hear how it is Baba's example of *manhood* as much if not more than Baba's political views that compel Iida. As a young man, Iida's deep interest in how other men display their manliness is probably unsurprising, but it should also remind us of the complicated multiple uses of gender identity. When we consider his identification with Baba and Baba's cause as, in some part, his identification with a vision of admirable manhood, we can see that frequent enemy, gender identity, doing its work as an ethics teacher.

The education Iida-san receives by falling a little too much in love with the subject of his reporting is, I think, provocative for scholars and teachers of social science. Social science has always had within it competing missions. One of those missions is the collection of "pure" knowledge about the ways human beings organize to manage their common endeavors (and the many reasons they might fail to do so). But we are also in the business of citizen education, striving to leave our students better prepared to act in and for the world. These knowledge-building and citizen education missions are not always happily married. At times, when we teach our students what we have learned about the powerful institutional structures and political, social, and economic trends that shape the sets of choices voters or political leaders face, we actually increase our students' cynicism and make it harder for them to feel responsible for the operation of power in the world around them.[2]

Observing Americans in the 1830s, Alexis de Tocqueville actually predicted this sort of problem as a result of the way intellectuals in democracies think. Tocqueville expresses concern about the larger social effects of the worldview of democratic historians (a category into which I think much of modern social science could be fit). Democratic historians discount the influence of single individuals on the course of history, he says, seeking causes in larger societal trends instead. Although Tocqueville praises democratic historians' capacity to see beyond individuals to find out the "general causes" in social change, he worries about the effect of their teaching on the behavior of democratic citizens: "Once the trace of the influence of individuals on the nations has been lost, we are often left with the sight of the world moving without anyone moving it."[3] Individuals come to believe they are caught up in a vast causal wave so much larger than themselves that they feel utterly powerless. "Thus historians who live in democratic times do not only refuse to admit that some citizens may influence the destiny of a people, but also take away from the peoples themselves the faculty of modifying their own lot."[4]

Tocqueville's point is that when individuals do not believe a good man can do good, when they cannot see their remainder of power amid the large social forces that shape their lives, they will have little reason to resist ill deeds done by those in power. This is a point very similar to that Vaclav Havel makes in the essay "The Power of the Powerless." I think Iida-san is a compelling example of the sort of teaching that might help to ameliorate the democratic citizens' disempowering sense that the "world [is] moving without anyone moving it." As a political reporter Iida is well-versed in the many forces that constrain the choices of the men (and occasionally women) about whom he writes, but as a man who credits another, mostly ordinary man a bit too fully with the power to change the world, Iida-san tempers his democrat's history with a sense of just how important a banal bit of good might be.

Iida-san's conversion to Baba-san's half-mat politics tells us something about what an unseemly partiality for the ordinary goodness of an ordinary man can teach a citizen about the importance of his power remainder. But what about me? What about the scholar who, partway through her research, puts down her books of demographic statistics to lug crates of beer and sake bottles and forgets her profession in the process of trying to shout a Japanese greeting like an ageing delivery-man? I suspect any of us who has done fieldwork has had his or her own moments of similar forgetfulness. I can be forgiven. (I hope I will be.) But right here, forgiveness is not what I am seeking. For this is what I know: If I hadn't carried that sake, hadn't finally accepted that a breakfast salad with a side of cigarette butts could be manageable for just a little while, hadn't come to be so wrongly, so wholly committed to one small town's affairs that I got angry when the predictable outcomes of the local electoral institutions undid the ideals of untutored democrats in predictable ways, I would not have been the person who could take Iida-san's confession over the beef tongue pot.

Of course my loss of perspective was also a loss. This past September, watching the Tokyo ward assemblyman Takada-san teach my small son and his smaller daughter how to join the other children carrying his neighborhood association's shrine through the streets of Shirakawa Ward in the annual festival, I felt how unfair I had been to him the morning he called me as I rode the campaign car in Takeno. I thought about Takada-san telling me years ago about the value of a community bound by obligations and deference to traditional hierarchies. I snapped my son's picture, and I marched along with him, watching the pleasure on the faces of the children and adults involved and watching Takada-san running from group to group, pushing the festival along. Takada-san respects traditions that lend support to parts of the Japanese political system I do not admire. But in his respect for those traditions, he is also sustaining a notion of community and, with his own hands, is building a place where young people might come to know their connectedness to each other and to the generations that have come before them. As he pushed the children's festival carts through the streets of a ward where every day more long shadows of isolating high-rise condominiums stretch across the landscape of single-family homes and smaller apartment buildings in which he grew up, I saw that Takada-san too was a small man fighting big power structures in ways I had never fully appreciated.

In the hot September sun I admitted to myself that my own notion of what a good man should do with his power remainder had not been generous enough. But that confession too came to me only after I got too far into my field, got lost in the details, smoked a horrible cigarette with real pleasure, and wanted desperately somehow to find a way to make one, not exactly ordinary man matter to an academy whose rules I had long ago forgotten.

Notes

PREFACE

1. Laura Miller translates derogatory references to *oyaji* as "old fart" in *Beauty Up: Exploring Contemporary Japanese Body Aesthetics* (Berkeley: University of California Press, 2006), 157.

INTRODUCTION

1. Vaclav Havel, "The Power of the Powerless," in *The Power of the Powerless: Citizens against the State in Central-Eastern Europe,* ed. John Keane (Armonk, NY: M. E. Sharpe, 1985), 23–96, 28, emphasis in original.

2. The names of people, places, and organizations, as well as some identifying details, have been changed to guard the privacy of my informants. The word *san* is an honorific commonly attached to Japanese names when one is talking directly with the named person. In Japanese it is preferable to speak to a person using his or her name rather than the second-person pronoun equivalent of the English "you." *San* might be translated as "Miss" or "Mr.," but *san* is used more often than we would use equivalent terms in English. I use the honorific frequently throughout the text as a reminder to readers that I am engaged in complicated social relations and conversations with my informants.

3. See, for example, Amy Waldman, "Bhopal Seethes, Pained and Poor 18 Years Later: Aftermath of Lethal Leak at Union Carbide Plant in 1984, India," *New York Times,* 21 September 2002, A3.

4. Information available on the City of Oak Ridge website, http://www .cortn.org/visitors/about-oak-ridge, accessed 14 April 2008.

5. Eliot Marshall, "The 'Lost' Mercury at Oak Ridge," *Science* 221, no. 4606 (1983): 130–132.

6. A report prepared by Gough's Union Carbide supervisors about their meeting of reprimand with him after the sampling indicates that he was upbraided for not "work[ing] through the system" and for taking samples for which he did not have authorization. A copy of the report is contained in the transcript of the hearing on the Oak Ridge mercury held by the U.S. House of Representatives. In the written testimony he submitted for the hearing Gough discusses his concerns about the effect his taking samples might have on his brother's job and explains his removal from consideration for a promotion. U.S. House, Subcommittee on Investigations and Oversight and the Subcommittee on Energy Research and Production of the Committee on Science and Technology, "The Impact of Mercury Releases at the Oak Ridge Complex," 98th Cong., 1st sess., 11 July 1983, 405, 406, 411.

7. This is documented in a memorandum about the sample returns from Steve Gough to his supervisor, 14 April 1982. Ibid., 434.

8. Documentation of the process by which Gough's questions led to further studies, growing discomfort within Oak Ridge National Laboratory, an investigation of management by the inspector general of the Department of Energy, and declassification of damning environmental assessment reports and other documents is available in the congressional hearing transcript.

9. "Shirakawa" is a pseudonym, as are the names used here for all individuals from my Shirakawa fieldwork.

10. Lam Peng Er, "Local Governance: The Role of Referenda and the Rise of Independent Governors," in Contested Governance in Japan: Sites and Issues, ed. Glenn Hook (New York: Routledge Curzon, 2005), 71–89, especially 81–82. Other recent political studies examine the rise and effect of referendum movements in a range of Japanese localities. For examples, see Numata Chieko, "Checking the Center: Popular Referenda in Japan," Social Science Japan Journal 9, no. 1 (2006): 19–31; Igarashi Akio, "Chokusetsu minshushugi no atarashii nami—jūmin tōhyō: maki machi no rei o chūshin ni," in Gendai shimin seiji ron, ed. Takabatake Michitoshi (Tokyo: Seori shobō, 2003), 139–170.

11. For works that treat the sense of social and political malaise in Japan in the 1990s, see Masuzoe Yōichi, ed., Years of Trial: Japan in the 1990s (Tokyo: Japan Echo, 2000); David Leheny, Think Global, Fear Local: Sex, Violence, and Anxiety in Contemporary Japan (Ithaca, NY: Cornell University Press, 2006). Jeff Kingston details the Lost Decade in the first chapter of Japan's Quiet Transformation: Social Change and Civil Society in the Twenty-first Century (New York: Routledge Curzon, 2004), 1–41. Public response to ageing demography and economic slowdown are treated in Leonard J. Schoppa, Race for the Exits: The Unraveling of Japan's System of Social Protection (Ithaca, NY: Cornell University Press, 2006).

12. Frances Rosenbluth, "The Political Economy of Low Fertility," in The Political Economy of Japan's Low Fertility, ed. Frances Rosenbluth (Stanford: Stanford University Press, 2007), 3.

13. For examples of this claim, see Tajima Yoshisuke, ed., Chihō bunken koto hajime (Tokyo: Iwanami shoten, 1996); Kikuchi Tetsuya and Fukuoka Masayuki, eds., Kore kara nihon o dōsuru (Tokyo: Nihon keizai shinbunsha, 1998).

14. A classic treatment of the "pipe" role played by local politicians is Haruhiro Fukui and Shigeko N. Fukai, "Pork Barrel Politics, Networks, and Local Economic Development in Contemporary Japan," *Asian Survey* 36, no. 3 (1996): 268–286.

15. Margaret McKean, *Environmental Protest and Citizen Politics in Japan* (Berkeley: University of California Press, 1981); Kurt Steiner, Ellis S. Krauss, and Scott C. Flanagan, eds., *Political Opposition and Local Politics in Japan* (Princeton, NJ: Princeton University Press, 1980). The collection of articles in Sheila A. Smith, ed., *Local Voices, National Issues: The Impact of Local Initiative in Japanese Policy-Making* (Ann Arbor: University of Michigan Press, 2000) does a fine job of capturing the increasingly contentious atmosphere in Japanese local politics from the early 1990s on. Similar terrain is covered in Shimizu Shūji, *Ninbii shindorōmu ko: Meiwaku shisetsu no seiji to keizai* (Tokyo: Tokyo Shinbun Shuppankyoku, 1999).

16. Small reductions in local assembly seat numbers in many towns in Japan have occurred since the beginning of my project. For example, the year of the election I observed, Shirakawa Ward Assembly seats were reduced from forty-four to forty. Seat reduction was mandated by a national law passed as part of a larger national initiative to streamline local governments.

17. Information from the websites of the City of Oak Ridge and the City of Oklahoma City: http://www.cortn.org/government/CityCouncil, accessed on 17 April 2008; http://www.okc.gov/council/index.html, accessed on 17 April 2008.

18. Scholars have argued that new demands would be placed on local assemblies as some types of policy decision making and implementation previously controlled by the national government were devolved to local governments. See Satō Atsushi, "Bunken shakai/seijuku shakai no shimin sanka," *Toshi Mondai* 90, no. 2 (1999): 3–14; Ōmori Wataru, *Bunken kaikaku to chihō gikai* [Devolution Reform and Local Assemblies] (Tokyo: Gyōsei, 1998).

19. Nearly 25 percent of all House members fit the category of politicians who inherited a base from a relative. Naoko Taniguchi, "Keeping It in the Family: Hereditary Politics and Democracy in Japan," in *Democratic Reform in Japan: Assessing the Impact,* ed. Sherry Martin and Gill Steel (New York: Lynne Reinner, 2008), 65–99.

20. The way the Japanese state works to avoid or resolve NIMBY struggles is the subject of Daniel P. Aldrich's *Site Fights: Divisive Facilities and Civil Society in Japan and the West* (Ithaca, NY: Cornell University Press, 2008). See also Shimizu, *Ninbii shindorōmu ko.*

21. I have changed the name of the company.

22. Among scholars there is some degree of confusion about the reasons why the Japanese government did not use what some analysts describe as extensive eminent domain powers to take the remaining land for the power plant from its owners. "Though expropriation and other forms of coercion are legal, and the state [has] relied on those policy instruments in handling opposition to other controversial facilities, the government never used them in siting any nuclear power plant," says the political scientist Daniel Aldrich. According to Aldrich, some officials at the former Ministry of International Trade

and Industry (MITI), the ministry charged with energy policy, argued that nuclear power plants were rightly viewed as "public enterprises" and that the government could expropriate the necessary land. Aldrich speculates that this has never been done in the case of nuclear power because bureaucrats fear the political fallout from doing so. See Aldrich, *Site Fights,* 120, 139–140. However, Heyden Lesbirel claims, "Private utilities cannot use eminent domain powers vested in the state to bypass or override local opposition." S. Heyden Lesbirel, *NIMBY Politics in Japan: Energy Siting and the Management of Environmental Conflict* (Ithaca, NY: Cornell University Press, 1998), 32.

The Japanese political scientist Shimizu Shuji seems to agree that political fallout can be a real barrier to land expropriation. He describes nuclear power plant construction as having been stalled by utility companies' failure to purchase land. Shimizu does not explain whether the government has the legal power to take land on behalf of a utility company, but in his treatment of land expropriation (actually "leasing") for the use of U.S. military bases he suggests that political friction has real costs. For example, he says that Okinawa government officials who refuse to sign in place of landowners who refuse to lease land for the use of the U.S. military have "no legal hope whatsoever of winning," but such resistance "is not always a political waste." The expropriation process takes so long that, in the case of U.S. bases, leases have sometimes run out briefly. Then the landowners enjoy at least a temporary right to enter the bases freely, which they have done. See Shimizu, *Ninbii shindoromu kō,* 113, 233.

A Japanese lawyer involved in the movement fighting the nuclear power plant in Takeno explained the situation to me differently. He and other plant opponents had long held a small piece of land on the planned site. (Eventually the site was replanned to exclude that piece of land, but the site could not be reworked to exclude the municipality's piece of land.) The lawyer said that for a long time he had assumed the land he originally held would be expropriated. He had simply hoped to win public attention to the issue through the expropriation process. However, expropriation proceedings were never started. Later he learned that was because, in order for the government to use the legal process for taking land on behalf of a power plant company, the plant plan must be fully certified under a separate law governing power plants. The law governing power plants allows full certification only for "executable" plans, and a requirement for deeming a plan executable is that the company own the land on which it plans to build. In other words, the combination of the power plant law and the takings law puts utility companies seeking to acquire land in a catch-22 situation. He learned about the legal barrier to expropriation in power plant cases during a visit with MITI officials.

23. The sort of public works corruption that took place in Takeno is a familiar feature of Japanese politics treated in detail in Brian Woodall, *Japan under Construction: Corruption, Politics, and Public Works* (Berkeley: University of California Press, 1996).

24. The House of Representatives electoral system change actually involved a combination of two types of districts: a single-seat district and a multiseat, party-list block. Voters now cast two ballots in each House election, one for their favorite candidate in the single-seat district, and one for their favorite

party in the party-list block. The important point is that candidates from the LDP no longer compete against each other in an effort to win multiple seats in the same district.

25. Unfortunately I cannot share the citation information for these numbers without revealing the real name of Takeno-machi, and that would endanger the privacy of my informants.

26. The political scientist Aurelia George Mulgan found that beer coupons were used in a similar way in an electoral district in southwestern Japan. See Aurelia George Mulgan, *Power and Pork: A Japanese Political Life* (Canberra: ANU E Press and Asia Pacific Press, 2006), 29.

27. For examples, see Schoppa, *Race for the Exits;* Steven R. Reed, ed., *Japanese Electoral Politics: Creating a New Party System* (New York: Routledge Curzon, 2003); Ethan Scheiner, *Democracy without Competition in Japan: Opposition Failure in a One-Party Dominant State* (New York: Cambridge University Press, 2006); Yusaku Horiuchi, *Institutions, Incentives and Electoral Participation in Japan: Cross-Level and Cross-National Perspectives* (New York: Routledge Curzon, 2005).

28. Robin M. LeBlanc, *Bicycle Citizens: The Political World of the Japanese Housewife* (Berkeley: University of California Press, 1999).

29. Examples of the growing body of work on women in Japanese politics are Sherry Martin, "Keeping Women in Their Place: Penetrating Male-dominated Urban and Rural Assemblies," in *Democratic Reform in Japan: Assessing the Impact,* ed. Sherry L. Martin and Gill Steel (Boulder, CO: Lynne Reinner, 2008), 125–149; Gill Steel, "Gender and Political Behaviour in Japan," *Social Science Japan Journal* 7 (2004): 223–244; Sherry Martin, "Alienated, Independent and Female: Lessons from the Japanese Electorate," *Social Science Japan Journal* 7 (2004): 1–19; Ogai Tokuko,"Japanese Women and Political Institutions: Why Are Women Politically Underrepresented?,"*PS: Political Science and Politics* 34, no. 2(2001):207–211; Mikanagi Yūmiko, *Josei to seiji* (Tokyo: Shinhyōron, 1999); Kunihiro Yōko, "Josei no seiji sanka no nyūwēbu," in *Toshi to josei no shakaigaku,* ed. Yazawa Nobuko (Tokyo: Saiensu Sha, 1993); Aoki Taeko, *Yoron minshushugi: Josei to seiji* (Tokyo: Waseda Daigaku Shuppanbu, 1991).

30. Mikanagi Yumiko, "Jendā to kokusai kankei: Nihon no anzenho-shō seisaku o megute" *Seijigaku: Nihon seiji gakkai nenpō* (2003): 73–88; Mikanagi Yumiko, "Nihon anzenhoshō seisaku to jendaa," *Kōkyō seisaku kenkyū, Tokushū: Shiminshakai no kōkyō seisakugaku* 5 (2005): 108–119; Jason G. Karlin, "The Gender of Nationalism: Competing Masculinities in Meiji Japan," *Journal of Japanese Studies* 28, no. 1 (2002): 41–77.

31. I have written a small one. See Robin M. LeBlanc, "Why Women Are Representing Men in a Japanese Town Assembly: A Little Tale about Gender Politics," *Kokusai jendā gakkai shi* 2 (2004): 35–70.

32. Seungsook Moon, *Militarized Modernity and Gendered Citizenship in South Korea* (Durham, NC: Duke University Press, 2005).

33. Of course I am not the only person to have thought this. Michel de Certeau uses the term "remainder" to describe that part of ordinary life that is constructed as outside the realm of investigation that can be conducted

according to scientific methods. He writes, "Ever since scientific work (*scientificité*) has given itself its own proper and appropriable places through rational projects capable of determining their procedures, with formal objects and specified conditions under which they are falsifiable, ever since it was founded as a plurality of limited and distinct fields, in short ever since it stopped being theological, it has constituted the *whole* as its *remainder;* this remainder has become what we call culture." Michel de Certeau, *The Practice of Everyday Life,* trans. Steven Rendell (Berkeley: University of California Press, 1984), 6, emphasis in original.

A student of environmental movements in Japan, Jeffrey Broadbent, has noted that polluted towns with successful environmental movements differed from other polluted towns because they were led by "local bosses" who had the "moral fiber to resist enticements and threats" and displayed an "activist leader morality." See Jeffrey Broadbent, "Movement in Context: Thick Networks and Japanese Environmental Protest," in *Social Movements and Networks: Relational Approaches to Collective Action,* ed. Mario Diani and Doug McAdam (New York: Oxford University Press, 2003) 204–229, quotation on 223. Broadbent makes a similar claim in another project in which he describes a local leader, Katayama, as seeing "a need to reframe popular attitudes toward authority." I am bothered, however, by Broadbent's claim that "people with strong internal morality like Katayama are perhaps more unusual in Japan than the United States." Aside from its disturbingly chauvinist quality, the remark also has the unfortunate effect of undercutting his assurances elsewhere that leaders such as Katayama are actually an important part of Japanese politics. Jeffrey Broadbent, *Environmental Politics in Japan: Networks of Power and Protest* (New York: Cambridge University Press, 1998), 145.

34. Robert A. Dahl, "The Concept of Power," *Behavioral Science* 2 (July 1957): 201–215, especially 202.

35. Clarissa Rile Hayward, *De-Facing Power* (New York: Cambridge University Press, 2000).

36. Ibid., 12.

37. The Foucauldian turn toward structure in the study of power is beautifully traced in Nicholas B. Dirks, Geoff Eley, and Sherry B. Ortner's introduction to *Culture/Power/History: A Reader in Contemporary Social Theory* (Princeton, NJ: Princeton University Press, 1994).

38. Michel Foucault, "The Subject and Power," trans. Leslie Sawyer, in *Art after Modernism: Rethinking Representation,* ed. Brian Wallis (New York: New Museum of Contemporary Art, 1984), 417–432. See 428.

39. Ibid., 421. Foucault actually says "modern Western state," but certainly Japanese theorists see Japan, a rich, capitalist nation with state institutions little different from those in Europe, as fitting Foucault's definition.

40. Hayward, *De-Facing Power,* 30.

41. Ibid., especially 57–62.

42. Sugita Atsushi, *Kenryoku* (Tokyo: Iwanami Shoten, 2000). Sugita describes his intellectual heritage in detail in a bibliographical guide toward the end of his book, 103–107.

43. James C. Scott, *Domination and the Arts of Resistance: Hidden Tran-*

scripts (New Haven, CT: Yale University Press, 1990); James C. Scott, *Weapons of the Weak: Everyday Forms of Peasant Resistance* (New Haven, CT: Yale University Press, 1985).

44. LeBlanc, *Bicycle Citizens,* 24–25.

45. See also the work by the American theorist Iris Marion Young, *Justice and the Politics of Difference* (Princeton, NJ: Princeton University Press), especially 192–225.

46. Dirks, et al., introduction, 14.

47. Linda Alcoff, "Cultural Feminism versus Post-Structuralism: The Identity Crisis in Feminist Theory," in *Culture/Power/History: A Reader in Contemporary Social Theory,* ed. Nicholas B. Dirks, Geoff Eley, and Sherry B. Ortner (Princeton, NJ: Princeton University Press, 1994), 105.

48. Sugita, *Kenryoku,* 86. Translations are mine.

49. I am not the only social scientist trying to see power by following individuals very closely. The linguist Miyako Inoue examines how individual women develop unique strategies of speaking Japanese "women's language" as a means of enhancing their status and power in the workplace. Inoue also argues that these individualized language strategies are locations for observing agency. Miyako Inoue, *Vicarious Language: Gender and Linguistic Modernity in Japan* (Berkeley: University of California Press, 2006), especially 251–277. George Mulgan has used a close reading of a single national-level politician's career as a means of portraying power dynamics in the Japanese political system, but her work does not involve any examination of how her research subject understands his own agency. She purposely avoided direct contact with him. See *Power and Pork,* 3. Despite these two examples, individualized studies of power are still quite rare.

50. Certeau, *The Practice of Everyday Life,* 35.

51. For example, see Scott, *Domination and the Arts of Resistance,* 70.

52. The sociologist Anthony Giddens also makes this argument. He writes, "All forms of dependence offer some resources whereby those who are subordinate can influence the activities of their superiors. This is what I call the *dialectic of control* in social systems." In many ways Giddens's notion of structuration points at the space between the dubious idea of a fully autonomous A who uses power and the tendency of structuralist thinkers to overlook the tactics of everyday life to which Certeau draws our attention. However, Giddens does not bring his theories to the ground on which ordinary people enact everyday life in a sustained way, as I try to do here. See Anthony Giddens, *The Constitution of Society* (Berkeley: University of California Press, 1984), quotation on 16.

CHAPTER 1

1. I use "election campaign" more loosely here than a Japanese politician would use the Japanese equivalent. That is because Japanese election law prohibits campaigning except within a very limited number of days prior to the election. However, most candidates admit that the bulk of the work necessary to get elected—developing alliances, raising money, establishing name recogni-

tion, and winning supporters—has been done in the months *prior* to the official campaign period. These activities are usually referred to as "encouragement" (*hagemasu*) or "support" (*ōen*) activities, but I call all of them election activities because the coming election is the sole reason for their taking place. When I am speaking about the legally recognized official campaign period, I write "formal campaign" or "official campaign." Takada-san's office could not properly be called a campaign office prior to the official campaign period. Instead, it was technically a *kōenkai* (constituency support organization) office. I use "campaign" office here because the goal of winning a seat was its sole reason for existence.

2. I found this on the Kyōdō Tsūshin website on 19 June 2007. "Chōsongi, josei 8 %: sōmushō ga kaihyō kekka happyō," http://topics.kyodo.co.jp/feature 47/archives/2007/04/post_140.html, originally posted on 23 April 2007.

Sherry Martin notes that since 1990, despite higher social and institutional barriers than expected in urban areas, women are making some surprising gains in representation on rural local assemblies dominated by conservatives. She suggests this may be partly the result of how women's electoral strategies capitalize on the electorate's growing expectations for the role everyday people should play in politics. Sherry L. Martin, "Keeping Women in Their Place: Penetrating Male-dominated Urban and Rural Assemblies," in *Democratic Reform in Japan: Assessing the Impact,* ed. Sherry L. Martin and Gill Steel (Boulder, CO: Lynne Reinner, 2008), 125–149, especially 146–147.

3. In her study of Tibetan Buddhist monastic life, Sherry Ortner discusses how our attention to the gender differences between men and women can obscure other sorts of structured social differences, such as those among men, which can be as important in shaping individual lives. See Sherry B. Ortner, *Making Gender: The Politics and Erotics of Culture* (Boston: Beacon Press, 1996), especially 116–138. Others have pointed out that conflicts over the specific nature of hegemonic masculinity can pit men against each other in competitions in which expectations about gender roles silence some men. See Mark Maier and James W. Messerschmidt, "Commonalities, Conflicts and Contradictions in Organizational Masculinities: Exploring the Gendered Genesis of the Challenger Disaster," *Canadian Review of Sociology and Anthropology* 35 (1998): 3–44.

4. The best known theorist of gender as performance is Judith Butler, *Bodies That Matter: On the Discursive Limits of "Sex"* (New York: Routledge, 1993). See also Candace West and Don H. Zimmerman, "Doing Gender," *Gender and Society* 1, no. 2 (1987): 125–151. For performative notions of gender applied to men's public presentations of themselves as men, see Hugh Campbell, "The Glass Phallus: Pub(lic) Masculinity and Drinking in Rural New Zealand," *Rural Sociology* 65, no. 4 (2000): 562–581.

5. Robin LeBlanc, *Bicycle Citizens: The Political World of the Japanese Housewife* (Berkeley: University of California Press, 1999).

6. Ibid.

7. Robin LeBlanc, "What Every Political Scientist Should Know about Housewives: Notes from the Japanese Case," *Journal of Pacific Asia* 5 (1999): 23–57.

8. For examples, see Aoki Taeko, "Shufu pawā no rekishiteki tojō: Midori to jendāgyappu," *Gendai no riron* 210 (1985): 68–77; Aoki Taeko, *Yoron minshushugi: Josei to seiji* (Tokyo: Waseda Daigaku Shuppanbu, 1991); Sumiko Iwao, *The Japanese Woman: Traditional Image and Changing Reality* (New York: Free Press, 1993); Kunihiro Yōko "Josei no seijisanka no nyūwēbu," in *Toshi to josei no shakai gaku*, ed. Yazawa Sumiko (Tokyo: Saiensusha, 1993), 215–254; LeBlanc, *Bicycle Citizens;* Mikanagi Yumiko, *Josei to seiji* (Tokyo: Shinhyōron 1999); Patricia L. Maclachlan, *Consumer Politics in Postwar Japan: The Institutional Boundaries of Citizen Activism* (New York: Columbia University Press, 2002).

9. For examples, see Itō Kimio, *"Otokorashisa" no yukue: Dansei gaku no bunka shakai gaku* (Tokyo: Shinyōsha, 1993); Itō Kimio, *Danseigaku nyūmon* (Tokyo: Sakuhinsha, 1996); Nishikawa Yūko and Ogino Miho, eds., *Kyōdō kenkyū danseiron* (Kyoto: Jinbun shosha, 1999); Taga Futoshi, *Dansei no jendā keisei: "Otokorashisa" no yuragki no naka de* (Tokyo: Tōyōkan, 2001); Taga Futoshi, *Otokorashisa no shakaigaku: Yuragu otoko no raifu kōsu* (Kyoto: Sekaishisō Seminar, 2006); Amano Masako, ed., *Dankaisedai shinron: "Kankei jiritsu" o hiraku* (Tokyo: Yūshindō, 2001); James E. Roberson and Nobue Suzuki, eds., *Men and Masculinities in Contemporary Japan: Dislocating the Salaryman Doxa* (New York: Routledge Curzon, 2003).

10. For examples, see Joanne Nagel, "Masculinity and Nationalism: Gender and Sexuality in the Making of Nations," *Ethnic and Racial Studies* 21 (1998): 242–269; Robert D. Dean, "Masculinity as Ideology: John F. Kennedy and the Domestic Politics of Foreign Policy," *Diplomatic History* 22 (1998): 29–62; K. A. Cuordileone, "'Politics in an Age of Anxiety': Cold War Political Culture and the Crisis of American Masculinity, 1949–1960," *Journal of American History* 87 (2000): 515–545. These are all treatments of masculinity and politics in the United States. I do not know of specific treatments of the relationship between masculinity and men's political participation in contemporary Japan, but some works do touch obliquely on the question of visions of manhood among political elites. One of these describes the masculinization of the Meiji emperor: Osa Shizue, "Tenshi no jendā: Kindai tennō zō ni miru 'otokorashisa,'" in Nishikawa and Ogino, *Kyōdō kenkyū danseiron*, 275–276. Another explores the vision of masculinity embodied in changing public discourse about housing: Nishikawa Yūko, "Otoko no kaishō to shite no ie zukuri," also in Nishikawa and Ogino, 245–274. Work by Yumiko Mikanagi and Jason G. Karlin examines how popular notions of Japanese manhood have shifted in correspondence with reconceptualizations of the Japanese state through the modern era. See Yumiko Mikanagi, "Jendā to kokusai kankei: Nihon no anzenhoshō seisaku o megute," *Seijigaku: Nihon seiji gakkai nenpō* (2003): 73–88; Yumiko Mikanagi, "Nihon anzenhoshō seisaku to jendā," *Kōkyō seisaku kenkyū, tokushū: Shiminshakai no kōkyō seisakugaku* 5 (2005): 108–119; Jason G. Karlin, "The Gender of Nationalism: Competing Masculinities in Meiji Japan," *Journal of Japanese Studies* 28, no. 1 (2002): 41–77.

11. "Josei shigi hyakunin toppa: Tokorozawa wa jūnin," *Asahi shinbun*, Saitama ed., 27 April 1999; Kunihiro Yōko, "Chiiki ni okeru 'shufu' no seijiteki shutaika: Dairinin undō sankasha no aidentitii bunseki kara," *Chiiki*

shakaigaku gakkai nenpō dai 7 shū: Chiiki shakaigaku no shinsōten 7 (1995): 121–148.

12. "Josei shigi hyakunin toppa," *Asahi shinbun.*

13. "Josei genki: Shigi sennindai," *Niigata nippō,* 26 April 1999.

14. Kuramae Katsuhisa, "Chiiki de katsudō, nakama ga 'jiban,'" *Asahi shinbun,* 16 July 2003.

15. Ibid.

16. "Josei shigi hyakunin toppa," *Asahi shinbun.*

17. Aoki, "Shufu pawā no rekishiteki tojō."

18. Imai Hajime, *Jūmin tōhyō Q & A* (Tokyo: Iwanami Shoten, 1998).

19. The term "referendum alliance" is my own. Among antiplant activists was a diverse range of formal and informal group alliances with a range of names and overlapping memberships.

20. Women referendum alliance candidates dominated in 2003 as well, but that election is outside the scope of my fieldwork.

21. Given the sometimes personal nature of the conversations I have recorded in order to examine the role of masculinity ethics in individuals' choices about political behavior, I have worked to hide the identity of the town of Takeno and the activists there. This strategy has, regrettably, made it impossible for me to cite scholarly articles that support some of my claims. However, anthropologists and sociologists have documented similar intensity in other towns that have held referenda. For examples, see Yamamuro Atsushi, "Genshiryoku hatsudensho kensetsu mondai ni okeru jūmin no ishi hyōji: Niigata makimachi o jirei ni," *Kankyō shakaigaku kenkyū* 4 (1998): 188–203; Arasaki Moriteru, Douglas Lummis, "Jūmin tōhyō wa minshushugi no gakkō: Taidan," *Sekai* 53, no. 1 (1999): 113–124; Watanabe Noboru, "Chiiki ni okeru 'shimin' no kanōsei: Niigata ken makimachi ni okeru shimin jichi no kokoromi kara," *Toshi mondai* 88, no. 2 (1997): 3–21.

22. Yamazaki Tetsuya, "Dankai dansei no jendā ishiki: Kawaru tatemae, kawaranu honne," in *"Dankai sedai shinron: kankeiteki jiritsu" o hiraku,* ed. Amano Masako (Tokyo: Yūshindō Kōbunsha, 2001), 85–146; Itō, *Danseigaku nyūmon,* especially 288–293; Taga, *Otokorashisa no shakaigaku,* especially, 121–143.

23. Amano, *Dankai sedai shinron,* 40.

24. Yamazaki, "Dankai dansei no jendā ishiki," 106.

25. See James E. Roberson and Nobue Suzuki, introduction to *Men and Masculinities in Contemporary Japan,* 1–19. See also Taga Futoshi, "East Asian Masculinities," in *Handbook of Studies on Men and Masculinities,* ed. Michael S. Kimmel, Jeff Hearn, and R. W. Connell. (Thousand Oaks, CA: Sage, 2005), 129–140; Gordon Mathews, "Can 'a Real Man' Live for His Family?," in Roberson and Suzuki, *Men and Masculinities in Contemporary Japan,* 109–125; Tom Gill, "When Pillars Evaporate: Structuring Masculinity on the Japanese Margins," in Roberson and Suzuki, *Men and Masculinities in Contemporary Japan,* 144–161; Tom Gill, "Yoseba no otokotachi: Kaisha, kekkon nashi no seikatsusha," in Nishikawa and Ogino, *Kyōdō kenkyū danseiron,* 17–43.

26. "Sarariiman kohō fusen: 'Rikkohō kyūshoku' rikai nao susumazu,"

Asahi Shinbun, online ed., 23 April 2007, http://www2.asahi.com/senkyo 2007t/news/TKY200704230093.html, accessed 20 June 2007.

27. According to Takeno-machi's town records, more than 2,000 people were employed in construction in 1995. That made construction third, after manufacturing and wholesale and retail sales, which employed a little more than 3,000 each. The total labor force for the same year was estimated at 15,752. As some substantial portion of those in sales, services, and other sectors of employment were serving customers in the construction field, the portion of the workforce directly affected by the preferences of leaders in construction is considerably higher than the number employed in that sector suggests. This phenomenon is described beautifully by Jacob M. Schlesinger in *Shadow Shoguns: The Rise and Fall of Japan's Postwar Political Machine* (Palo Alto, CA: Stanford University Press, 1999) and in the *Niigata Nippō* collection *Genpatsu o kobanda machi: Makimachi no mini o ou* (Tokyo: Iwanami Shoten, 1997).

28. LeBlanc, "What Every Political Scientist Should Know about Housewives."

29. The predominance of the salaryman image, including the business suit, is discussed in Roberson and Suzuki, introduction; Taga, "East Asian Masculinities"; R.W. Connell, "Globalization, Imperialism, and Masculinities," in Kimmel et al., *Handbook of Studies on Men and Masculinities.* See also Dorinne Kondo's discussion of Japanese suits and globalized masculinity in *About Face: Performing Race in Fashion and Theater* (New York: Routledge, 1997), 157–170.

30. Iwane Kunio, *Atarashii shakai undō no yohanseki: Seikatsu kurabu-dairinin undō* (Tokyo: Kyōdō Tosho Sābisu, 1993).

31. Natsume Sōseki, *Botchan,* trans. J. Cohn (Tokyo: Kodansha International, 2005).

CHAPTER 2

1. I am well aware that many English-speaking scholars would hesitate to use the words "ethical" and "moral" interchangeably. However, I do so here for two reasons. The first is that Takada-san's conversations with me were entirely in Japanese, and there are no two words in colloquial Japanese that correspond exactly to the words "ethical" and "moral." Japanese translators of some Western philosophy doubtless make choices about these differences, but discourse is not so disciplined in the sort of lived politics I seek here to understand. The second reason for using both of these terms is that, as English words, each conveys a part of the multitude of senses in which Takada-san discussed values, a discussion that ranged from the meaning of life and the definition of humanity to questions of professional relationships and basic etiquette.

2. The best known theorist of gender as performance is Judith Butler, *Bodies That Matter: On the Discursive Limits of "Sex"* (New York: Routledge, 1993). See also Candace West and Don H. Zimmerman, "Doing Gender," *Gender and Society* 1, no. 2 (1987): 125–151. For performative notions of gender applied to men's public presentations of themselves as men, see Hugh Campbell, "The

Glass Phallus: Pub(lic) Masculinity and Drinking in Rural New Zealand,"
Rural Sociology 65, no. 4 (2000): 562–581.

3. This phenomenon is thoroughly treated by Naoko Taniguchi in "Keeping It in the Family: Hereditary Politics and Democracy in Japan," in *Democratic Reform in Japan: Assessing the Impact,* ed. Sherry Martin and Gill Steel
(New York: Lynne Reinner, 2008), 65–99.

4. Changes to the Local Autonomy Law in 1999 reduced the maximum
number of seats allowable in a given local assembly. The maximum allowable
is determined on the basis of population. See Jichi shō, *Chihō jichihō zenbun:
Kaisei* (Tokyo: Gyōsei, 2000), 22–23. The new law reduced the maximum
allowable assembly seats 12.3 percent for assemblies at the city and ward levels.
Shirakawa Ward was one of forty-eight cities and wards with seat numbers
over the maximum. See "Chihō giin sū no hōteisei haishi," *Asahi shinbun,*
10 February 1999. Statistics for Shirakawa Ward Assembly member salaries
come from a report published by the ward office in December 2002. I cannot
specify the publication information for the report without possibly revealing
the true identity of my informant. The total annual salary as I have calculated
it includes both a monthly salary of approximately 590,000 yen and an added
subsidy system equivalent to 3.85 times the monthly salary. This subsidy is the
equivalent of the bonuses regularly paid in the private workforce. The salary in
2002 was actually lower than the salary when Takada-san first ran for office
in 1999 because, in a time of financial crisis in the ward, the assembly members
had voted to reduce their base salaries, as well as the base salary of the ward
mayor, top bureaucratic official, and other political leaders. The ward assembly member base salary is about 100,000 yen more than the average salary of a
ward civil service employee on the general track, the track most likely to lead to
policy-making positions of importance; however, ward civil service employees
are likely to qualify for a variety of other subsidies and benefits that assembly
members do not receive, raising the total average bureaucrat's compensation to
a level similar to or higher than that of an assembly member.

5. Whether that claim was partly rhetoric designed to bolster the energy with
which supporters worked for candidates is unclear, but the changing assembly
size probably did increase incumbents' sense of electoral insecurity.

6. Shozo Ota and Kahei Rokumoto, "Issues of the Lawyer Population:
Japan," *Case Western Reserve Law Review* 25, no. 2 (1993), http://search
.ebscohost.com/login.aspx?direct = true&db = a9h&AN = 9706165989$site
= ehost-live.

7. Fewer than 47 percent of eligible voters went to the polls in Takada-
san's ward for his election, but turnout was up slightly over the previous ward
assembly election turnout four years earlier.

8. In the past few years the population of Shirakawa Ward, like most other
urban wards, has begun to grow again with the building of new high-rise
residential developments.

9. In many local assembly elections, such as the town assembly election in
Takeno, conservatives run as independents. Almost all are actually members
of the LDP; in Takeno I know that several of the independent conservatives
actually played key parts in LDP campaign organizations in the prefectural

assembly elections, for example. The custom of running as independents accomplishes two things: it keeps the LDP from having to choose among candidates competing for endorsement, and it helps to support a fiction of public-spirited nonpartisanship at the local level. In Tokyo ward assemblies, however, most (not all) candidates do run with a party endorsement. Even when conservatives are running as independents, they usually engage in some *chiku wari,* or informal dividing of the single, at-large district into individual territories, that is, unless the reason the candidate is running without party endorsement is because he or she hopes to challenge another conservative running in the same *jimoto.* The failure of the Referendum Association to practice *chiku wari* in the Takeno Assembly elections cost them seats, a problem I discuss in chapter 5.

10. Yamamoto Shinichirō, *Wakariyasui kōshoku senkyo hō: Jitsumu to kenshū no tame no* (Tokyo: Gyōsei, 1998).

11. For the usefulness of inherited *kōenkai,* as well as the growing importance of *kōenkai* to the voter mobilization activities of politicians, at least at the Diet level, see Otake Hideo, "How a Diet Member's Koenkai Adapts to Social and Political Changes," in *How Electoral Reform Boomeranged,* ed. Otake Hideo (New York: Japan Center for International Exchange, 1998), 1–31.

12. The best work treating LDP campaigns remains Gerald L. Curtis, *Election Campaigning Japanese Style* (New York: Kodansha, 1971).

13. Filial piety is still an important concept in contemporary Japan. See Akiko Hashimoto, "Culture, Power, and the Discourse of Filial Piety in Japan: The Disempowerment of Youth and Its Social Consequences," in *Filial Piety: Practice and Discourse in Contemporary East Asia,* ed. Charlotte Ikels (Stanford: Stanford University Press, 2004).

14. An example of this is found in the *Analects,* section 10.3: "When summoned by his lord to receive a guest to the court, his countenance would change visibly and his legs would bend. He would salute the others standing in attendance, gesturing his clasped hands to the right and to the left, and with his flowing robes swaying front and back with his movements, he would glide forward briskly." *The Analects of Confucius: A Philosophical Translation,* trans. Roger T. Ames and Henry Rosemont Jr. (New York: Ballantine Books, 1998.), 134.

15. One reason these groups have such odd names is that the names are usually a pun on the meaning of the characters that make up the name of the politician for whose support the group has been formed. The names also try to capitalize as much as possible on traditionally auspicious images and words that convey conviviality. It's probably fair to say that the creators and members of these groups are a bit tongue-in-cheek about the symbolic qualities of the group name, but then they continue to do those things, such as visit shrines traditionally considered especially powerful, that might be expected to lend the politician some supernatural assistance, should it happen to be available.

16. Giving chocolates on Valentine's Day in Japan is done only by women, and is usually as much related to professional or obligatory social relationships as it is to the love relationships Americans think of in connection with the day. I discuss obligatory chocolates briefly in the next chapter, but the topic is treated most thoroughly in Yuko Ogasawara, *Office Ladies and Salaried*

Men: Power, Gender, and Work in Japanese Companies (Berkeley: University of California Press, 1998), 98–113.

17. A social scientist who becomes a leader in the campaign she is studying is in obvious danger of losing her objectivity. But a participant observer who makes it clear to her research subjects that she is indifferent to or uninvolved in their pursuit immediately loses access to riches of information. I pursue these problems in detail in the conclusion.

CHAPTER 3

1. Although most scholars of Confucian texts and concepts would employ romanized Chinese terms to discuss the character *jin* (*ren* in romanized Chinese), I am using the romanized Japanese here because this discussion is intended to shed light on the Confucianism of a contemporary Japanese conversation, not to take a position in the scholarly debate about the *Analects* and the idea of *ren*. "Benevolence" is the term used for *jin* in D. C. Lau's translation of the *Analects,* (New York: Penguin, 1979). "Authoritative person" is the concept with which *jin* is described in David L. Hall and Roger T. Ames, *Thinking through Confucius* (Albany: State University of New York Press, 1987). The same translation is used in *The Analects of Confucius: A Philosophical Translation,* trans. Roger T. Ames and Henry Rosemont Jr. (New York: Ballantine Books, 1998). "Nobleness" comes from *The Analects of Confucius: A New-Millennium Translation,* trans. David H. Li (Bethesda, MD: Premier Publishing, 1999). For comments on these translations, the use of "humanity" and "humaneness," and other ideas for translating the term, see the excellent discussions in Hall and Ames, 110–114, and Ames and Rosemont, 48–51, as well as the remarks in Li, 11.

2. Ishikawa Tadashi, *Kōshi no tetsugaku: "Jin" to wa nani ka* (Tokyo: Kawade shobō shinsha, 2003). See also Hall and Ames, *Thinking through Confucius,* and Ames and Rosemont, *The Analects of Confucius: A Philosophical Translation.*

3. These passages were originally quoted in Ishikawa, *Kōshi no tetsugaku,* 10, 12–13. The English for all translations in my text is from the Ames and Rosemont translation, *The Analects of Confucius: A Philosophical Translation.* These are not the most elegant translations I have read, but I am convinced that Ames and Rosemont have been helpfully exacting about the way they substitute English terms for the Chinese. The parenthetical citations embedded in my main text refer to the book and aphorism numbers for the passage as found in the text Ames and Rosemont used for their translation. Book and aphorism numbers of many passages match across different translations; however, the numbers of the aphorism do not always match those used by the Japanese translation on which Ishikawa relies. In those cases I have matched them by their content.

4. This passage was quoted in Ishikawa, *Kōshi no tetsugaku,* 14. Ishikawa treats the ordinariness of the virtue described in this passage on 12–16.

5. Ishikawa's interpretation of *jin,* which draws on both Japanese and American scholars of the *Analects* as well as an array of Western philoso-

phers, has much in common with the interpretation offered by David Hall, Roger Ames, and Henry Rosemont, who coined the term "authoritative personhood" to translate *jin*. Hall and Ames and later Ames and Rosement argue that *jin* is really a process-oriented concept of developed humanity such as in "person-making" or "human becoming." See Hall and Ames, *Thinking through Confucius*, 114–124; Ames and Rosemont, *The Analects: A Philosophical Translation*, 49. Like Ishikawa, Ames and his coauthors believe *jin* is not a "one-dimensional" moral vision. But they add a communal element to a person's search for *jin* becoming that Ishikawa does not stress as strongly: "Authoritative personhood is a calculus of 'taking in' the selves of others and exercising one's own developing judgment in trying to effect what is most appropriate for all concerned." Hall and Ames, *Thinking through Confucius*, 119.

6. Hall and Ames write, "*Yi [gi]* is frequently divided into two concepts and translated alternatively as 'righteousness' or 'meaning.' It is because this specific concept is so important and yet has been so sorely misunderstood that we shall hold its translation in abeyance and . . . [let] context speak for itself" (*Thinking through Confucius*, 89–90). *Yi* is the Chinese pronunciation of the character that is read in Japanese as *gi*.

7. For a rich discussion of this sense of *giri*, see Yuko Ogasawara, *Office Ladies and Salaried Men: Power, Gender, and Work in Japanese Companies* (Berkeley: University of California Press, 1998), 98–113.

8. For a discussion of Nitobe's posthumous popularity in Japanese society, see Michael A. Schneider, "The Intellectual Origins of Colonial Trusteeship in East Asia: Nitobe Inazō, Paul Reinsch and the End of Empire," *American Asian Review* 17, no. 1 (1999): 7–8.

9. Nitobe Inazo, *Bushido: The Soul of Japan*, 10th ed. (New York: G. P. Putnam's Sons, 1907), 25–26.

10. Ibid., 27.

11. Ames and Rosemont translation. This passage features the advice not of Confucius but of Master You, a prominent disciple of his, yet it fits seamlessly into other statements Confucius makes on filiality.

12. I find the most helpful English translation and annotation of this passage in Li, *The Analects of Confucius*, 4.18, notes on 50.

13. In the Chinese tradition the Confucian values of loyalty to one's ruler and filiality were at times in conflict with each other, with filiality often winning the upper hand. In Japan, however, Tokugawa-era scholars argued that when the demands of office conflict with the needs of one's parents, the most filial response is to gratify the parents by achieving a reputation for punctilious service on behalf of one's office. I. J. McMullen, "Rulers or Fathers? A Casuistical Problem in Early Modern Japanese Thought," in *Past and Present*, no. 116 (August 1987): 56–97.

14. In Japan followers of Confucius have been blamed for the oppression of women at least since the late nineteenth century, when the modernizer Fukuzawa Yūkichi wrote scathing criticism of the treatise by the neo-Confucianist Kaibara Ekken (1630–1714) on the education of women, *Onna Daigaku*. See Fukuzawa Yūkichi, *Fukuzawa Yukichi on Japanese Women: Selected Works*,

trans. Eiichi Kiyooka (Tokyo: University of Tokyo Press, 1988); Carmen Blacker, "Fukuzawa Yukichi on Family Relationships," *Monumenta Nipponica* 14, no. 12 (1958): 40–60. An English version of the *Onna Daigaku* is available in Kaibara Ekken, "Women and Wisdom of Japan," in *The Way of Contentment and Women and Wisdom of Japan,* trans. Shingoro Takaishi (1905; reprint, 2 vols. in 1, Washington, DC: University Publications of America, 1979).

Kaibara Ekken is widely regarded as an important transmitter and elaborator of neo-Confucian thinking in early modern Japan. See, for example, Tetsuo Najita, "Intellectual Change in Early Eighteenth-Century Tokugawa Confucianism," *Journal of Asian Studies* 34, no. 4 (1975): 931–944; Masao Maruyama, *Studies in the Intellectual History of Tokugawa Japan,* trans. Mikiso Hane (Princeton, NJ: Princeton University Press, 1974), 61–67; Mary Evelyn Tucker, *Moral and Spiritual Cultivation in Japanese Neo-Confucianism: The Life and Thought of Kaibara Ekken (1630–1714)* (Albany: State University of New York Press, 1989).

Some have argued that Confucianism did not mean unmitigated oppression for women. Kathleen Uno makes the point that Confucian hierarchies could benefit older women in a family in "Women and Changes in the Household Division of Labor," in *Recreating Japanese Women, 1600–1945,* ed. Gail Lee Berstein (Berkeley: University of California Press, 1991), 17–41, especially 24. Uno also argues that the spread of ideas about women's duties such as those in Kaibara's *Onna Daigaku* encouraged women's participation in the economy of the household (30).

For evidence of the great degree of diversity in the customs regarding gender expectations for women in Confucian Japan, see also Anne Walthall, "The Life Cycle of Farm Women in Tokugawa Japan," in Lee, *Recreating Japanese Women,* 42–70. Confucian dictates about filiality gave elderly mothers a certain position within the family, for instance, and Japanese families were not always perfectly Confucian at any rate. Some scholars have pointed out that the exclusion of women from politics in the twentieth century was based on views and policies that were essentially new, despite their claims to reflect Japanese tradition. Sheldon Garon, "Women's Groups and the Japanese State: Contending Approaches to Political Integration, 1890–1945," *Journal of Japanese Studies* 19, no. 1 (1993): 5–41; Sharon H. Nolte and Sally Ann Hastings, "The Meiji State's Policy toward Women, 1890–1910," in Lee, *Recreating Japanese Women,* 151–174; Kathleen S. Uno, "The Death of 'Good Wife, Wise Mother'?," in *Postwar Japan as History,* ed. Andrew Gordon (Berkeley: University of California Press, 1993), 293–322.

15. Detailed accounts of famous LDP politicians involved in huge scandals with connections to organized crimes are available in Jacob M. Schlesinger, *Shadow Shoguns: The Rise and Fall of Japan's Postwar Political Machine* (Palo Alto, CA: Stanford University Press, 1999).

16. *Jīsan* can be thought of as related to the colloquial term *oyaji,* used in the Ozawa Ichirō Democratic Party campaign poster I described in the preface.

17. Among the best known of these arguments is made by Robert D. Putnam with Robert Leonardi and Rafaella Y. Nanetti, *Making Democracy*

Work: Civic Traditions in Modern Italy (Princeton, NJ: Princeton University Press, 1993). Scholars who have used Putnam's framework to examine the Japanese case have argued that Japan lacks both the generalized trust and the robust organizational life in civil society that he sees as essential supports for high-quality democratic government. For examples, see Robert Pekkanen, *Japan's Dual Civil Society: Members without Advocates* (Stanford: Stanford University Press, 2006); Toshio Yamagishi, Karen S. Cook, and Motoki Watanabe, "Uncertainty, Trust, and Commitment Formation in the United States and Japan," *American Journal of Sociology* 104, no. 1 (1998): 165–194; Robert D. Putnam, Susan J. Pharr, and Russell J. Dalton, "Introduction: What's Troubling the Trilateral Democracies," in *Disaffected Democracies: What's Troubling the Trilateral Countries*, ed. Susan J. Pharr and Robert D. Putnam (Princeton, NJ: Princeton University Press, 2000), 3–27.

18. This view of members of Congress received its now classic presentation in David Mayhew, *Congress: The Electoral Connection* (New Haven, CT: Yale University Press, 1974).

19. See, for example, Bruce Cain, John Ferejohn, and Morris Fiorina, *The Personal Vote: Constituency Service and Electoral Independence* (Cambridge, MA: Harvard University Press, 1987).

20. Kasaya Kazuhiko, *Bushidō no shisō: Nihongata soshiki to kojin no jiritsu* (Tokyo: PHP Kenkyū, 2002).

21. Ibid., 41–57.

22. Kasaya Kazuhiko, *Bushidō to gendai: Edo ni manabu nihon no saisei hinto* (Tokyo: Sankei Shinbunsha, 2002), 41, translation mine. Work by Eiko Ikegami draws some similar conclusions about samurai honor but sees this development in the *bushidō* ethic as a modernizing adaptation of the original ethic. See Eiko Ikegami, *The Taming of the Samurai: Honorific Individualism and the Making of Modern Japan* (Cambridge, MA: Harvard University Press, 1995), especially her treatment of Yoshida Shōin's notion of loyalty, 324.

23. Kasaya's accompanying text for his NHK lecture series includes a photo of investigators entering a meat-processing plant to investigate the fraudulent labeling of meat and a photo of a bureaucrat from the Ministry of Foreign Affairs (MFA) bowing low in apology for a scandal involving the misuse of public funds. Kasaya describes the MFA scandal (which included a cover-up scheme) as an example of the misinterpretation of the *bushidō* ethic of loyalty. Kasaya, *Bushidō no shisō*, 18–19.

24. H. D. Harootunian, *Toward Restoration: The Growth of Political Consciousness in Tokugawa Japan* (Berkeley: University of California Press, 1970), 197. See also the description of Yoshida Shōin's school in Donald Roden, "Thoughts on the Early Meiji Gentleman," in *Gendering Modern Japanese History*, ed. Barbara Molony and Kathleen Uno (Cambridge, MA: Harvard University Asia Center, 2005). Roden writes, "Shōin in particular insisted upon building a spiritual union among students and teachers; and toward that end he studiously avoided the imposition of any bureaucratic regulations regarding admission, promotion, evaluation, and even the scheduling of classes" (69).

25. I treat the literature on power as a structural phenomenon in the introduction. See Clarissa Rile Hayward, *De-Facing Power* (New York: Cambridge

University Press, 2000); Nicholas B. Dirks, Geoff Eley, and Sherry B. Ortner, introduction to *Culture/Power/History: A Reader in Contemporary Social Theory,* ed. Nicholas B. Dirks, Geoff Eley, and Sherry B. Ortner (Princeton, NJ: Princeton University Press, 1994).

CHAPTER 4

1. This table arrangement, called a *kotatsu,* is standard in Japanese homes in the winter because most of them are not centrally heated. Baba's house certainly was not.

2. As I have discussed in earlier chapters, prior to getting a commitment from the local assembly and mayor to hold a town-sponsored referendum, the Referendum Association held its own, unofficial referendum, sending invitations to all of Takeno's registered voters. Despite efforts by supporters of the nuclear power plant to call for a boycott of the unofficial referendum, more than 45 percent of the voters turned out.

3. Readers unfamiliar with Japanese local politics may be confused. In many towns, such as Takeno, even LDP members run for office as independents because excessive partisanship is considered unseemly in community affairs. But in Shirakawa Ward most candidates express party affiliations when running for office. Moreover there is a difference between independents who are recognized by fellow LDP members as LDP men and "real independents," or in other words, those candidates toward whom LDP members have no fellow feeling. Real independents can expect to face the unwelcome challenge of an LDP candidate campaigning in the same *jimoto,* or home territory, whereas LDP independents are under some party pressure to avoid trampling overmuch in each other's *jimoto.*

4. Although he explains that their power has gradually been declining, the political scientist Gerald Curtis claims, "Farmers enjoy a well deserved reputation for political clout within the LDP. Although they comprise no more than 5 percent of the labor force, farmers exercise political influence far greater than their numbers might suggest." Gerald L. Curtis, *The Logic of Japanese Politics: Leaders, Institutions, and the Limits of Change* (New York: Columbia University Press, 1999), 46–47. Electoral system changes, redistricting, and the growing importance of imported agricultural products to the Japanese diet were all beginning to erode farmer power in the LDP at the time of the Takeno election I observed, but farmers are nonetheless very important players in the party, as is attested to in Aurelia George Mulgan's recent study, *Power and Pork: A Political Life* (Canberra: ANU E Press, 2006).

5. A similar account of "manly" tears shed by a citizens' movement leader can be found in a collection of essays about a movement to turn garbage in a small town into fertilizer and to rebuild local agriculture. See Takeda Giichi, "Chiiki no tasukiwatashi o mezashite," in *Daidokoro to nōgyō o tsunagu,* ed. Ono Kazuoki (Tokyo: Sōshinsha, 2001), 26–94, especially 82.

6. Most research on gender and Japanese-language usage has been focused on women. But one study suggests that men are quite conscious of and know how to use "masculine" ways of speaking (particular words or sentence end-

ings) to demonstrate camaraderie or anger with other men. See Cindi Sturtz Streetharan, "Japanese Men's Linguistic Stereotypes and Realities: Conversations from the Kansai and Kanto Regions," in *Japanese Language, Gender, and Ideology: Cultural Models and Real People,* ed. Shigeko Smith Okamoto and Janet S. Shibamoto (New York: Oxford University Press, 2004), 275–289. For rich treatment of the way women self-consciously manipulate gender markers in Japanese language as a means of accessing power in work situations, see Miyako Inoue, *Vicarious Language: Gender and Linguistic Modernity in Japan* (Berkeley: University of California Press, 2006).

7. Furumaya Tadao, *Ura Nihon: Kindai Nihon o toinaosu* (Tokyo: Iwanami Shoten, 1997).

8. For an examination of how powerful the salaryman image is in Japan's popular consciousness, see James E. Roberson and Nobue Suzuki, eds., *Men and Masculinities in Contemporary Japan: Dislocating the Salaryman Doxa* (New York: Routledge Curzon, 2003).

CHAPTER 5

1. The volunteer staff, according to both my own observations and Katō's description, consisted of elected officials from other regions who had won office with Katō's assistance in other areas of Japan as well as men and women with an interest in developing an alternative to political party organization who had financial independence or flexible terms of employment. I have written about Katō's organization and philosophy elsewhere: Robin M. LeBlanc, "The Potential and Limits of Anti-Party Electoral Movements in Japanese Local Politics," in *Democratic Reform in Japan: Assessing the Impact,* ed. Gill Steel and Sherry Martin (New York: Lynne Reinner, 2008), 175–192.

2. By "true political independent" I mean to say that Ochi had no affiliation with established parties, not even an informal one. "Homemade" (*tezukuri*) is a term widely used in Japan for campaigns in which the bulk of the work is done by unpaid volunteers, strategies focus on least-cost options (such as sending out the plain campaign postcards supplied by the local government rather than glossier candidate-produced postcards), and much of the funding comes from small donations.

3. This search was performed with the Japanese characters in the search line on 7 July 2007 at 2:55 P.M. On an earlier search (March 2006) I found as many as 120,000 references.

4. See http://www.tackns.net/mixed/aun_yasukuni.html. This was a blog posted on 15 June 2005 as part of a series titled "Shisōka 'T'-shi ga kataru" on a larger blog site titled "Tack'ns Since 1996," http://www.tackns.net/index .html. Sites were accessed on 7 July 2007.

5. A radical challenger of gender distinction is Judith Butler. As she admits, she has been criticized for her insistence that sex/gender distinctions are unfounded and unnecessary discursive categories. However, the criticism most gender scholars levy toward her work is not directed at the persuasiveness of her claim that sex/gender distinctions are unfounded in any prediscursive reality but at the practical politics of proceeding as if gendered identities are

easily discarded. As Butler points out, admitting that gendered identities are both hard to change and in fact sometimes useful in organizing interventions against gender oppression is not a challenge to her main claim that gendered identities ought to be radically challenged. See Judith Butler, "Performative Acts and Gender Constitution: An Essay in Phenomenology and Feminist Theory," in *Writing on the Body: Female Embodiment and Feminist Theory,* ed. Katie Conboy, Nadia Medina, and Sarah Stanbury (New York: Columbia University Press, 1997), 401–417.

6. Versions of this sort of position in U.S. politics would be those taken by Amy Gutmann and Iris Marion Young when they argue for political recognition of and procedural protections for marginalized groups such as women and people of minority races. They seek to build a more explicit consultative process into political discourse precisely because dominant men benefit from their unacknowledged and unexamined (or gut-level) affinities for people like themselves. See Amy Gutmann, *Identity in Democracy* (Princeton, NJ: Princeton University Press, 2003); Iris Marion Young, *Justice and the Politics of Difference* (Princeton, NJ: Princeton University Press, 1990).

7. See Robin LeBlanc, *Bicycle Citizens: The Political World of the Japanese Housewife* (Berkeley: University of California Press, 1999).

8. A good example of the place of such narrative practices is discussed in my treatment of the electoral movement of the Seikatsu-sha Nettowāku. See ibid., 121–163, especially 132.

9. Robin M. LeBlanc, "Why Women Are Representing Men in a Japanese Town Assembly: A Little Tale about Gender Politics," *Kokusai jendā gakkai shi* 2 (2004): 35–70. See also chapter 1 in this book.

10. For further discussions of this problem, see my treatment of this issue in an LDP woman's campaign for the House of Councillors in *Bicycle Citizens,* 164–193.

11. Takada-san was alluding to an American social science classic: David Riesman, Reuel Denney, and Nathan Glazer, *The Lonely Crowd: A Study of the Changing American Character* (New Haven, CT: Yale University Press, 1950).

12. Compared to Americans, Japanese are believed to tolerate longer silences in conversation and to generally employ a hesitancy about speaking in ways that might cause conflict. Research on the use of silence by Japanese men has also emphasized its often punishing character. See Tomohiro Hasegawa and William B. Gudykunst, "Silence in Japan and the United States," *Journal of Cross-Cultural Psychology* 29, no. 5 (1998): 668–685; Susan K. Tomita, "The Consideration of Cultural Factors in the Research of Elder Mistreatment with an In-depth Look at the Japanese," *Journal of Cross-Cultural Gerontology* 9, no. 1 (1994): 39–52.

13. Door-to-door vote seeking is technically illegal under Japanese campaign laws. However, it is not illegal for a candidate to visit supporters on official business (such as an incumbent delivering a newsletter about assembly activities prior to the beginning of the official campaign period) or for a candidate to visit a home where one friend hopes to introduce him or her to

another. If the friend happens to mention that the individual is running for office, so much the better. The practice the Takeno candidates used did not vary substantially from Takada-san's practice of making New Year's greeting visits to the homes of likely supporters.

14. This general point is also made by Adam Jaworski, who argues that powerful men can use strategic silences to enhance their power while also "silencing" others, who thus lose an opportunity for challenging those in power. Importantly, however, Jaworski assumes that the power of silence is in its tendency to support the status quo. In Baba's case, silence is used to undo the status quo. See Adam Jaworski, *The Power of Silence: Social and Pragmatic Perspectives* (Newbury Park, CA: Sage, 1993).

15. Young, *Justice and the Politics of Difference.*

16. Simone de Beauvoir makes a famous version of this claim in *The Second Sex,* trans. and ed. H. M. Parshley (New York: Knopf, 1989), xv.

17. The notion of hegemonic masculinity is elaborated by R. W. Connell in *Masculinities,* 2nd ed. (Berkeley: University of California Press, 2005), xviii, 76–81. James Roberson and Nobue Suzuki describe a hegemonic notion of Japanese manhood, what they call the "salaryman doxa," in the introduction to *Men and Masculinities in Contemporary Japan: Dislocating the Salaryman Doxa,* ed. James E. Roberson and Nobue Suzuki (New York: Routledge Curzon, 2003). I have treated related literature and discussed the hegemony of notions of Japanese men as breadwinners in LeBlanc, "Why Women Are Representing Men in a Japanese Town Assembly." See also Itō Kimio, *Otokorashisa no yukue: Danseigaku no bunka shakaigaku* (Tokyo: Shinyōsha, 1993).

18. This has been documented in a variety of different settings. For examples, see Hugh Campbell, "The Glass Phallus: Pub(lic) Masculinity and Drinking in Rural New Zealand," *Rural Sociology* 65, no. 4 (2000): 562–581; Mark Maier and James W. Messerschmidt, "Commonalities, Conflicts and Contradictions in Organized Masculinities: Exploring the Gendered Genesis of the Challenger Disaster," *Canadian Review of Sociology and Anthropology* 35, no. 3 (1998): 325–345.

19. Young, *Justice and the Politics of Difference,* 131.

20. A good example of this in the case of Japanese studies of masculinity is Asai Haruo, "Dansei keisei ron gaisetsu," in *Nihon no otoko wa doko kara kite, doko e iku no ka* (Tokyo: Jūgetsu sha, 2001). Asai calls on men to develop a masculinity in which they can admit their weakness, cultivate their "feminine" traits, and truly enjoy a shared life with women.

21. I have written elsewhere about the attachment of Baba and others in his community to the male breadwinner image. I do think that some sorts of men would be excluded from political power even in a politics more to Baba's liking. LeBlanc "Why Women Are Representing Men in a Japanese Town Assembly."

22. Patricia L. Maclachlan, "Information Disclosure and the Center-Local Relationship in Japan," in *Local Voices, National Issues: The Impact of Local Initiative in Japanese Policy-Making,* ed. Sheila A. Smith (Ann Arbor: Center for Japanese Studies, University of Michigan, 2000).

CONCLUSION

1. I am not sure where Baba learned this saying, but according to my colleague Winston Davis, professor emeritus of Japanese religion at Washington and Lee University, something like this "half-mat" philosophy is used by a Japanese Buddhist group established by Nishida Tenkō. In an e-mail Davis wrote, "I first heard this saying (or something like it) when I was shown one of the small homes (huts) that one of the older members lived in at Itōen. It was called the 'One and a Half Mat House' because of Tenkō-san's saying that you need one mat for sleeping and only half a mat when you are awake" (28 July 2003). Davis suggested the saying may have originated with the nineteenth-century agrarian reformer Ninomiya Sontoku. In the 1850s Sontoku advocated revitalization of agrarian villages threatened by the developing market economy with a combination of "practical programs that taught that hard work, frugality, and filial piety were essential to individual success and happiness," as well as financial support for families who agreed to return fallow land to cultivation. See David L. Howell, "Hard Times in the Kanto: Economic Change and Village Life in Late Tokugawa Japan," *Modern Asian Studies* 23, no. 2 (1989): 349–371, especially 368. Although as far as I know Baba is unfamiliar with both Itōen and Ninomiya Sontoku, I find it fascinating that he regularly uses a saying that may come from a man who lived in the same period of Japanese history as one of Takada-san's heroes, Yoshida Shōin.

2. A treatment of the very long history of the divide between pure scholarship and citizen education in political science is Raymond Seidelman with the assistance of Edward J. Harpham, *Disenchanted Realists: Political Science and the American Crisis, 1884–1984* (Albany: State University of New York Press, 1985).

3. Alexis de Tocqueville, *Democracy in America,* trans. George Lawrence, ed. J. P. Mayer (New York: Harper & Row, 1988), 495. See also Hindy Lauer Schachter,"Civic Education: Three Early American Political Science Association Committees and Their Relevance for Our Times,"*PS: Political Science and Politics*31, no. 3(1998):631–635.

4. Tocqueville, *Democracy in America,* 496.

Index

Text:	10/13 Sabon
Display:	Sabon
Compositor:	BookMatters, Berkeley
Indexer:	Andrew Christenson
Printer & Binder:	Maple-Vail Book Manufacturing Group